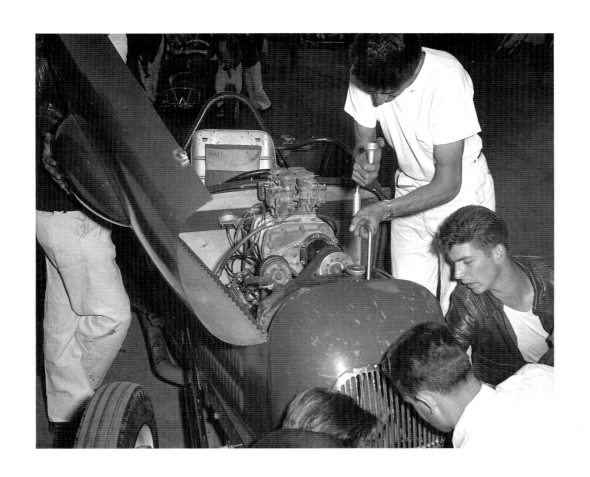

DRY LAKES AND DRAG STRIPS
THE AMERICAN HOT ROD

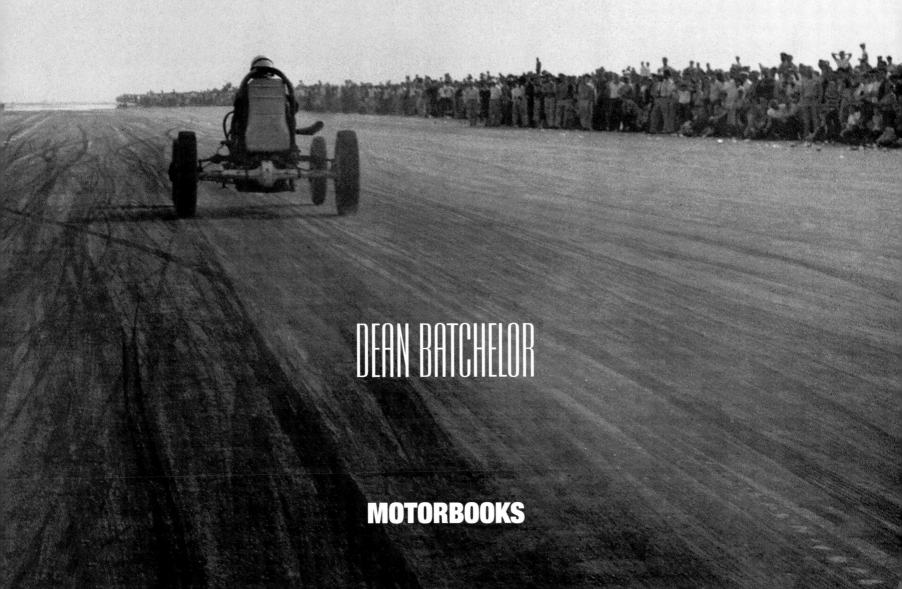

DEAN BATCHELOR

MOTORBOOKS

This edition published in 2002 by Motorbooks, an imprint of MBI Publishing Company, Galtier Plaza, Suite 200, 380 Jackson Street, St. Paul, MN 55101-3885 USA

Motorbooks titles are also available at discounts in bulk quantity for industrial or sales-promotional use. For details write to Special Sales Manager at MBI Publishing Company, Galtier Plaza, Suite 200, 380 Jackson Street, St. Paul, MN 55101-3885 USA

ISBN 0-7603-1216-8

Front and back cover photos courtesy of Greg Sharp collection.

On the frontispiece: Barney Navarro (with speed wrench) and friends work on a supercharged flathead track roadster, circa 1950. *Greg Sharp collection*

On the title page: An early drag race at Bakersfield in 1954. Crowd control and safety took a back seat to the racing in the early days. *Author photo*

Printed in Hong Kong

Contents

Dean Batchelor
Tribute

Dean in his '32 Ford Roadster at El Mirage Dry Lake, in 1948.
Author collection

If this reads more like a biography than the usual book preface, it's meant to be. This was the story Dean Batchelor talked about writing for years, his dream book. And shortly after finishing the manuscript he passed away. Dean was only seventy-two and in apparent good health, and we'd planned on having him around for many years to come—a friend, a mentor, an inspiration, and historian extraordinare. So while this book certainly wasn't meant to be a postscript to Dean's life, it became a very fitting one.

For too long, automotive enthusiasts were split into "us" and "them" camps. Hot rodders in one section. Sports car "teabaggers" in another. Indianapolis racers were at the pinnacle of the midget sprint-car hierarchy. NASCAR stockers were a different breed. Drag racers had their own game to play. What few people were ready to admit was that they were all, at heart, the same "motorheads."

Dean was one of the rare ones who comfortably bridged that gap.

Moving to California from Emporia, Kansas, in 1927, Dean grew up in a era still talked of dreamily by older Californians. It was a milk-and-honey period in the Golden State, an era of expansion led by the automobile, which became a necessity to connect the widely spread communities.

Influenced by many factors—from this new-and-evolving culture to balmy weather to the local aircraft industry to the nearby dry lakes that made perfect race tracks—the modifying of automobiles was a natural. Right in the middle of it all was young Dean Batchelor, a hot rodder before the term was popularized, a member of the Road Runners car club working with the now-famous Southern California Timing Association.

This was in the years leading up to World War II, years of flathead Fords, comp coupes, highboy roadsters, and dusty days on the lakes, a noisy but peaceful time compared to the world war so many of the racers were about to experience. Dean ended up as a B-17 radio operator on those dangerous air missions to Germany and back. Like so many brave flyers, Dean didn't make it back to England after one flight, shot down in Germany where he became a prisoner.

Dean loved to tell the story about his first journey back to Germany many years later on a BMW press trip near Munich. His German host asked, "So, you have been to Germany before?"

Dean: "Yes, I was shot down here during the war."

A pause from the tactful German. Then, "Oh, I'm sorry."

Ever inquisitive, Dean discovered English automotive literature while stationed in that country, and it became part of his culture.

Back in California, Dean earned his degree in industrial design at Los Angeles' Chouinard Art Institute, and remained the hot rodder, driving his '32 Ford highboy roadster to school each day. With another well-known hot rodding pioneer, Alex Xydias, Dean created the *So-Cal Special*, a Ford flathead V-8-powered streamliner he drove to 193mph, while Bill Dailey later took it to a 208mph average at Bonneville. Dean designed both the frame and aerodynamic body for the Mal Hooper/Shadoff Chrysler Special, a machine as pretty as it was fast, setting numerous U.S. and International top speed records during the 1950s.

His reputation within the growing hot rod business led to a short stint as an advertising salesman, but Dean quickly switched to the editorial side, becoming editor of *Hop Up* magazine in 1952, before moving to *Motor Life* in 1956.

Dean the hot rodder was making a transition, however, moving to the teabagger side of the business. In 1958, he went to work for *Road & Track* where he would become editor and, later, editorial director. Sports cars were now his passion, with Ferraris his speciality; he would go on to write four books on the subject. And he would marry his loving wife, Pat. Leaving *Road & Track* in 1975, Dean went to Harrah's famous automobile collection in Reno, Nevada, where he was technical assistant to the director and general manager.

After his time at Harrah's, Dean wrote a very comprehensive book on the collection, and I had the pleasure of working with him as the photographer on the project. That experience was when I first began to truly appreciate the no-nonsense, dogged manner of Dean's research. No assumptions, no presumptions, he wanted the facts in black and white. No truth was ever stretched in a Dean Batchelor story. We worked together again on *Cunningham: The Life and Cars of Briggs Cunningham* a project that became, for a variety of reasons, long and drawn out. But Dean's faith in the need to tell Briggs Cunningham's story was so strong he never wavered from his belief that the book must be finished and done properly. Which it was.

For many of us, our last memory of Dean is from a weekend honoring Briggs at the Palm Springs vintage races. I'll always remember Dean at the formal dinner, dressed in his tuxedo with a tartan tie and cummerbund for a splash of color. It was just a few days before he died. Dean was delighted, because this book was finished. The man who had risen to the heights of his industry, who had edited the most famous sports car magazine in

America, who had delighted in driving his Ferrari 340 Mexico coupe along the twisty roads above Reno, had finished the book he wanted to write more than any other. Not about the glamour of rubbing elbows with the world's top automotive executives or being wined and dined in foreign capitals, but about where it all began. Looking for a little more speed down on the dry lakes.

These days, of course, it's accepted that a man can have a Duesenberg, a Cobra, and a lakester in the same automotive collection—that a highly tuned flathead Ford V-8 is as interesting an engine as a six-carb Ferrari V-12. It's an accepted fact that many of the men who established America's road racing power, influenced Indy cars, and designed and engineered many of America's production cars, had their beginnings in the hot rod movement of Southern California.

Dean Batchelor knew it all along.

— *John Lamm*

A young Dean (left) and Alex Xydias pose with their streamliner at Bonneville in 1949. The racer posted the two fastest averages for the meet: 156.39mph average with a V-8 60, and 189.745mph average with a Merc, with a top one-way of 193.54mph. *Greg Sharp collection*

Dean with his Ferrari 340 Mexico at Laguna Seca, in 1974. *Gordon Martin*

What Is A Hot Rod?

Typical dry lake roadster of the 1940s, this one Riley V-8-powered. Jim Kurten owned the chassis, Gene Von Arx claimed the engine, and the car was driven by Bill Spalding. *Edlebrock collection*

"Hot rod," "Hot rodding," "Hot rodder," "Hot rodded." Words, terms, phrases that can be, and have been, used in both the affectionate and the pejorative sense. The term "hot rod" and its variations, however, are fairly new additions to our lexicon.

During the two years I spent researching material for this book, I found no concrete evidence suggesting the exact date the term was first used , but I believe it to be early in 1945.

No magazines, racing newspapers, or racing programs I've found mentioned the words until after WWII, and my own memory—which is pretty good—fails to guide me in claiming the term's date of first use.

Pre-WWII literature referred to cars we would today call hot rods by their body styles—roadster, coupe, pickup, phaeton—or in some instances in racing programs as "hot irons," or "hop-ups," but I've yet to find a prewar reference to anything being a "hot rod."

Before we proceed, I should define what is to be considered a hot rod within the pages and parameters of this book. The discussion—the seeking of a true definition of the term—has been going on for years, and the arguments have ranged from the reasonable to the ridiculous.

One advantage an author has is the opportunity to establish his own rules—at least insofar as his book is concerned. Establishing my definition will probably do little to end the argument, but that's okay. I don't know of any rule that says my definition must be accepted by everyone. However, for my purpose in this book, a hot rod is any production vehicle which has been modified to provide more performance.

I realize this is a broader definition than most enthusiasts would use, but I believe that, while hot rodders

may well have influenced other forms of motor racing, hot rodders themselves were also influenced by other forms of motor racing. Even though competition cars are set up differently for their tracks or circuits—Bonneville, oval track, drag racing, or road racing—there are too many overlapping similarities to ignore one in favor of the others.

One goal I set for myself was to dispel some of the myths surrounding hot rodding, and try to set the record straight on who did what first, and when and where. While researching this book my own perceptions have been rearranged and, in a few instances, completely changed.

Many hot rodding enthusiasts think it all started in California—particularly in the Los Angeles area. I think it can be safely said that hot rodding, as we know it today, developed in southern California, and grew faster there than it did elsewhere; but it did not start there, strictly speaking.

My own perception has been that the modification of production engines started about the same time in the Northeast, Midwest, and West—the difference being that those engines built in the East and Midwest went into sprint cars to be raced on oval tracks, while the engines built up in the West typically went into street cars.

The good roads, good weather, and proximity to the dry lakes of southern California made a good argument for the "it all started in California" premise, and my research convinced me there is some truth in it. But that didn't turn out to be the whole story, as you shall see.

Finally, in spite of my currently held belief that hot rodding—that is, the modification of production engine and chassis—started about the same time all over the U.S., there is a distinct western bias to this book. I make no excuse for that. I grew up in southern California, became interested in cars there, created customs and hot rods there (and helped others do so), and then became an automotive writer working in the burgeoning automotive magazine business in southern California.

Aside from the western slant to this book, I have also arbitrarily decided that the contents will include primarily the first fifty years of hot rodding as I view it: 1920 to 1970. Those were the pioneering and the formative years when the hot rod builder really had to do it himself.

Whether pursued as a sport, hobby, or business, the activity we now call hot rodding grew out of its infancy and matured in those fifty years into a multimillion dollar-per-year industry.

It also brought automotive fame, glory, and financial success to southern California automotive entrepreneurs before spreading to other parts of the U.S. (and the world). It was a great time, and I regret missing the first twenty years, having gotten active in this sport/hobby/business in 1940.

But the time from 1940 on is one that I know from experience, and had I not been a part of this automotive arena I would never have spent the past forty-three years writing about and working on cars—and this book would have been written by someone else who had "been there." I'm pleased that I was, and that I'm able to share my experiences, knowledge, and enthusiasm for this activity with you.

Bob McClure's B class Lakester is pushed to starting speed at El Mirage Dry Lake, May 1952. *Ralph Poole photo, author collection*

The Hewitt & Ballanger Wayne-Chevy-powered Modified Roadster ran 144.46mph at Bonneville in 1952. The entry was from Whittier, California. *Ralph Poole photo, author collection*

CHAPTER 1

Before "The War"
They Didn't Call Them Hot Rods

*Street racing, dry lakes racing,
and prowling junkyards for parts.
It was a time of innovation.*

The bucolic atmosphere of Mint Canyon, through which California State Highway 6 (it has since been replaced by Highway 14) offered the most direct path from Los Angeles to the Mojave Desert, was shattered by the sound of unmuffled motorcycles. It was 1927, and these strange-looking machines, so unlike the Harley-Davidsons, Indians, and Henderson cycles usually seen on the streets of southern California, were thundering up the two-lane concrete road with, quite obviously, some purpose in the minds of their riders.

Thirteen year-old Charles W. Scott came running out of the family home near the highway to take in this bewildering array of machinery.

A few weeks later the quiet of this rural community was broken once again; this time by cars. Like the cycles Scott had seen earlier, these cars were strange as well. Some of them were being driven. Some were towed behind another car, and almost all of them were stripped of fenders, running boards, lights, bumpers, and anything else unnecessary .

The cars being driven created a terrible racket. Young Scott was awestruck. This was something he wanted to know more about. Running back to the house, he asked his mother if he could take the family car, a 1922 Chevrolet Touring, and follow them. Scott had gotten a driver's license at the age of twelve, so that he could drive his little sister and brother and a half-dozen of their classmates to grammar school each day.

His mother agreed that he could follow them, but only if she went along. Though Charlie was only thirteen, he could handle the car well enough, but neither he nor his mother had any idea how far these cars were going, or where they would stop.

The adventurous pair fell behind some stragglers and followed them to Palmdale, and then north through Lancaster to a tiny town named Rosamond, where they turned east about three miles to find the entrance to Rosamond Dry Lake. A course and crude timing equipment had been set up, and the cars were lining up, each ready for a run through the timing traps.

Scott discovered that the group would accept entries on the spot. For what he now remembers as a fifty-cent fee, he would be able to drive the Chevy through the timing lights. Heart in mouth but foot on the floor, young Charlie wheeled the Chevy through the time traps at what he thought would be about 100mph. The disappointment was almost overwhelming as they wrote down 69mph for his first-ever run on a dry lake.

Twenty-six years later, in 1953, Charles W. Scott's Ardun-Ford-powered B-Class Lakester, driven by Leroy Holmes, would be the first open-wheeled hot rod to average better than 200mph on the Bonneville Salt Flats. But we're ahead of our story; see chapter ten for more on that.

Few of us had the luxury of being able to drive at thirteen, and no one I know had a mother who would drop everything to accompany her son on some kind of mechanical wild goose chase and then get out of the car—the family car—so the kid could see how fast it would go.

Skip-it was built in 1934, for 14 year-old George "Skip" Rubsch, by his father and the men at George senior's A-1 Autobody in Los Angeles. They were emulating the style and flair of the aftermarket speedster bodies for Model T Fords. The car was rebuilt in 1936, and again in 1938 when it acquired the cream and red flame paint job and the modified 1938 Oldsmobile Six grille. Power was a Model B Ford four with a Model C crankshaft, Cragar overhead valves, a Winfield carburetor, and a re-worked Mallory distributor. The frame was Model A Ford, and Ford axles were used front and rear. Because of the body type, *Skip-it* had to run as a streamliner at Muroc. *Frederick A. Usher photo*

Opposite page, his Riley V-8-powered roadster was a group entry; the chassis was owned by Jim Kurten, the sohc Riley V-8 engine belonged to Gene Von Arx, and Bill Spalding entered the car and drove it. Bill Spalding is standing, and Gene Von Arx is kneeling in front of the roadster. George Riley was noted for his ohv conversions for the Ford Models A, B, and C four-cylinder engines and for the flathead V-8. He also made a few 225ci single overhead camshaft V-8 racing engines for the 225 Class hydroplanes. The crankshaft, connecting rods, and oil pan were from an early Ford V-8 flathead, and Riley designed and made the rest of the engine. *Eldebrock collection*

Dry Lakebed Locations

The dry lakebeds in southern California are located in the Antelope Valley of the Mojave Desert at an elevation of approximately 2,800ft above sea level. This area is euphemistically called the "high desert" to differentiate it from the Palm Springs and Salton Sea area which are the "low desert." Contrary to many published reports, these dry lakes are not salt flats—only Utah's Bonneville Salt Flats fit that description, at least in the United States. California's dry lakes are dried-mud flats formed by the desert's natural drainage.

Muroc Dry Lake, because of its large area and hard surface, was the favorite for speed trials from the late 1920s, continuing until 1942. The U.S. Army Air Corps ejected the racers from the lake in June, 1938, but relented and allowed sporadic use of the lakebed through 1942. That area is now Rogers Dry Lake and the Edwards Air Force test base.

Harper Dry Lake was used, intermittently with Muroc, from 1938 through 1942, and then as an alternative to El Mirage through 1946. Rosamond Dry Lake, the most accessible but least practical (small available area and poor surface) of the dry lakes saw action from the mid-1920s until 1948, particularly from motorcycle timing groups.

El Mirage Dry Lake came into constant use in 1945 and continues as a venue for summer weekend time trials and TV commercials. One excursion was made by the SCTA to Cuddeback Lake in about 1950 but proved to be a disaster. The lengthy washboard dirt road into the lake almost shook the cars to pieces, and then the lake surface was soft, and no significant speeds were recorded.

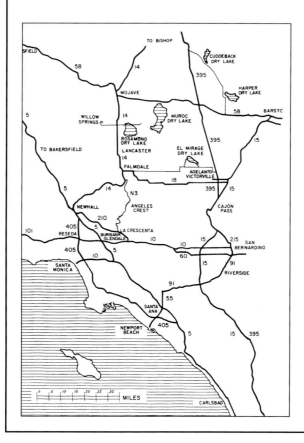

Jack Harvey, of the SCTA Road Runners Club built this Ford Model B (with Cragar overhead valves) streamliner in 1939. It was too heavy, and too big—with a lot of frontal area—but achieved a credible 115.38mph. This wasn't fast enough to excite other competitors to build aerodynamic bodies for their cars. *Eldon Snapp photo, author collection*

But things were different in 1927. There were no freeways or expressways, but then there wasn't much traffic either. One could drive from Los Angeles to one of the dry lakes in not much more time than it takes today; a bit over two hours today, a little under two and a half hours then.

Highway 6, the Mint Canyon (Sierra Highway) road where Scott lived, wasn't the only route from L.A. to the high desert, it was simply the one most used by Los Angelenos headed for the dry lakes. Those who lived in Orange, Riverside, and San Bernardino counties went over Cajon Pass, on Route 66 from San Bernardino to Victorville, and then north on 395 to Kramer Junction—a.k.a. four-corners—and west to Muroc, or Rosamond, or east to Harper Dry Lakes (see map).

The Mint Canyon road was preferred if you were towing a car. We all ended up at the same place, but the ascent through Mint Canyon was more gradual and therefore easier on the tow car; rising from about 1,200-feet elevation at Saugus and Newhall, to 3,179 feet at the summit before Palmdale, a rise of about 2,000 feet in thirty miles.

The route over Cajon Pass climbed from 1,040 feet at San Bernardino to 4,190 feet at the summit, a rise of 3,100-plus feet in less than twenty miles.

Besides, going up Highway 6, we could stop at the Solemint store (where Mint Canyon and Soledad Canyon crossed) and get the best root beer in the world—served in those giant frosted mugs that made the drink so refreshing—at ten cents a mug.

The cars and their engines that Scott saw at Rosamond Dry Lake in 1927, and those seen in subsequent years up to WWII were marvelous examples of youthful ingenuity. Any-one building or modifying a car in the 1920s or 1930s had only his own imagination, and that of his friends, to go on.

The only automotive magazines published then were either trade magazines, which described in boring detail manufacturing or service problems related to the auto industry, or racing publications, which covered primarily oval-track racing and were sold at race meets. There were no how-to magazines.

There were also very few speed shops where one could go to learn the esoteric methods of race car preparation. Lee Chapel established one of the first, if not the first, speed shops in the country, on San Fernando Road in Los Angeles, and George Wight started Bell Auto Parts in Bell, California—both in the early 1930s.

The first speed equipment for modifying production engines seems to have originated in Indiana, and was made for oval-track racing cars powered by Ford Model T, Chevy, or Dodge four-cylinder engines. As early as 1920 one could buy a sixteen-valve head (advertised as a "Peugeot type" head) for the Ford, Chevy, or Dodge engines. They were made by Robert Roof in Anderson, Indiana, and by Morton & Brett and Craig-Hunt, both in Indianapolis.

Roof's head was a pushrod and rocker-arm set-up, the Craig-Hunt head was a chain-driven single overhead camshaft job with rocker arms to inclined valves, and the Morton & Brett was a double overhead-camshaft head. These racing components (dual intake manifolds and welded tubular exhaust headers were also available) were sold directly from the manufacturer to the racer via magazine and race program advertisements.

Eddie "Bud" Meyer brought the first mid-engined (the twenty-one-stud flathead V-8 was behind the driver) roadster to the dry lakes on May 19, 1940. Bud, is in the cockpit, and his father, Eddie Meyer, is standing on the front frame horns. On this initial outing, which was also the first time Meyer had run alcohol for fuel, the roadster turned 121.95mph—the fastest time ever made by a roadster at the dry lakes at that time. On a two-way record run the car averaged 118.66.
Gus Rollins photo

In the early 1930s, Wight's Bell Auto Parts was selling overhead valve set-ups for the Ford A and B engines, made by both George Riley and Crane Gartz (Cragar), each Los Angeles based, and Winfield carburetors from Ed Winfield's small shop on Treadwell Street in Los Angeles. Winfield also ground racing camshafts and would soon offer them for street use as well as track use. For specifics on speed equipment, see chapters two, three, and four.

For engine components not specifically made for racing, the local junkyard was the source of choice. Some pieces could be obtained from the parts departments at auto dealerships, but this wasn't too satisfactory

in the early days. Parts department guys didn't understand racing, and the parts were too costly for the racers during those depression years.

Junkyard research is the reason why so many engines ran crankshafts, rods, carburetors, and other odds and ends that weren't generic to the make of engine. Even rods from WWI-era Curtiss OX-5 aircraft engines found their way into quite a few car engines. Bob Rufi, for example, paid thirty-five cents each for four OX-5 rods for his record-setting Chevy four-cylinder streamliner.

While the junkyards offered engine and chassis parts, the "midnight auto supply" furnished a substan-

Sheitlin's Fargo four-Port.
Author photo

Sheitlin, left, and Geroge Wight, owner of Bell Auto Parts. Wight helped Sheitlin with the car at the lakes.

A Legend in His Own Time

Frank Sheitlin, a.k.a. "Blind Slim," was one of the legends of early dry lakes racing. A mechanic by trade, Sheitlin lost his eyesight, partly from welding without using safety goggles. Because of his previous experience as a "sighted" mechanic, he continued to port and relieve cylinder heads and blocks.

Using a portable grinder, Slim would check his work by feel. When his friends would visit his backyard garage at night he would turn on the lights so they could see, all the time making rude remarks about guys who needed eyes to see where they were going.

If Slim took his engine apart, he could then reassemble it because he remembered where he had put all the pieces. He could, and did, overhaul, a carburetor or an engine with equal ease and was able to tune the engine by listening to it run.

Frank was a member of the SCTA 90 MPH Club. His car, a Modified class car with a Ford Model B block and Fargo four-port ohv cylinder head and four Winfield sidedraft carburetors, was driven by a fellow club member at 106.63mph on Harper Dry Lake on May 19, 1940.

One of the prettiest modifieds ever to run at the lakes was built by Dustin "Dusty" Campbell, who ran a four-cylinder before installing a V-8 (and adding a 1939 La Salle grille) in 1939. Campbell sold the modified to Danny Sakai, who ran a Mal-Ord-built V-8—the engine equipped with Ord's cylinder heads, dual intake manifold, and ignition. The car's wire wheels are from a mid-1930s Packard. With Sakai at the wheel, the modified consistently topped 120mph, and the best run we can attribute to the car was 126.58mph at the September 28, 1941, SCTA meet at Muroc Dry Lake. Sakai unfortunately lost his life on October 17, 1941, while riding fellow Walkers Club member Bob West's motorcycle.
Author photos

tial number of body parts. While researching this book, I mentioned to Chuck Spurgin that the Whippet radiator seemed to be popular with both dry lakes racers and sprint car builders. Chuck said that in the 1930s there was hardly a Whippet on the streets of Los Angeles which still had its original radiator.

Life at the Lakes

Competition classes for dry lakes racing were established almost as soon as the hop-up artists started using that venue for their speed trials, and these classes have changed considerably over the years. A program from a 1933 Muroc Racing Association meet lists the following:

Class A: 70–80mph
Class B: 80–90mph
Class C: 90–100mph
Class D: Six- and Eight-Cylinder cars
Class E: Modified Roadster Bodies
Class F: Stock Roadster Bodies over 100mph

After the cars had run through the timing traps and established their speed capability, they were assigned to one of the appropriate classes. At that point the match racing started.

Two or three cars, usually, but occasionally up to five cars were sent off from a slow rolling start for what amounted to a drag race, although it wasn't called a drag race then. That term, like "hot rod," came later.

Match races had a tremendous appeal for the spectators as well as the racers, but they were dangerous, and it's a miracle they didn't cause multiple crashes and injuries. The lead car had no problem, but those following were driving in swirling dust sometimes so thick the drivers couldn't see where they were going.

Dry lakes problems in those days may not have been helped by advertisements such as this one, which appeared in the 1933 Muroc Racing Association program:

Art Chrisman at Pomona in the Harvey/Leman/Caruthers/Neumayer/Chrisman car.
Author photo

Evolution of a Dry Lakes/Drag Racing Car

This Harry Lewis-built Modified, patterned after an early sprint car with Franklin tubular front axle and semi-elliptic springs and Ford rear axle with transverse-leaf spring, started life in the mid-1930s with a Rajo T engine. However, by the time Jack Harvey raced it at the dry lakes in 1938 and early '39, it was Model A Ford Cragar-powered. Jack sold it to his brother George, who joined with Ernie McAfee to race it through the rest of the '39 season with a Ford V-8 engine. Jack, George, and Ernie were all members of the SCTA Road Runners Club.

Up to this point the car had always run with a white paint job, but when it was sold to Jack Lehman, who ran it as the Lehman-Schwartzrock entry with the SCTA Albata Club, it acquired a "fire engine red" color as reported by the *SCTA Racing News*. As the L-S entry it turned 123.96mph on Harper Dry Lake at the June 14, 1942, SCTA meet.

The car was subsequently sold to Doug Caruthers (who ran it with a black paint job), which brought it back into the Road Runners Club once more. Doug ran the car under his own name, then as the Johnny Johnson-Doug Caruthers entry—all in B Modified Class. Caruthers also fitted lights and mufflers and drove it on the street on special occasions.

Caruthers sold the Modified to LeRoy Neumayer, who used it as a dragster mostly at Santa Ana but occasionally on other southern California strips. Art Chrisman purchased it from Neumayer, and it gained its greatest fame as the "Chrisman No. 25 Dragster." Art had lengthened the chassis, mounted Ford disc wheels in place of the Kelsey-Hayes wire wheels, and fitted drag racing slicks to the rear wheels. As Chrisman ran it, and as it sits now, it is painted bronze with gold leaf trim.

Match races were abandoned after the Southern California Timing Association (SCTA) was formed November 29, 1937. The first organized SCTA meet was at Muroc Dry Lake on May 15, 1938, and it ushered in a new era of dry lakes racing.

New classes were formed, based on the type of car, and included Roadster, Modified, Streamliner, and Unlimited. The Roadster class meant just that; the car had to wear a stock roadster body. Modifieds could be either one-man or two-man cars, usually made from the cockpit "bucket" of a roadster (narrowed for the one-man cars) with no bodywork behind the bucket, and had to have at least 400sq-in of roughly flat area behind the driver. Streamliners were any

cars which had pointed or rounded tails at the rear of the body, and Unlimited cars were those with V-16 engines (Cadillac, Marmon, etc.) or cars with supercharged engines.

In the early days of dry lakes time trials the timing equipment was hand-held stopwatches; one to record when the car entered the quarter mile and the other to indicate when the car had completed the distance. As time went by hand-held stopwatches gave way to stopwatches activated by wires stretched across the course—at the beginning and end of the quarter mile—a few inches off the ground so the car's front wheels would trip the mechanism. Rubber hoses, as we used to see in gas stations, were also tried but inasmuch

Frank Morimoto, of the SCTA Mobilers Club, was a regular entrant at race meets through the latter half of the 1930s. This is his Moller 4-Port-powered Model A phaeton at Muroc in 1937. That's Frank, wearing an aviator's helmet sitting on the front wheel of the '29 and surrounded by his buddies. No matter what Morimoto brought to the dry lakes, it was always one of the top runners.
Tom Medley collection

Outrider club member Hank Rollins' Model A phaeton, with early flathead V-8 engine and 1935 Ford grille and shell, at Harper Dry Lake on July 23, 1939. They're in what appears to be a very long line of cars waiting to make their timed runs.
Gus Rollins photo

as they relied on air pressure to activate the timing, the errors in speed could be enormous. This last timing method was short lived.

In the mid-1930s, a young Los Angeles City College engineering student named Walter Nass designed and built the first electric timing equipment used at the dry lakes. Nass wasn't a racer, nor was he tempted to be one; he had been asked by a friend, Ernie Clover, to design an accurate and reliable timing system for the cars. Nass thought this a challenge worthy of an engineering student so he obliged his friend.

The system that Walter Nass designed, built, and operated at the dry lake meets still used a trip-wire across the course at the start and finish, but instead of mechanically operating a stopwatch, the retracting wire closed an electrical switch. The current from the closed switch energized a solenoid which operated a paper punch.

This punch, when activated, punched a small hole in a rotating heavy-paper disc about six inches in diameter. Each paper disc, replaced by a new one after each run, carried only two bits of information—the time the passing car tripped the first wire, and the time when it tripped the second wire.

The elapsed time was determined by the distance between the two punched holes, measured by radial grad-

uations printed on the discs to facilitate quick and easy reading. The most important component of this system, however, was a thermostatically-heated tuning fork, which maintained the accuracy and consistency of the system.

Walter Nass transferred to the University of Southern California to complete his mechanical engineering degree, and sold his timing equipment to the SCTA to be operated by a new official timer. The Nass system

Dry lakes time trials were some of the safest racing venues anywhere—if all participants and spectators were reasonably careful. Unfortunately, too many of these young men, particularly from the spectator ranks in the early days, let their enthusiasm outrun their common sense. The results were predictable and often tragic. When an accident occurred, injured parties were taken to a hospital in Palmdale or Victorville, and the car owners hoped their friends would look after the wreck for them—otherwise it would be stripped in a matter of hours. *Vince Cimino and Tom Gosch photo*

Ernie McAfee, in car 24, was the victor in this heat race at Harper Dry Lake in 1939. The '30 Model A roadster (76) is the Farmer-Ingersoll entry with a McDowell ohv head on an A block, the '32 (47) is Karl Orr's roadster with milled heads and dual manifold. McAfee was driving a four-cylinder modified of unknown engine type. *Eldon Snapp photo*

Muroc Dry Lake, 1933. Frankie Lyons (24), Riley 4-Port Model A, and Hi Halfhill in the Claud Neal/Hi Halfhill 2-Port Riley, watch each other to get an equal start in their match race.
Greg Sharp collection

The Spalding brothers, Bill and Tom, built this streamliner in 1939. The powerplant was an early Ford V-8 twenty-one-stud flathead, with milled heads, Harman camshaft, and dual intake manifold and ignition made by the Spaldings. The car was big and heavy, and, because it ran on gasoline with minimal speed modifications, it had too little horsepower to make it perform well. In spite of its handicaps, it managed a run of 128.75mph on October 29 at Rosamond Dry Lake. The frame was made of channel iron bought at a junkyard, the axles were Ford with transverse leaf springs, and the body was sheet steel. While the brothers were in the military service during WWII, their parents gave the car to the scrap drive. The Spaldings were members of the Mobilers Club of SCTA.
Eldon Snapp photo

was used by the SCTA from May 1938 until June 1940 when J. Otto Crocker became the timer. At that time the SCTA switched to Crocker's timing system.

Street Racing

When the racers weren't at the dry lakes, which was most of the time, actually, as each timing association usually ran from three to six lakes meets each summer, they could be found at any of several hangouts in the Los Angeles area. Two of the most popular places were The Twin Barrels, "Headquarters of Club Muroc," at 7227 Beverly Boulevard and The Frying Pan, "Where the Race Gang Hangs Out—See Our Collection of Lakes Photos," 1164 South La Brea.

These and other gathering places served food and provided a great place to see one's friends and bench race, but they also functioned as the planning areas for street racing. If one couldn't drum up a race at one eatery, he could drive to one of the others and find someone willing to "try it out."

In contrast to the impromptu races, which could happen anyplace two cars found themselves side by side, the races organized at the various car club hang-outs were serious affairs—quite often with money riding on the outcome. Occasionally races were for "pink slips," and the car itself changed hands after a defeat. The California vehicle registration system used a white slip when the car was financed and owned by the bank, but the real ownership title was pink. Obviously it wouldn't pay to race for white slips, but if you could win the pink slip you owned the car.

The most popular race sites were Sepulveda Boulevard just south of San Fernando Road, alongside the Van Norman Dam and reservoir; Lincoln Boulevard just west of Sepulveda and next to Mines Field (which became Los Angeles International Airport); Foothill Boulevard near the Santa Anita horse-race track in Arcadia; Glenoaks Boulevard just west of the Burbank city limits (the Burbank police couldn't touch the racers and the L.A. police had to come from the Van Nuys substation), and Peck Road in El Monte. There were other locations, but these were prime time, with straight, level, smooth surfaces and no cross traffic.

Although illegal, racing on these sites was reasonably safe. The absence of cross traffic and a late night rendezvous when there was little or no traffic

When the SCTA started running lakes meets in 1938, clubs took turns providing crews and cars for safety patrol to prevent activity that would threaten the safety of the members and spectators. This 1936 Ford convertible, almost a new car at the time, was a Road Runners Club car, and that's Eldon Snapp (his photos appear throughout this book) sitting on the back of the front seat. *Author collection*

Ralph Schenck's beautiful "Golden Submarine"-type streamliner made its debut at the May 19, 1940, SCTA meet at Harper Dry Lake. A Chevy four with an Olds 3-Port head provided the power. The June 30 SCTA *Racing News* stated, "The car itself is an enclosed cockpit job of aircraft type construction and an aluminum body." Schenck's car achieved 118.57mph in its initial dry lakes appearance.
Eldon Snapp photo

eliminated a large part of the danger. But street racing at other sites and at other times of day could be extremely hazardous.

Phil Weiand, noted designer and manufacturer of speed equipment, became a paraplegic because of a street racing accident in the 1930s. His car, a hopped up Model T Ford, was approaching a curve when his passenger, panicked that Phil might not negotiate the curve, grabbed the centrally-located parking brake handle, throwing the roadster out of control. They were both thrown out when the car flipped.

A Simpler Time

During WWII racing of all kinds was put on hold. There were more important things to occupy the time and minds of young men. Gas rationing and tire rationing didn't allow this sort of activity even if the boys had the time to do it.

Before the war, Wally Parks and Eldon Snapp produced the SCTA monthly newsletter, a mimeographed bulletin of four, six, or eight pages depending on the amount of club business and news to be published. The SCTA *Racing News*, as it was called, was five cents a copy but was mailed to all SCTA members.

When Parks and Snapp went off to war, Veda Orr took over publication of the *Racing News* and filled the void left in the lives of dry lakes racers. The newsletters published from 1943 to 1945 were filled with letters from SCTA members writing from Europe, North Africa, and the Pacific Theater of operations; all maintaining their ties with their chosen hobby and their racing buddies. And it was obvious that these guys were eager to get home and build a car if they hadn't already, or race the one they left behind.

Going to the dry lakes in the 1930s (and to some degree, after WWII) was like having our own fraternity

or country club. These were eagerly anticipated events, and we made every effort to not miss one. After a while you got to know everybody, and even if you weren't on a first-name basis with the hot-shoes, you knew who they were and could recognize them instantly. If you wanted to be a competitor, you joined one of the clubs that were part of the SCTA.

I was an outsider in those days. I had a '39 Merc sedan which had an Edelbrock "slingshot" dual manifold on the engine but nothing else. In 1941, while working the swing shift at Lockheed Aircraft, I met Will Donovan and Fred "Tiger" Baymiller who worked in the same plant area that I did. Fred was a member of the Bungholers Club and Will belonged to the Centuries—both SCTA affiliates.

They were my pipeline to what was going on in southern California racing (today we call it "networking"), and they would let me know when and where the next meet was to be held. The swing shift got off at 12:30 A.M., unless we worked overtime. After leaving work Saturday night (Sunday morning, actually) I would go home, change clothes, pick up my buddies Bill and Charlie Faris, Ray Charbonneau, and sometimes Clark Stone and Gene Savant, and we'd head for the desert in my Merc.

Leaving Burbank, where we all lived, about two or three in the morning we had time to eat breakfast in Palmdale or Lancaster and then head east to the lakebed in daylight. We'd stay on the lakebed until mid-Sunday afternoon or until they stopped running cars, drive home, and after I dropped my pals off at their homes I'd wash the Merc, take a shower, put on my good clothes and head for the Hollywood Palladium to see whatever big band was playing there.

This meant that I would have been up from Saturday morning until past midnight on Sunday, but as I

Ernie McAfee built this springless streamliner—powered by a Winfield-flathead-equipped Model B Ford four—and became the 1938 SCTA season champion. Ernie's best time, set at the last SCTA meet in 1938, was 137.41mph. McAfee sold the car to Karl Orr at the end of the season, and Karl installed another Model B Ford engine but equipped with a Cragar ohv cylinder head. Ernie was a member of the Road Runners Club; Karl belonged to the Albata Club. *Eldon Snapp photo*

Between the large number of competitors and the tremendous number of spectators, the crowd at dry lakes meets was sometimes unmanageable. This is a scene from the mid-1930s. That almost-new 1934 Ford roadster is sitting in front of a Pratt & Whitney engine crate which is being used for the timer's (Walter Nass) desk. Ted Cannon can be seen behind the roadster's front wheel, back to camera, wearing a Throttlers Club coverall. Walter Nass, wearing a hat, is at the top of the photo. *Walter Nass collection photo*

was nineteen at the time, and in excellent physical condition, I made the most of the one day a week I had off.

In those days the bands I usually saw were Tommy or Jimmy Dorsey, Harry James, Woody Herman, Gene Krupa, or Glenn Miller. Stan Kenton was a bit far out for the Palladium then, and he had a good gig going at the Rendezvous Ballroom on the Balboa peninsula in Newport Beach anyway.

The black bands, such as Count Basie, Duke Ellington, Cab Calloway, and Earl Hines, weren't hired to play at the Palladium. I think it likely had something to do with a Los Angeles city ordinance that allowed black patrons to attend if there was black entertainment on the stage. If we wanted to see these bands we went to the Trianon, Meadowbrook, or Ocean Park Pier ballrooms.

Looking back on my dry lakes experience before

the war, bigotry or other social stigmas just didn't exist there. It wasn't a case of being politically or socially correct, it was simply a non-issue.

Many Japanese boys and a few blacks were competitors—Yam and Harry Oka, Frank Morimoto, Danny Sakai, and Mel Leighton's names come quickly to mind—and there was no racial conflict. You were judged by your car, not your color. If you had a fast car, you were deemed okay. If you had a really fast car, you were somebody to know, and it didn't make any difference where you came from. On the other hand, if your car was a dog, you were ignored—or maybe helped if you were already a friend.

Those were great times and growing up in this environment was a great experience. We were enjoying the best life had to offer a car nut and, unfortunately, I don't think we really appreciated it as we should have.

A 1932 photo of what we believe was the first speed shop in California, if not the nation. It was owned by Lee Chapel and located at 3263 San Fernando Road in Los Angeles. The shop shared space with a junkyard office. In 1933, Chapel moved his shop to 4557 Alhambra Avenue, Los Angeles. It remained at that location until 1937 when Lee closed the shop to spend two years touring the country with a midget race car. In 1939, he opened a speed shop at 1143 East 14th Street in Oakland, California. Chapel's 1924 Chevy four roadster, at the right in this photo, with an Olds 3-Port head was timed at 111mph at Muroc Dry Lake in 1930.

Jack Lehman, of the SCTA Albata Club, stops at the timing stand to have his time (123.96) written on his entry sticker by the official. It was June 14, 1942, and this beautiful, red modified, which displayed more chrome than ordinarily seen at a dry lakes meet, would later be owned by Doug Caruthers, LeRoy Neumayer, and Art Chrisman—who still owns the car. *Author photo*

Marvin Lee's 2-Port Riley-powered '29 Model A roadster had a fabric bellypan, rear deck cover, and tonneau cover over the cockpit—all painted silver to match the body color. Unfortunately, a fuel leak deposited fuel in the canvas bellypan and that, combined with a hot exhaust pipe, set the car on fire. While spectators watched—none had a fire extinguisher—the car burned to the ground.
Eldon Snapp photo

A member of the Glendale Sidewinders Club has attracted the attention of one of Glendale's "finest," and they've stopped on North Brand Boulevard, to discuss their differences. It's in the late 1930s, and the old Pacific Electric tracks are still in use, proving that the Los Angeles area really did have a public transportation system.
Tom Medley collection

This roadster carried a full custom body. Gene Von Arx, of the SCTA Outriders Club built the frame, using two early Chevrolet frames to utilize the frame kick-ups so the rails could sit lower. Ford axles were used front and rear, but the typical Ford transverse leaf springs were replaced by four semi-elliptic springs. The engine was a flathead Ford V-8 with a Riley overhead valve conversion fed by two Chandler-Groves carburetors. Gene Von Arx, Sr., who had worked at the Walter M. Murphy coach-builders and the Don Lee Cadillac custom shop, built the roadster body for his son. The body material is steel and the senior Von Arx designed the car as he went along. The front wheel fenders are attached to the backing plate on the inside and the spindle on the outside. The top and upholstery (the latter, Lincoln Bronze leather) was made by two men who worked in the California Metal Shaping shop in Los Angeles. The 3100lb roadster rode on a 94in wheelbase, and the black lacquer was nicely set off by the chrome grille bars made from half-round naval brass extrusions. Von Arx completed his car in 1939.
Gene Von Arx photo

Left, Harper Dry Lake July 23, 1939. A typical line of cars waiting to "run the traps." Car 213 is Road Ramblers club member Horace Achterman's Edmunds-equipped '34 V-8 roadster, car 54 is Road Runners club member Orville "Snuffy" Welchel's two-port Riley modified, and 204 is the Hornets Club Lockwood-Tyler Chevy four with Olds three-port head. Number 102 wasn't listed in the program.
Gus Rollins photo

Walter Nass and his timing crew are safely ensconced in the bed of a 1-1/2-ton dump truck, which puts them above the crowd for good vision, and out of harm's way if a driver loses control of his car. The disc (see text) has space for the entrant's name, car club, car number, time, and speed. Not visible here are the circumferential graduations into which the punch will set the time for a speed calculation. These photos were taken on May 15, 1938, at the first-ever SCTA meet, held at Muroc Dry Lake.
Walter Nass collection

Regg and Dolores Schlemmer, in Tom McIntire's 1931 Model A Ford, arrive at Muroc on April 30, 1933 for a run through the Muroc Racing Association timer. After removing fenders, windshield, lights, luggage, and spare tire, the Winfield-equipped (Yellow head and downdraft carburetor) roadster ran a flat 100mph. In addition to the Winfield-equipped engine, Tom had added Packard wheels, special hood sides with vent doors, and a Ruckstell Dual High transmission.
Tom McIntire photo/Don Montgomery collection

Below, Arnold Birner, of the SCTA Bungholers Club, ran this modified with a Riley four-port ohv conversion on a B block. At the May 17, 1942, meet he clocked 124.65mph, and at the June 14, 1942, meet he turned 125.69mph.
Vince Cimino photo/author collection

CHAPTER 2

The Model T Ford

*Created as a car for the masses,
it became a car for the racers.*

Twenty year-old Bob Estes was about ready for the 10:00 P.M. closing of the Union gas station where he worked—the northeast corner of Pico and Sepulveda in west Los Angeles—when a sleek, black Packard Convertible Coupe drove up to the gas pumps. Behind the wheel was Clark Gable, even then (spring of 1933) one of the top movie idols and soon to become the greatest box office draw of his era.

While Bob filled the Packard's tank, Gable noticed a shiny black '25 Ford Model T roadster parked beside the station office, and remarked "I see we both like black cars." The T was Estes' pride and joy and, typical of car nuts, he kept the car spotless and in perfect running order.

Estes replied "Yes, but it's too bad your Packard won't go like that T."

"What?" then, "Can I take a look at it?"

"Sure, go ahead."

Then Gable said, "Would you start it up?"

"Sure, I'm about to close the station, and I always start it before I close to get the oil warmed up before I take it on the road."

Estes and Gable talked a bit, and Gable then said, "Do you really think your car is faster than my Packard?" To which Estes replied, "Well, put it out on the street and we'll run between here and Santa Monica [Boulevard] and we'll find out. We have to bet a little money, like five bucks, so just wait while I turn off the [station] lights."

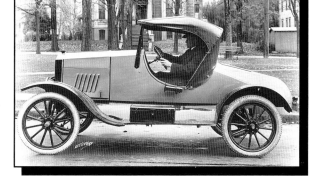

As Bob put it while relating the story, "I cleaned his clock in a hurry, and after we got to Santa Monica I suggested, for another five bucks, that we go the other direction. And I beat him again."

A few days later actress Carole Lombard came into the station and said she wanted to buy Bob's T to give Gable for his birthday, explaining, "Clark has talked about nothing but that car for two days." Bob had owned the T for about four years at that point, and it was finally fixed up and running to suit him, and he was in no mood to sell it. When Miss Lombard was informed of this she raised the offer, and after still being rebuffed asked if she could copy it. Bob said, "Sure, why not, but you can't take it away from the station." A few days later two men came to the station to measure the car and take photos.

A duplicate was made, but Estes remembers it as being a disaster; not at all like his T. Estes' Model T Ford was equipped with a Frontenac SR rocker-arm ohv cylinder head, single Winfield downdraft carburetor, and a crankshaft from a 1922 Wills Sainte Claire V-8 adapted to fit the Model T block. This not only provided a tremendous increase in crankshaft strength and stiffness but allowed for full oil pressure to the main and rods. A Rocky Mountain three-speed transmission was fitted behind the stock T two-speed transmission, and a Ruckstell two-speed rear axle had been installed.

The Maxwell body (not the Maxwell car company) for the Model T Ford was one of the many sporty styles available in 1919. The body, and a matching radiator, bolted onto the Ford frame using the same attaching holes as a stock body. The driver of this sporty model probably entered from the passenger side rather than climb over the running-board-mounted tool box, ah-ooga horn, and the no-door body side. *Jarvis Erickson collection*

Opposite page, Roy "Multy" Aldrich, long-time member of the Bonneville Nationals technical Committee, built this Model T roadster in the 1930s. The frame, for which Roy paid $1.00, is from a 1913 model. The engine, of unknown year, has a Rajo ohv set-up with twin Stromberg carburetors, and Nash-derived twin ignition driven from the 1925 Chevy generator via Durant gears. The hood, body, and rear deck all came from different cars. Roy drove it from his home in Mentone, California, to Wendover, Utah—a round trip of about 1,300 miles—for the speed trials, and ran it through the traps once, at 85.06mph. Multy typifies the spirit of the "Salt Bears" who came to the flats each year, camping out in tents to save the expense of motel rooms. *Author photo*

INDIANAPOLIS MOTOR SPEEDWAY ANNUAL 500 MILE RACE 1924
Driver FRED S. HARDER. Car FORD.
KIRKPATRICK PHOTO # 6624.
619 W. WASH ST.

PEUGEOT TYPE CYLINDER HEADS FOR FORDS

16 OVERHEAD VALVES

1918

PATENTED
MANUFACTURED BY

THE LAUREL MOTORS CORPORATION, ANDERSON, INDIANA

Successors to ROOF AUTO SPECIALTY COMPANY

~~$85.00 F.O.B.~~
$100.00 F. O. B.

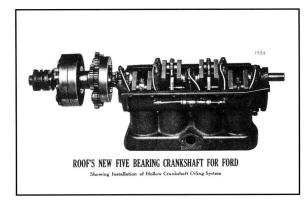

ROOF'S NEW FIVE BEARING CRANKSHAFT FOR FORD
Showing Installation of Hollow Crankshaft Oiling System

The T, stripped of fenders, bumpers, running boards and top had been run a few years earlier at Muroc Dry Lake at more than 100mph so Bob knew what he was doing when he had challenged Gable's Packard.

Estes may not be your typical youth of the 1930s, but he did display the entrepreneurial spirit prevailing in some young men of the Depression era. Within two years Estes had left his job with Union and had bought two Tide Water Associated stations—the first at Third and Serrano, the second at Eighth and Western. He built the business at these two stations to the point where he had the two highest volume Associated stations in the Los Angeles area. Then Associated pulled

Top, a 1918 advertisement for the Robert Roof "Peugeot Type" sixteen-valve head for the Ford Model T. Roof's designs were marketed under the name Laurel Motors Corporation, Anderson, Indiana, successors to Roof Auto Specialty Company. The price on this ohv head conversion was $100 F.O.B

Bottom far left, the Wills Sainte Claire V-8 crankshaft fitted to Bob Estes' Model T engine. Because the bore-centers of the Wills engine didn't line up with the centers of the Model T engine, the crank throws had to be ground off-center to place the rods in line with the T cylinders. The crank throws were ground slightly undersize to accommodate the T rods, and being ground only to the width of the T rod, it kept them in alignment with the bore centers. *Bob Estes photo*

Bottom left, after developing both eight- and sixteen-valve cylinder heads for the Model T, Robert Roof built this special crankshaft to run in the three original Ford main bearings with the addition of two auxiliary main bearings. A 1924 circular sent by the Robert Roof company "to you and some other well-known racing drivers" advertised the new five main-bearing, full lubricated crankshafts for the Model T engine at $125 each. "Providing we get an acceptance from you on this proposition and a deposit of $25 as a guarantee that the equipment will be taken—delivery in approximately fifty to seventy-five days, or in ample time for installation in your car before the season opens." The flier went on to say "There's no profit for us in this proposition whatever . . . but we are making the above proposition, believing it will be an aid generally to the racing parts department of our business."

Oppposite page, three Fords ran in the 1924 Indianapolis 500, all entered by the Barber-Warnock Ford dealership in Indianapolis. All three ran double overhead camshaft Frontenac cylinder heads (unlike the 1923 entry which had an overhead valve Fronty engine), and they finished 14th (Bill Hunt), 16th (Alfred E. Moss—father of Stirling Moss), and 17th (Fred Harder). The exhaust and intake sides (with a Winfield Model V updraft carburetor) of the Harder entry is shown. *Indy 500 photo, Indianapolis Motor Speedway Corp.*

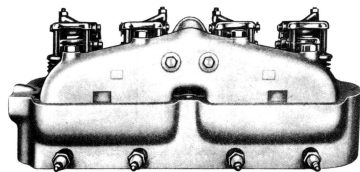
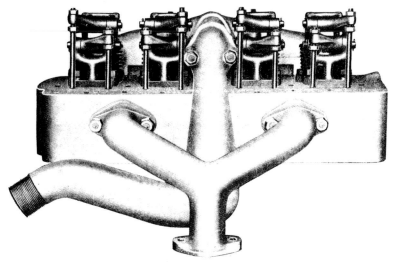
By 1919, the Roof-designed sixteen-valve Laurel Motors head had new intake and exhaust manifolding. The four-port exhaust was retained, but fed to a crossover pipe placed next to the intake for the two ports—a system for heating the intake mixture to ensure smooth running at low speeds and increased fuel mileage.

the plug and assumed ownership and control of all their stations in the area. Within a year they were all gone, victims of poor management.

On the other hand, this budding young businessman was on the wrong side of the law much of the time because of his driving habits—that is, go as fast as you can whenever you can—and his involvement in street racing. The hopped up T, in addition to providing daily transportation, was the ideal tool to practice his race-whenever-you-can philosophy.

It finally reached the point where he was followed by the police almost everywhere he drove. He knew this impasse would come to a head, so Estes invited the confrontation by letting the word out that he always closed his station at 10:00 P.M. and would be going up Pico Boulevard and the police were welcome to catch him—if they could.

One night he saw the police cruise by his station several times so he thought this was the night they would be waiting for him. He called his girlfriend, Elaine Brownley, and said "If you hear sirens, open the garage door, I'm coming in."

In a few days before this "meeting" Bob had fitted an amber lens in the right spotlight on the T, and installed a blue light bulb behind it. The combination gave a red glow almost as bright as the red lights used by the police.

When Estes left the station that night, he hadn't gone more than a few blocks when he saw red lights in his rear view mirror. Bob gunned it and they took off. Estes knew all the streets in the area, perhaps as well or better than the police, and at the corner of Pico and Hauser there was always water on the pavement.

With the sirens behind him, and the red light on his car, what few motorists were out moved out of his way, thinking he was one of the chasers rather than the chasee. Bob took the corner at Hauser and Pico in fine style, having practiced it many times (it was on the way to his girlfriend's house), but one of the cycles slipped on the wet pavement and the officer went over the curb and into a store front, putting him in the hospital. The other went straight ahead, and Bob was able to get to Elaine's house where she had the garage doors open and he scooted in, quickly closing the doors behind him.

That wasn't quite the end of the episode, however. He left the T in Elaine's garage for about a week before finally taking it home, but less than a month later Bob was cornered by the cops, hit on the head with a truncheon, and knocked unconscious before being taken to jail. When he appeared in court the judge confiscated his car "to be sold to keep this menace off the streets" and the money from the sale (Bob remembers it as a fraction of the car's worth) was given to Estes.

What made Bob's court appearance look really bad was that he, as was his usual nightly practice, had a bag full of cash from the station's cash register. In spite of the fact that he was wearing his gas station uniform, with his name on the front, the police insisted he had stolen the money. In Depression-era Los Angeles, Bob never left money in the station overnight, but this time it added to his troubles rather than eliminating them.

Estes' experiences as he related them to me for this book probably weren't typical of southern California, but his car was. This was a time when those who liked cars, but couldn't afford Packards, Duesenbergs, Lincolns, or Cadillacs, had to improvise. And what better car could they pick than the Model T Ford?

Model Ts were plentiful and cheap, and most speed equipment that was available was made for the Ford engine. All through the 1920s and well into the 1930s, the Model T engine was a favorite with both track racers and street racers.

Both George Riley and Waukasha-Ricardo made high compression (about 6:1 then) flat heads for the T, and overhead-valve heads were available from Rajo (an acronym for Racine, Wisconsin, where they were made, and Joe Jagersberger, who made them); Frontenac (two of the three Chevrolet brothers, Arthur and Louis), made in Indianapolis, Indiana; Robert Roof, in Ander-son, Indiana, who was probably the real pioneer in Model T Ford racing equipment; and Akron "C," named for the city in which the head was made.

The Akron head may well be the most interesting design of all the overhead valve conversions—the valve actuation was certainly unique. The "C" in the designation indicates the inclusion of eight seamless steel tubes, bent in the shape of a lying-down C.

One end of each tube was directly over the upper end of a pushrod, the other end of the C-shaped tube was directly over a valve. Inside these tubes were ball bearings, the outer diameter of each a sliding fit to the inside of the tubing. As the pushrod, raised by the cam lobe, moved the nearest ball bearing it, in turn, moved the line of bearings leading to the valve tip. The idea worked much better in theory than it did in practice, and the Akron C-Head had a short commercial life.

Bob Estes' 1925 Model T roadster had some of the usual additions—Hartford friction shock absorbers, and S & M spotlights— plus a few items unique to this car. The hand-operated pressure pump, on the outside of the driver's door, provided fuel tank pressure to ensure fuel flow. The all-black car had white piping around the edges of the top and that, along with the nickel-plated windshield, radiator, and spotlights, was the only relief from the all-black look. Estes fitted Rocky Mountain external cable-operated contracting brakes on the rear wheels to augment the single stock brake band in the transmission. A Rocky Mountain three-speed transmission was fitted behind the T two-speed.
Bob Estes photo

This ohv—four intake, four exhaust—Frontenac head is the work of C.W. Van Ranst, an engineer who is perhaps better remembered for the front-wheel drive systems of L-29 Cords, Ruxtons, and the 1931 Packard experimental fwd. This particular engine is set up with twin Zenith carburetors and a special water pump. In 1923, L.L. Corum, driving a Barber-Warnock-entered Fronty T with a similar engine, finished fifth overall in the Indianapolis 500 averaging 82.58mph. *Author photo, Harrah's Auto Collection.*

Bottom left, Frontenac dohc, eight-valve head on a 1922 Model T block, also has Fronty oil and water pumps, Bosch magneto, Fronty flywheel & clutch, and twin Winfield model S carburetors. The Frontenac twin-cam heads were designed by a Japanese-American named James Sakayama and had four 49mm (1.93) diameter valves per cylinder, placed at 60 degrees from intake to exhaust included angle, and chain cam drive. *Author photo, Harrah's Automobile Collection.*

Bottom right, Rajo cylinder heads got their name from Racine, Wisconsin, where they were made, and Joe Jagersburger, the man who made them. This one, on a 1922 Model T block, is the eight-valve design, with a Delco distributor, Apco water pump, Faithful Oiler, and Zenith carburetor. The cast-iron manifold includes both the two-port intake system and the four-port exhaust headers. These conversions, and the Fronty rocker-arm heads, were sold by the thousands to racers and those who simply wanted a faster street car, but couldn't afford Duesenbergs, Packards, etc. *Author photo, Harrah's Automobile Collection*

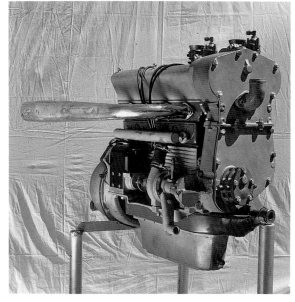

Ed Winfield

Ed Winfield's early fame came from his carburetors, but his later, and more lasting fame came from his racing camshaft grinds. Every cam grinder in the business today owes a debt of gratitude to Winfield; he not only led the way, he was the first with the best. He was the pioneer in racing camshaft design. He was also a pioneer in innovative ideas for coaxing more power from an engine and more speed from the car.

One episode is typical of Winfield thinking. Because of the firing order of a Model T (1-2-4-3) combined with the two-port intake system, number one and four each got a full charge of fuel every time, but two and three received only partial filling of the compression chamber. A stock Model T crankshaft has a 180-degree crankshaft with the two center throws up when the end throws are down.

Winfield made a billet crank with numbers one and two up and numbers three and four down. He slso redesigned the camshaft so that the firing order was 1-3-2-4, and this separated each intake pulse so that all cylinders were fueled equally. It did, however, create balancing problems and Winfield admitted "it had a little vibration."

But did it go! Running one of his own Winfield flatheads, his own cam grind, the "two-up, two-down" crankshaft, and his own carburetors, and driving the car himself, Winfield beat a field of overhead valve and overhead cam engines, including Frontenac and Miller at Ascot Speedway in January 1928. Arthur Chevrolet, who was one of the defeated driving a Fronty T, said, "I saw it, but I still don't believe it."

A Model T race car, the Barber-Warnock entry driven by L.L. Corum, finished fifth in the 1923 Indianapolis 500. Its engine was equipped with a Frontenac SR overhead valve set-up and a Winfield carburetor. For the 1924 Indy 500 the same car had a double overhead camshaft Fronty. Bill Hunt drove it, and was flagged off the track at 191 laps while running in fourteenth place.

The four cars ahead of Corum's Model T in 1923 were all Millers, and in 1924—the race won by L.L. Corum in a Duesenberg—the only cars ahead of Hunt were two Duesenbergs and eleven Millers.

The prodigious amount of racing equipment made for the Model T Ford engine included flathead, overhead valve, single overhead camshaft and double overhead camshaft cylinder heads, reground camshafts, special connecting rods, counter-balanced crankshafts (including some five main-bearing conversions), pistons, clutches, carburetors, pressure oiling systems, and ignitions—really anything one could want or need to go racing or to create a very rapid street usable car.

The vast majority of this equipment was developed in the Midwest, primarily around the Indianapolis area, for out-and-out racing cars. The fact that customers soon started buying racing equipment to install on cars that were street-driven and would never see a race track, except the parking lot, probably surprised the speed equipment manufacturers. However, anyone ca-

Some lucky kid, between the ages of eleven and fifteen, won this snappy Model T Ford Speedster (body by Bub, Milwaukee, Wisconsin) in 1923. It was a promotional tie-in between the California State Fair and the *Sacramento Union* newspaper. It's unknown if the dog was part of the prize or was simply being used to promote the contest.
 Jarvis Erickson Collection.

pable of creating this equipment had to be resourceful, so it wasn't long before they took advantage of this bonanza and began advertising in both trade and racing publications for milder-tuned race car parts for your sports model.

It wasn't difficult to adapt racing equipment to street use. A little less cam timing, a little lower compression ratio, maybe a single carburetor instead of two, a little heavier flywheel for smoother engine operation, and soon you had an engine that produced more than twice the stock horsepower, but was tractable enough for easy driving.

Concurrently with the advent of racing equipment for Ford, Chevrolet, and Dodge cars (there was equipment made for other makes, but these were the Big Three in those days), a large business developed in building speedster-type bodies to fit these frames.

These were ultrasimple bodies with few creature comforts or other amenities, but they enabled the impecunious driver to emulate the factory-built speedsters. And, with the lighter weight of these special bodies, and a bit better aerodynamics, a Ford Speedster with a hopped-up engine was a pretty fast car; many of them were able to top 100mph which, in the 1920s and '30s was a tremendous feat.

If one wanted to make an issue of who was first and did the most in the race to make the Model T into everyman's race or sports car, the nod would have to go to states east of the Mississippi River. I've seen advertisements for fourteen different (and this is by no means all of them, I'm sure) speedster-type bodies manufactured between 1915 and 1925, and they were made in Chicago, Illinois; Indianapolis, Indiana; Lexington, Owensboro, and Louisville, Kentucky; and New York City.

Above, Johnny Walker, of the SCTA Albata Club, built the body for his streamliner by stretching doped fabric over a metal framework. The engine, mounted behind the driver, is a Model T Ford equipped with a George Riley two-spark-plug-per-cylinder flathead. The car later ran a Winfield-equipped Model B engine. *Vince Cimino photo*

Bob Estes and his father, at Muroc Dry Lake in about 1930. This is the car in which he defeated Clark Gable in an impromptu race on Sepulveda Boulevard a few years later (see text). The '25 T roadster had a Frontenac SR ohv cylinder head, a single Winfield downdraft carburetor, and a crankshaft from a Wills Sainte Claire V-8 adapted to the T block. A Rocky Mountain three-speed transmission and a Ruckstell two-speed rear axle made the car both faster and easier to drive. Bob topped 107mph at Muroc, with fenders, lights, and windshield removed. *Bob Estes collection*

Not a happy way to go home. The roadster was made up from an assortment of parts (typical for the era)—Model T engine with a model BB Rajo cylinder head (which had four exhaust ports on the left side) and what looks like a Frontenac SR valve cover. The BB Rajo could be set up with either single or dual ignition. The car also has a Whippet radiator, Franklin tubular front axle, and 18in wire wheels. A hand pressure pump can be seen on the driver's door below the rear axle and brake assembly resting across the cockpit. The tow car is a 1935 Ford sedan. *Walter Nass collection*

Genuine racing equipment for the T engine was made in Peoria, Chicago, and Rantoul, Illinois; Indianapolis, Anderson, and Muncie, Indiana; Racine, Milwaukee, and Waukesha, Wisconsin; Dayton and Akron, Ohio; Saginaw, Michigan; Philadelphia, Pennsylvania; Clarinda, Iowa, and New York City. George Riley of Los Angeles made a device called the "Multilift" to increase valve lift in Model T engines, Ruckstell Mfg. Co. in Berkeley made two-speed axles for the T, and the W.O. Thompson Co. in Pasadena, California, made a Model T engine oiling system. Those three were about the extent of Model T Ford performance items made on the West Coast before 1920.

The Model T Ford gained a reputation as a "tin lizzie" and worse—a car that Ford's competitors, and many of the driving public, put down as worthless. Some even said that FORD was simply an acronym for Fix Or Repair Daily.

In spite of the jokes made about the Model T Fords, it was one of the most important automotive de-velopments in the world. Ts put the masses on wheels (considering traffic today, there are those who argue that Henry Ford was wrong), and the model became the backbone of early American racing.

The first commercially available racing equipment to hop-up a production car was made for the Model T, and the cars were used successfully for all types of racing—from Indianapolis to board tracks to dirt tracks to dry lakes and street racing. In 1923, a modified Ford Model T finished fourteenth in the first 24 Hours of Le Mans, in France. That car had over-head valves in a head designed and built by Montier, in Paris. It had a single intake port on the left, and three exhaust ports on the right, and the engine drove through a four-speed French-made transmission. Not all Ford speed equipment was made in California, or even in America.

The Model T may well have been created as a car for the masses, but it became a car for the racers.

Ruckstell 2 Speed Axle

The Ruckstell Equipped Ford

is the only Light Weight American Car with

FOUR FORWARD SPEEDS

Proved in Service

By 6000 enthusiastic owners in the State of California alone.

The installation of the *Ruckstell Axle* unit, as an integral part of the Ford car, in no way alters nor affects any rotating part of the Ford mechanism—such installation being the equivalent of factory construction.

Order through your Ford Dealer.   No agents or distributors solicited.

$62.40

F. O. B. Berkeley, California, Tax paid.

RUCKSTELL SALES & MFG. CO.

819 Snyder Ave., Berkeley, Cal.

Ruckstell's two-speed rear axle was a valuable asset for overcoming the handicap of the Model T two-speed transmission. Many modified Ts were equipped with this unit. The *Ford Owner and Dealer* magazine was one of the best places to promote these parts.

CHAPTER 3

Models A, B, and C Fords

Eight for show, Four for go.

If bumper stickers had been popular in the immediate post-WWII era, I'm sure we would have seen them carrying the above message. The four-cylinder guys didn't care much for the V-8 crowd, or their cars, and never missed a chance to rub some flathead V-8 driver's nose in it if they could.

I remember one night in 1946 when my buddies Ray Charbonneau and Charlie Faris were in Larry and Carl's Pasadena, California, drive-in. They were sitting in Ray's 1929 Model A roadster; a really grungy-looking car that, except for the '40 Ford disc wheels and new tires (6.00x16 and 7.00x16), looked like a junkyard fugitive. The dark blue paint, brushed on probably five or more years earlier, was burned off the top of the hood, the result of an engine fire one night out on the Mint Canyon Road. There was no upholstery, and the only instrumentation was a tachometer and an oil pressure gauge; both hung on wires from the cowl.

Underneath the jalopy-look it was a different story. Hydraulic brakes, from the same 1940 Ford which provided the wheels, had been fitted, and the engine was a Model B Ford with a 4-port Riley head, complete with Winfield camshaft, Mallory ignition, and a long manifold with four Stromberg Model 48 carburetors. The engine had been built by Mal Ord for a sprint car, and Ray had bought it from Bell Auto Parts, but had built the four-carb manifold himself. The car also had twin pipes, cylinders one and four to one side, two and three on the other.

More important, Ray's Riley had never lost a race. Those who have never seen a good-running four-banger come off the line just haven't seen acceleration (we're talking 1940s and '50s, not 1990s). At this point, Charbonneau hadn't run at the dry lakes because he didn't belong to a club.

While Ray and Charlie were eating their burgers and fries, a clean-looking '32 roadster backed into the slot next to them. The high-boy wasn't flashy, but it looked solid, sounded good, and was a very tidy and purposeful machine. A car that probably was a real runner. The two guys in the Deuce finished their coffee about the same time my friends finished their burgers, and the passenger in the other roadster leaned over and, with just a touch of humor in his voice, asked "Wanna try it out?"

Ray didn't need any more invitation than that, so he turned on his lights to attract the car hop, who came to retrieve her tray, and Ray said "You bet, let's go."

I need to digress a moment here. In those days the drive-in "wanna-bes" and "posers" had a ploy. These types had cars that were stock, or nearly so, but didn't want anyone to know it. So the gambit was to pull into a drive in, set the hand brake, depress the clutch, put the transmission in second gear, then let out the clutch just as the key was turned of. The combination of ignition off and the clutch dragging against the flywheel served to stop the engine very quickly. Now everyone knew that race cars had higher compression for more power and had light flywheels for quicker engine response, ergo if your engine stopped immediately you must be a racer.

Gene Savant in the Model B Winfield flathead-powered '29 A roadster he bought from Roger Blanche. Carter Covert is walking across the street in this 1941 shot taken on Verdugo Avenue in Burbank, California. A group of us were on our way to a street-race rendezvous. This roadster was one of those cars which came out of the gate as if shot from a cannon, and there weren't many cars that could stay with it for the first 300 yards. The engine was built up by Willie Utzmann, and Blanche had run it 117mph at the dry lakes as a member of the Glendale Sidewinders Club of the SCTA. Savant subsequently sold the car to Charlie Faris who ran it as a member of the SCTA Road Runners Club. *Author photo*

Opposite page, a Cragar ohv setup on a Ford B block in a Bonneville car. The Winfield SR carburetors are mounted on an over-the-counter cast-aluminum intake manifold. An auxiliary case on the front of the engine carries a drive to the Eisemann aircraft magneto just barely visible under the exhaust and to a water pump in front of the engine. The small tank at the right is a radiator catch-tank to keep radiator overflow from spilling onto the course. *Author photo*

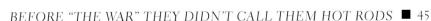

Jack McAfee, who would later gain fame road racing Ferraris and Porsches, ran this D.O. Hal-powered sprint car in the track and at the dry lakes with the SCTA Throttlers Club. He clocked 122.95mph in 1947 when this photo was taken at El Mirage Dry Lake. The Hal twin-cam cylinder head was mounted on a Ford Model B block and carried two Winfield downdraft carburetors. *Author photo*

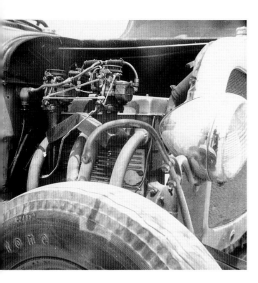

Above, one of the rare Murphy ohv conversions for the four-cylinder Ford Model A block, with two Stromberg carburetors sitting on a home-made intake manifold. The Murphy head, like the Miller-Schofield/ Cragar and the 2-Port Riley, had both intake and exhaust on the same side.
Gus Rollins photo

Right, June 30, 1940, Rollin White of the SCTA 90mph Club brought this Winfield flathead model B Ford—with a pair of Winfield carburetors—to Harper Dry Lake. Judging from the photo, White ran the car with the hood's top and left side, but without the right side so it wouldn't interfere with the dry lakes exhaust headers.
Edelbrock collection

Opposite page, one of the best-looking, as well as one of the fastest, ohv conversions for the Ford Model A, B, and C was the 4-Port Riley. The Riley design was an F-head, meaning the intake valves were in the head (eight, in this case, as the pushrods activated forked rocker arms and there were two small intake valves per cylinder) and the stock exhaust valves in the block were used. This engine, with what looks like a Wico magneto, and two Winfield carburetors on a log-type manifold, has a set of headers that have been used on a flathead A, B, and C as the header flanges are bolted to a long plate which has plugs (between cylinders 1 and 2 and 3 and 4) to cover the stock intake ports.
Author photo

Well, Ray didn't need to go through that routine because his engine had about 10:1 compression ratio, and the flywheel was turned down so much it barely had metal to hold the starter ring gear. As soon as the car hop had picked up her tray, Ray hit the starter button and all hell broke loose. He goosed the throttle and the WAP, WAP of those twin pipes caused every head in the drive-in to spin around. The eyebrows on the pair in the '32 arched a bit more, and they began to think this might be a real race after all.

They decided to "have it out" on Washington Boulevard, in east Los Angeles, about twenty minutes away. Once there, They squared off, decided on a slow rolling start, and were ready to go. Surprisingly not many spectators had followed them, which was unusual.

When each driver nailed it, the Riley led by a car length through first gear, but in second the V-8 caught up and they ran side by side to over 100mph. Both drivers were completely baffled at this point, because the V-8 had never lost a race either; here were two unbeaten cars that seemed to be completely equal. They turned around and started back the other direction and Ray missed the shift to second and lost not only the race but half the transmission.

Ray and Charlie limped home to Burbank with only high gear operable, using a lot of secondary streets to avoid stop signs or crowded thoroughfares. There were no freeways then, and it was a long and arduous trip home.

A few days later Ray and Charlie were back at Larry and Carl's, but without the Riley, and they ran into the '32 again. After introducing themselves, their racing adversary proved to be a known name in dry lakes racing, Randy Shinn, a member of the Road Runners Club of SCTA, who would finish number one in SCTA season championship points for 1946, and number two in 1947.

Randy asked them if they would consider joining the Road Runners. Charlie had a Winfield flathead Model B-powered '29 roadster at home in the garage, so they were both eager to join a good club. This later led to Charlie's brother Bill, myself, and Lute Eldridge also joining the Road Runners Club.

Above, a Riley 2-Port (a pre-WWII shot of Jack McGrath's engine) with the valve covers off shows the forked rocker arm set-up used with the eight intake valves in the head. The Riley 2-Port had the intake on the right, the 4-Port on the left. Jack has fitted a '32 Ford radiator shell on his '27 T-bodied roadster.
Bill Phy photo

Wes Cooper and Bob Hayes ran this Fargo 4-Port with the Glendale Sidewinders Club of the SCTA. The '27 T body featured a cast-aluminum grille and a hammered aluminum shell and hood, all made by Art Ingels. The best run for the car was at an SCTA meet on May 8, 1949, when the Lakester turned 142.18mph. (After the 1948 season the Roadster class was divided into stock body and Lakester—which included any roadster that was channeled or had full bellypan or custom work ahead of the firewall.)
Tom Medley collection

Enter the Model A

As I've already noted, engine speed modifications in the U.S. really began with the Ford Model T engines—the equipment made for track use but then migrating to the street. When the Model A Ford was introduced for the 1928 model year, speed merchants saw a quantum leap in both original specifications and in hop-up potential.

Engine displacement was greater in the Model A: 200.5ci compared to the T's 176.7 (the T had a 3.75x4.00in bore and stroke while the A measured 3.875x4.25in). The stock horsepower rating doubled to 40bhp rather than the T's 20bhp, and every moving component in the engine was stiffer and stronger. Model T main and rod bearings were 1.250in in diameter, but the new Model A had rods that measured 1.500in, and the mains were 1.625in in diameter.

Early racers thought they'd died and gone to heaven. The techniques used in hopping up the A were similar to those used on the T, but the beefier components offered a far greater, more reliable, potential than those artisans of speed had ever imagined.

When Ford Motor Company brought out the V-8 in 1932, which was to be a low-priced sport model with

plenty of speed, the company realized it couldn't forget the buyers who had supported the company through the Model T and Model A eras, consequently the Model B was introduced at the same time.

The B had the same body and trim as the V-8, but used a still further upgraded version of the Model A engine. Stock, it had ten more horsepower (50bhp now, instead of 40), but more important to the racers was the lower-end; rod bearing size was now 1.875in, and main bearings were 2.000in in diameter, the crankshaft was counterbalanced, and there was oil pressure to the main bearings. Enterprising hop-up artists drilled the crank to get pressure to the rod bearings, then sawed or ground off the rod dipper scoops (welding the holes shut) because they were no longer needed.

A further advantage to the racers was the fact that almost every piece of bolt-on speed equipment—cylinder heads, intake manifolds, ignitions, camshafts, and exhaust headers—that would fit the Model A could also be used on the B. Main and rod bearings were still poured babbit, but that didn't pose a problem and, in

Above, depending on which racing program you look at in 1939 this was either the Jack Stebles or the Hurst-Allen entry—both agree on the Winfield flathead Ford four engine however. The car's Bugatti radiator set it well apart from its competitors, at least visually. An SCTA Throttlers Club plate is plainly visible on the front. It would seem, also, that the exhaust was hidden under the car at some point in its life.
Vince Cimino and Mark Dees photo

Johnny Junkin's Cragar Ford four Modified at Muroc Dry Lake in the mid-1930s is typical of the cars that would be built well into the late 1940s for this class—ultra simple, ultra light, and as streamlined as it could be without being moved out of the Modified and into the Streamliner class. The barely visible Whippet radiator was one of the most popular items to be added to any Modified car.
Greg Sharp collection

Above, the 4-Port Riley Model B engine in Ray Charbonneau's '29 roadster (see text) was originally built by Mal Ord for a sprint car. Ray bought it from Bell Auto Parts for his roadster. The log intake manifold had been built for two Winfield Carburetors, but Ray reworked it to carry four Strombergs. Like most four-bangers it was a very strong engine up to about 5500rpm. On July 7, 1946, Ray ran the car on El Mirage Dry Lake at 115.23mph, and Randy Shinn—his adversary on Washington Boulevard—turned 119.52.
Charlie Faris photo

fact, it furnished a continuity that was probably appealing to most engine builders—at least they were familiar with the engine, because Model A experience could be carried over to the B.

In 1933, the Model C Ford engine was introduced, and was like the B except that it had steel exhaust valve inserts. This was the last of the Ford fours, and by the time the 1933 models came out, buyers were so infatuated with the V-8 that only a handful of four-cylinder Model Cs were sold.

The End of the Four-Cylinder Era

The choice of ready-made and over-the-counter available speed equipment for the four-cylinder Fords was staggering. Available Model T cylinders heads, for example, numbered at least a dozen each for flathead, overhead valve, and overhead camshaft designs, and those numbers almost doubled for the A, B, and C engine.

Not only were the "normal " flathead, ohv, and ohc heads produced, but odd configurations such as having a single overhead camshaft for the intake valves while retaining the stock (location—the cam lobes were reground for lift and timing) camshaft in the block for the exhaust valves. This resulted in having eight intake valves and eight exhaust valves. And then there was the

Top and left, July 19, 1942, Charles Beck, of the SCTA Centuries Club turned 131.96 in this Ford B Winfield-flathead streamliner. The car is the ex-Bob Rufi Chevy 'liner rebuilt after Bob's crash at Harper Dry Lake on November 17, 1940, and with a Model B Ford replacing the Rufi Chevy four. The chassis was almost identical to that run by Rufi in 1940, but the body received a different configuration when it was rebuilt after the wreck. The WWI Jenny wheel covers are still there, however. In the background of the profile photo is the Chuck Spurgin Chevy four roadster which turned 112.50 at this meet.
Author photos

Frontenac dohc "stagger-valve" head which had five ports on each side—with two intake and three exhaust ports on each side of the head.

Usually there were still eight valves for the conversions, but the Riley F head used eight intakes in the head (via forked rocker arms operated by each push

Right, Mark Craven's Fargo 4-Port Model B Ford engine in his 1929 Model A roadster in 1947. The four Stromberg carburetors are sitting on adapters to a log manifold made for four Winfield carburetors. Typically, a '32 Ford radiator shell has been adapted to the A. The driver grasps the end of the tow rope which is attached to the front frame cross tube. Top speed of the car in 1947 was 112.64mph.
Wally Wilson photo

Bottom, Ed Winfield, more noted for his carburetors and camshafts, also made cylinder heads. This one is an overhead valve conversion for the Model A, B, or C and has, naturally, a pair of Winfield carburetors. It is a cross-flow design with two intake ports on the left, and four exhaust ports on the right, with eight valves in a row.
Al Drake photo

rod) and four exhaust valves in the block. Some of the dohc designs were straightforward eight-valve (two per cylinder) and some were sixteen-valve designs. Most of the ohv heads for the four-cylinder Ford had the intake and exhaust ports on the same side; these designs were probably made for commercial use , but the more successful ohv conversions were cross-flow heads with the intake on one side and exhaust on the other.

The racers' ingenuity became strikingly obvious when they started adapting five-main-bearing crankshafts to the three-main A, B, or C block by bolting or welding a bearing web to support the additional bearings between cylinders one and two, and three and four.

This had also been done with Model T engines, but with the advent of the A it became far simpler to make the conversion. It wasn't necessary to build a completely new crankshaft because the local junkyard furnished anything you wanted—if you knew what to look for. The Buda diesel (models DA and DB), Leroy, Hercules, Scramm, and Waukesha four-cylinder engines all had five-main bearing crankshafts which would fit the Ford B engines with a minimum of machine work.

Some racers used 1936 Pontiac six-cylinder connecting rods, which had insert bearings and would fit the Model B crankshaft throw. When these were used, metal had to be ground from the side of the rod big-end to keep it from hitting the camshaft in the block. If a sohc or dohc head was used, it eliminated that problem because the camshaft(s) had moved "upstairs."

It was also determined by the hop-up guys that a 0.625in reamer could be run through the A or B valve lifter bore, and then adjustable lifters from other engines would fit. No need to get these replacement parts from the dealer's parts department, the local junkyard was a superb place to find parts that would work. It took time, and a diligent search, but it paid off. And the parts were cheap.

Finding speed equipment to bolt on to your Model A or B was no problem. By the time the hobby came to a temporary halt at the start of WWII, you could find replacement flatheads made by Acme, Duray, and Winfield. Overhead valve conversions were made by Alexander, Ambler, Cragar, Gemsa, McDowell, Miller-Schofield (which became Cragar), Moller, Murphy, Riley, Rutherford, Sparks, and Winfield.

For the really serious racer, single overhead camshaft conversions were made by Gemsa, Hal, McDowell, Miller, and Morales. Double overhead camshaft set-ups were available from Cragar, Gemsa, Hal, Frontenac, Dreyer, McDowell, Miller, and Lyons.

Ignition systems were furnished by Bosch, Scintilla, and Mallory, but some conversions from aircraft or marine units were made by the racers. Manifolds, of course, were readily available over the counter, although these components seemed to be favorites of the amateur fabricator. It was a fairly simple matter to make up your own exhaust headers and, from what was seen at the races, a great number of lakes racers made their own intake manifolds as well.

These owner-built, fabricated manifolds were the result of two factors: It was cheaper to build your own, and there was always the feeling that "I can do it better."

Even after the V-8 came out in 1932, the four-cylinder Fords remained popular with racers. This can be attributed to several factors—familiarity with existing components, resistance to change, availability of a large amount of existing speed equipment and, in some cases, stubborn loyalty to a known entity.

The puzzling fact that little bolt-on speed equipment was available for the V-8 until it had been in production for seven or eight years undoubtedly contributed to the four-cylinder engine's longevity as a viable racing powerplant.

As more speed equipment became available for the Ford V-8, the four bangers started to be replaced by the newer engine. Surprisingly, only a few manufacturers of four-cylinder equipment tried to make the change to building V-8 equipment—George Riley and Col. Alexander both made ohv heads for the Ford flathead V-8, and Art Sparks made a few flathead cylinder heads. Cam grinders and carburetor and ignition makers could easily adapt to the V-8 but I haven't found other manufacturers of heads who did.

The number of racers favoring the four-cylinder Fords continued to dwindle, but never did and never will fade out completely. There's something beautiful about these antique assemblies of iron—the look, the sound, and the performance of the engines brings a glint to the eyes of the "True Believers."

Rosamond Dry Lake, October 29, the last SCTA meet of 1939. A Cragar Model A roadster burns while spectators, unable to help because no one had a fire extinguisher, watch the fire burn itself out after destroying the engine. The SCTA didn't insist that on-board fire extinguishers be carried until 1947. *Frederick Usher photo*

CHAPTER 4

Drive-Ins, Dry Lakes, and Drag Racing

*We did it all,
and we'll never see times like these again.*

May 7, 1950. The last thing I remember on that Sunday afternoon at El Mirage dry lake was starting my return record run in the So-Cal streamliner. We (Alex Xydias and I) were running a Ford V-8 60 for power, and I had qualified for a record run the day before by clocking 152.28mph.

I don't know how fast I was running on this return run, but inasmuch as the existing record, which I had set the previous July, was 138.74, I was trying to do about 140. We were trying to move the record up about 2mph at each successive lakes meet so we could gain enough points to win the season championship. Having already turned a 152, I thought this would be an easy way to get the needed points.

Unfortunately, when we turned the car around at the east end of the course to start back on the second leg of the record run, a cross-wind had come up and was blowing from my left at about 45 degrees to my path of travel. Because the streamliner was so light (a little more than 1,300lb with driver, fuel, and water) with about 65 percent of the weight on the rear wheels, it wasn't stable in a cross-wind.

I got a good start from the push car, and the little "60" was pulling well, but I had a premonition that something was wrong. I didn't know what, but it bothered me, and I considered aborting the run. I should have paid attention to my premonition.

I was correcting for the quartering wind by steering a bit to the left. Suddenly the wind let off and the

car took a dive to the left. In spite of my frantic steering correction to the right, it was too late and the car went completely sideways, skating up the lakebed full broadside to the course until the right wheels dug in, and the car did a complete barrel roll in the middle of the time traps.

I am only here to write about this because the car landed on its wheels. We had a good safety belt and an on-board fire extinguisher, but that was it for the safety equipment. We had no roll bar. If the car had landed on its top instead of its wheels, my head would have been ground off to my shoulders.

Further, we had no floorboards, relying on the streamlined body's bellypan to serve that purpose. When the car went over, the riveted-on pan came off like a tossed frisbee. By losing the belly pan/floorboards, my feet could have fallen through that gaping hole when the car came down and I could have lost both legs.

Additionally, our throttle control was a device used with outboard motors for trolling: When you squeezed it you could move it, but letting go of it locked it in place. When the car went over and the wheels were in the air, rpm picked up from 6,200 to more than 8,000 and it came down running wide open and headed for the crowd at the finish line.

Several things happened at that point, none of which I had control over as I had been knocked unconscious when my head hit the steering wheel, gashing my forehead above my right eye.

Brothers Bob and Dick Pierson entered this chopped '34 three-window coupe at Bonneville in 1950 and at El Mirage in 1951, running with the Russetta Coupes Club and the SCTA Road Runners. At Bonneville, they set two records—149.005mph with their own C class engine and 146.365 with a B class engine borrowed from Bill Likes (he also ran both engines in his '29 A V-8 roadster, setting a B record at 138.140 and a C record at 147.295—the latter entered as Hernandez & Meeks, though it was Bill's car). *Photo at El Mirage, 1951, by Bernie Couch*

Opposite page, Howie Wilson drove Stu Hilborn's streamliner after Stu's accident in 1947. It was the first hot rod to better 150mph in a timed top-speed run. At the July 17-18 SCTA meet at El Mirage Dry Lake, Wilson clocked 150.50mph one way and set a B streamliner two-way record of 146.470mph. *Greg Sharp collection*

Right and bottom, this is what dry lakes racing is all about; Bob McClure, a member of the Glendale Coupe & Roadster Club, starts a run in his B class Lakester. His push-truck moves him off at about 60mph and Bob stays to the left of the torn-up course, hoping for better traction. He'll thread his way through those hummocks that dot the El Mirage lake bed on a gradual left curve until he starts on the straight section. This was at a Russetta Timing Association meet on May 17, 1952. *Ralph Poole photos, author collection*

The impact with the ground broke the front engine mounts, which dropped the front of the engine about two inches, shearing the Kong ignition from the front of the engine when it hit a piece of angle iron which supported the tach drive. The engine quit running at that point, thus stopping the car.

The next thing I remember is regaining consciousness in Jack Purdy's ambulance which was going flat out down Cajon Pass toward San Bernardino. Purdy had guaranteed the SCTA that he would transport injured parties from El Mirage to St. Bernadine's Hospital in San Bernardino in forty-five minutes. It was about fifty-seven miles, as I recall, with the first few miles being a washboard dirt road from the lakebed to the paved road. I'm glad I was unconscious for most of the trip.

My first thought on coming to was where am I, followed by what am I doing here? The ambulance attendant explained that I had been in an accident, and

Proof that roadsters were used for more than just dry lakes racing or drive-in cruising. Ray Brown ran this Eddie Meyer-equipped '32 roadster as both transportation and weekend racer. In the winter of 1947-48, he and some friends ventured into the mountains near Lake Arrowhead and Big Bear Lake where conditions weren't exactly top-down, sun in the face driving. *Ray Brown and author photo*

they were taking me to the hospital. Then I thought, oh shit, the car is damaged, and we won't be able to run at the next meet. It's strange how one's priorities rearrange themselves in situations like this.

I should have been thinking about my eyesight (it all worked out, but there was a serious question for awhile about how much of it I would regain), and here I was worrying about running the car again.

As it turned out, I never drove the car again—by choice. Alex had a friend, Bill Dailey, who wanted to drive the car, and I had a friend, Ray Charbonneau, who also wanted to drive. We arranged to have them take turns, which worked out okay, but kept both out of the 200 MPH Club when it was formed two years later. While both had driven the 'liner over the 200mph mark several times, neither had made a two-way run at that speed to qualify for club membership.

A few weeks after my accident, we took the car apart in Alex's Speed Shop and found that both front spindles were broken, and the front axle was split from the right kingpin inward about eighteen inches. The rear axles had each made a full 360-degree twist before

Above, El Mirage Dry Lake, May 6, 1950—the first SCTA meet of the 1950 season. The So-Cal Streamliner makes its first dry lakes appearance with the new nose and larger front tires. In this configuration and with the 156ci V-8 60 engine installed, I drove the 'liner 152.28mph to qualify for a two-way record run.
John Faris photo

Manuel Butkie's Backwards T modified roadster. The class rules allowed some streamlining ahead of the firewall, but from the firewall to the back of the body, it had to be stock configuration. I suggested to Butkie that the '27 T body was better aerodynamically if it were turned around. He did it, and I drove the modified roadster 148mph at an SCTA meet. Manuel is shown here at a Russetta meet. The sight of the car seemingly running backward through the timing traps was a bit unsettling to the timing crew.
Author photo

shearing the axle keys. All these pieces were replaced, magnafluxed, and installed as before, retaining the ball-bearing races for wheel hubs, carrier and pinion bearings. The frame, a pair of Model T Ford rails, came through unscathed, and Valley Custom, in Burbank, which had built the body, repaired the body damage.

Looking back on all of this I wonder how I could have been so smart and so dumb at the same time; smart, because I was instrumental in creating a car that was about 30mph faster than anything in its class (and actually faster than any car on the dry lakes or at Bonneville—making it the fastest car in America at the time), and dumb, not to build more safety features into the car.

The SCTA technical committee, in its infinite wisdom, passed a rule that prohibited lock-on throttle controls, but didn't pass a rule requiring separate floorboards in addition to the underbody panel. Had they done this in 1950 (it was made a requirement later) it would probably have saved Fred Carrillo's foot at Bonneville in 1953 when the fiberglass body of his streamliner disintegrated during his accident there. Unfortunately, I think I was on the technical committee at the time so I can't blame someone else for the oversight.

August 10, 1947—Jack McAfee of the SCTA Throttlers Club climbs into his D.O. Hal Model B Ford sprint car for a run at El Mirage Dry Lake. His best time was 122.95miles per hour. Jack was running the car with the oval-track set up for tires.
Author photo

El Mirage Dry Lake, May 7, 1950—I learn why one should never drive a light, aerodynamic car with tail-heavy weight distribution in a cross wind. I had qualified for a record run on Saturday, and this Sunday morning I had made the downwind leg of the record run and was coming back into a quartering wind—the wind direction was from my left at about a 45-degree angle. I was correcting into the wind to keep the car straight, when the wind stopped and the car took a dive to the left. This brought the tail around, putting the car completely sideways, to the direction of travel. The car skidded briefly on all four wheels dug into the dirt, tipped up on two wheels (in this photo, the car is traveling to the left but pointed at the photographer), and then, did a complete barrel-roll, landing on its wheels.
Duane Steele photo

Fred Carrillo

Fred Carrillo with one of his famous connecting rods in hand. The engine is a 208ci, turbocharged AMC V-8 which powered a Carrillo-owned Indy car.

Fred Carrillo is a native Californian, born June 5, 1926, in Los Angeles. In the immediate post-WWII years, he was a member of the SCTA Road Runners Club, running a channeled '32 roadster before building a mid-engined '27 T Modified Roadster for Bonneville in 1951.

Carrillo had given up dry lakes racing by 1953 when he brought a radical Chrysler Hemi-powered streamliner to Bonneville. At the AAA/FIA runs in 1953, a week after the Nationals, Fred told the Firestone rep that he planned to run 300-mph. He was told, "our tires won't stand up to that speed." Fred replied "We're going for 300, and your name's on the tires, what do you propose we do?" The Firestone man's answer was to put 90psi in the tires (they had been running about 60psi).

The advice almost killed Carrillo. One of the cast-magnesium wheels was flawed, and the 90

pounds of pressure blew the left front wheel apart at better than 200mph. When the car came to a stop—a pile of rubble that looked as though a bomb had exploded inside the car—a half-mile down the course, Carrillo had lost a foot and had other, lesser injuries.

Rather than continue racing himself, he established a company to manufacture bullet-proof connecting rods. Carrillo rods were in the Ford GT40s which won Le Mans, the Brabham-Repco with which Jack Brabham won the World Driver's Championship in 1966, and they were in the Al Teague streamliner (a Roots-blown Keith Black Hemi V-8 provided the power) which set a new Land Speed Record in its class in 1993, at 409.986mph, with a best one-way run of 432mph.

Carrillo rods are also used in more classic and antique cars than anyone suspects—it pays to protect your investment.

The Vets Return

The hot rod movement (we could call them that now, as the term was first used in early 1945) exploded, figuratively speaking, of course, in the immediate post-WWII years. Most returning servicemen were overjoyed to get out of the service, out of uniform, and get on with their interrupted lives.

Some went back to school, some got married, some simply went back to the jobs they had left, and many came back to wives and families that had been left behind.

In my case, I wanted to go to school and did, studying Industrial Design on the G.I. Bill. But I also

wanted to buy a '32 roadster and get into hot rodding as a competitor instead of being the eternal spectator.

In July 1945, while I was home on a ninety-day RRR (Rest, Recovery, and Rehabilitation) leave, I bought a '32 roadster. It wasn't much as it sat, and I paid just $400 for it. The owner told me it had a Winfield camshaft in the engine, but it didn't run as though it did. When I discovered that two spark plug wires were crossed, we put them on the correct plugs, and the engine came to life.

Even with the cam, the roadster wasn't very fast—I later clocked an even 100mph after installing an Edel-

brock Super dual intake manifold. But by God I had a '32, and I was a happy GI. Out of the service (I was mustered out three months after buying the roadster) and into a hot rod. Life couldn't have been better.

Two of my buddies, Ray Charbonneau and Charlie Faris, got out of the service about the same time I did, and each had a '29 A roadster at home in the garage; Ray's had a 4-port Riley head, and Charlie's sported a Winfield flathead. They had joined the SCTA Road Runners Club and another friend, Lute Eldridge, and I followed them in joining the club. While Ray and Charlie's roadsters were primarily for the dry lakes, with

occasional forays onto the street for some racing closer to home, Lute's and my roadsters were primarily transportation with occasional dry lakes runs.

It was not only great to be free of military obligations, but it was a grand time for car nuts. The streets of southern California, particularly in Los Angeles County, were thick with interesting cars—hot rods, custom cars, and the occasional imported sports car. In those days we weren't terribly impressed with imported cars. Few of us thought much about handling, which was the sports car's strong suit. We judged a car by how fast it could get to the next traf-

SCTA Lancers Club member Jack Calori ran this handsome '29 roadster body on '32 rails 128.38mph on September 21, 1947, at El Mirage Dry Lake. His flathead Merc engine had Eddie Meyer heads, Weiand dual intake manifold, and a Clay Smith camshaft. Earlier in the year he had set a two-way average of 124.43mph for a new C class roadster record. *Author photo*

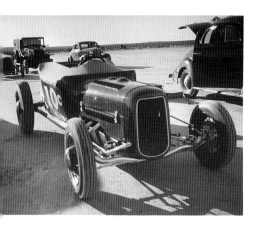

This page, three modified roadsters, three different looks, and three selections for the small front tires so popular with dry lakes racers: Top, Paul Schiefer (San Diego Roadster Club) ran Ward's Riverside 5.00-16in grooved tires on his '24 T; center, Bert Letner (Road Runners) favored 5.00-16 motorcycle tires on his '25 T; and, bottom, Wes Cooper and Bob Hayes (Glendale Sidewinders) used Firestone 5.50-16 grooved tires on the front of their '27 T. The Ward's and Firestone tires were made for the front of dirt-track sprint cars. The front tires on the three modified roadsters were often mistakenly called "implement," as in farm implement, tires. Actual implement tires, while extremely rugged, would not have held up to high rotational speeds; farm implement tires were never used in dry lakes racing. *Author photos*

Ray Brown

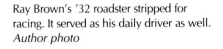

Ray Brown seemed your typical hot rodder in the 1940s. He worked at Eddie Meyer Engineering as an engine builder, drove a '32 Ford roadster on the street which, in a display of company loyalty, had Meyer equipment—heads, dual intake manifold, and ignition—on the flathead V-8 engine, was a member of the SCTA Road Runners Club, and ran his roadster at the dry lakes.

Brown started his own business in 1950—tune-ups, engine building, and speed equipment. His shop built the Chrysler engines (B and C Class) for Mal Hooper's Shadoff Chrysler Special, which set twelve U.S. and twelve International records at Bonneville. One of those engines went into a Mickey Thompson dragster—the one which started the "slingshot" seating position, and the narrowed rear track for better directional stability.

Ray's exploits with engines and speed are well known and certainly admired, but, in my opinion, these were not Brown's greatest automotive contribution. Shortly after starting his own shop, on Western Avenue in Los Angeles, he established the first company to produce seat belts for the public. Marketed under the name "Impact Auto Saf-Tee Belt," in 1951, Brown's company fought the lonely battle of selling safety to a skeptical and uncaring public.

Brown kept at it and by 1962 his company became the first contract supplier of auto safety belts to the U.S. Government. Brown sold his plant, property, and business to American Safety Equipment Co. in 1966, and stayed sixteen months as a consultant. Once he left ASE he was hired by Superior Industries, a multiproduct company which specializes in alloy road wheels, as senior vice president, acting as director of marketing and sales. With Brown's help, Superior became the largest manufacturer of alloy wheels in the world.

fic light, or how fast it would go at top speed, and there weren't many imports that could even stay close to a good roadster.

Most of the imports we saw on the streets then were MGs, Singers, and the like, but an increasing number of Jaguar XK-120s were appearing (we thought they were okay because they had twin overhead camshafts like our beloved Offy midgets and Indianapolis cars), and a few Porsches were being sold, but they weren't very fast. We cared not that a Porsche did it with less than 90ci; what counted was getting there first, not how you got there.

Hangouts and Speed Shops

Speed shops—Alex Xydias' So-Cal in Burbank, Karl Orr's in Culver City, Don Blair's in Pasadena, Roy Ricther's Bell Auto Parts in Bell, Barney Navarro's in Glendale, Phil Weiand's in L.A., the Miller brothers (Ak, Larry, and Zeke) in Whittier, Vic Edelbrock's and Eddie Meyer's in Hollywood, Smith & Jones (Clay & Dan) in Long Beach, and Paul Schiefer's in San Diego—were

Above, Bob Pierson, of the Russetta Coupes Club, ran this '36 three-window coupe in 1947 and '48, then chopped the top to run in '49 and '50. The car was a record setter, with a best average of 140.40mph. The engine was a flathead Merc with Edelbrock equipment, and the car served as daily transportation when not running at the dry lakes.

Don Towle, of the Russetta Timing Association Coupes Club ran this chopped '34 five-window coupe in 1948 and '49. The car was driven by Don Corwin, and the best run had been 117.80mph until he changed the bellypan to give more ground clearance and the speed went up to 135.85 on a two-way average. The engine was a flathead Merc equipped with a Kong ignition (popular with racers because it had a manual spark control), Winfield camshaft, and Edelbrock heads and triple intake manifold. *Author photo*

The SCTA timing stand was constructed on a two-wheeled trailer frame and when first built was hauled to and from each lake meet. Ultimately, it was stored at Bill Albright's Lazy A Ranch at the north end of El Mirage Dry Lake. Once a year it went to Bonneville to be on the salt flats during the National Speed Trials. Here at El Mirage in the early 1950s, Chief Timer Otto Crocker sits behind his timing equipment with recorders and observers alongside. Jack Purdy is in his ambulance hoping his service isn't needed.

where we hung out during the day, and the drive-in restaurants were our home away from home at night.

After WWII there were drive-ins everywhere, and you could probably find a roadster or custom car in any one of them at almost any time. Some, often for unknown reasons, became more popular than others. Bob's Big Boy in Glendale, Pasadena, Burbank, or Toluca Lake; Piccadilly in Culver City; Larry and Carl's and The Green Spot in Pasadena; Parker's Night Owl in Glendale; the Triangle in north L.A.; the Circle in Long Beach, and the Hula Hut in Whittier were some of the most popular.

Some clubs seemed to adopt a drive-in as their surrogate club house. You could find Outriders Club members at the Triangle, Glendale Coupe & Roadster Club guys at Parker's, and the Sidewinders were usually at one of the Bob's Big Boy restaurants. The Sidewinders' particular loyalty was probably somewhat chauvinistic , as Bob Wian started his first drive-in on Colorado Boulevard in Glendale, and the Glendale and Burbank club members liked what they found there.

If some members of the California state legislature had had their way, we might not have been doing any of this street cruising and hanging out. Assembly Bill #908 was introduced in early 1945 and referred to the Committee on Transportation and Commerce as an act to add to the Vehicle Code relating to equipment: "675.1 Fenders. Every motor vehicle shall be equipped with four fenders or mudguards."

And Assembly Bill #910, introduced at the same time, re "675.2 Prohibited Equipment. No equipment shall be installed upon a motor when it is used to propel a motor vehicle, which is designed to increase the horsepower of the motor above that which it had at the time it was manufactured."

All this came at a time when the Hearst Newspapers and the National Safety Council were trying to ban racing on the track and modified street cars. Fortunately cooler heads prevailed, and things stayed pretty much as they were. I think being hassled by the police was due more to how the car was being driven than the fact that it was a hot rod, or custom. In the three and a half years I drove my '32 on the streets, I received one ticket—for parking the wrong way in front of my house.

Mickey Thompson

Mickey Thompson was the renaissance man of motor racing—running at the dry lakes with a '36 Ford coupe, Bonneville with a twin-engined coupe in 1952 (194.34 Class D record), driving a stock Ford six in the Carrera Panamericana in 1953, building the first slingshot-seated dragster (and the first with narrow rear track for better directional stability) in 1955, back to Bonneville in 1958 with a twin Chrysler-engined streamliner to clock 294mph.

In 1959, he founded Mickey Thompson Equipment Co., set a drag boat quarter-mile record of 137.94mph with twin Pontiac V-8s. Then, in 1960, *Challenger I* ran 406.6mph at Bonneville (a broken drive shaft prevented completion of the record run).

Mickey stunned the racing world in 1963 by introducing a 12in-wide tire (designed by Thompson and Gene McMannis and built by Firestone) for Indy cars. Thompson seemed to be everywhere at once, operating drag strips (Long Beach and Fontana), setting endurance records at Bonneville with Danny Ongais (Ford Mach I Mustang), driving a Ford factory off-road pickup for Bill Stroppe in 1970, and founding the SCORE International off-road series; then starting, with partner Alex Xydias, the SCORE Trade Show.

Mickey, and his wife Trudy, met a tragic death in 1988 when they were murdered in front of their home in Bradbury, California. Mickey's son, Danny, now runs the family business.

Veda Orr, wife of Karl Orr and his partner in racing, was the first woman known to compete in organized time trails at the dry lakes. On May 25, 1947, when this photo was taken, she clocked 121.76mph. The Merc engine was equipped with Offenhauser heads and manifold and a Clay Smith camshaft. She and Karl ran as members of the SCTA Albata Club. *Bill Freeman photo, Don Montgomery collection*

Dry Lake Summers

Unlike the custom car crowd, who never took their cars off paved roads or to places where they could get dirty, hot rodders were drawn, as if by instinct, back to the dry lakes during the summer.

This would be more understandable if one had never been to the dry lakes. The Mojave Desert in California is a forbidding place. These dry lake beds are about 2,800 feet above sea level, and this "high desert" is a bit cooler (if you want to call 100 degrees in the shade cool) than the "low desert" around Palm Springs, Joshua Tree, and Blythe. And the lakes were dirty. That ultra-fine alkali dust got into everything—though I suppose you could make a case that the fine dust helped seat the rings in a new engine after it had been sucked into unfiltered carburetor intakes.

Enterprising concessionaires brought their "roach coaches" to the lakebed on race weekends to sell hot dogs, hamburgers, candy, gum, soft drinks, potato chips, and other delicacies. If it sounds crazy to eat salty food such as pota-

to chips in a place where we couldn't get enough to drink anyway, remember that in two days on the lakebed you would lose an enormous amount of body liquid through perspiration. We needed salt to balance our body chemistry, and junk food was more enjoyable than salt pills.

At various times we saw guys with small tank trailers selling water for ten cents a paper cup full. Others brought ice to sell. One guy appeared with a snow cone machine. As dull as a snow cone can be, it was refreshing on that inhospitable lakebed. Joe Goss came up with a variation on the theme; he brought a bottle of

Manischewitz wine and we poured that over the snow cones. Don't laugh, it's a lot better than drinking that sweet stuff, and it actually tasted pretty good. Of course you wouldn't want much of it.

I had heard stories about lakes meets with a thousand entries, and 10,000 spectators. Going through old lakes programs the largest entry I found (October 30-31, 1948) was 224 cars. I can attest to the fact, though, that there were thousands of spectators at some meets, and I have waited in line for several hours on more than one occasion just to get one run through the course.

Howard Johansen (Howard's Cams) built a catamaran-type streamliner for the dry lakes and ran it the first time at the 1949 Bonneville meet. The two "hulls" were made from the rounded nose and pointed tail of two aircraft auxiliary wing tanks with a straight section between. A flathead Merc V-8 sat in the right hull—the hole in the nose is for carburetor air intake—and the driver sat in the left side. Howard never got the bugs out, and the best the car did, was 147.54 at Bonneville in 1949. *Author photo*

Stuart Hilborn

Stuart Hilborn, born October 9, 1917, in Calgary, Alberta, Canada, moved with his family to Washington State, then Pasadena, and finally Santa Monica, California. His interest in cars began in 1938 when he went to watch the activity at Muroc Dry Lake, and was shocked by all those cars going so fast. Hilborn subsequently built a '29 A V-8 and began racing instead of spectating.

In 1941, Eddie Miller built a four-carburetor intake manifold for Stu's twenty-one-stud flathead V-8 which Hilborn ran until after WWII. In 1946, while still in the military, Hilborn designed his injection system. Knowledge gained from his occupation as a chemist for a paint company helped him plot fuel-flow requirements, although he admits a lot of testing was done before he was satisfied with it.

His Hilborn-injected flathead-powered streamliner was the first hot rod to top 150mph (Howie Wilson drove the 'liner 150.50mph on July 18, 1948). Hilborn's first made-for-sale injector was for Ed Haddad's Offy midget. Haddad was so successful that incoming orders caused Stu to quit his job and start his Fuel Injection Engineering Company, moving to Mission Viejo, California.

Before Cooper and Lotus came to Indianapolis, there were years when every entry on Memorial Day was equipped with Hilborn injectors, and it is safe to say that these injectors have been used in every type of racing in which they would be allowed—Bonneville, dry lakes, drag racing, motorcycles, hydroplanes, midgets, sprint cars, Indianapolis cars, and the Scarabs (both sports racing and Formula 1).

The years I ran my stock-bodied '32 roadster—1947 to 1948—the SCTA had only four engine classes: A=0-183ci, B=183-250ci, C=250-350ci, and D=350ci and over. There were two body classes: roadster and streamliner. Any application of a supercharger or overhead camshafts moved the car up one class.

The following year, 1949, after I had sold the roadster to build the streamliner with Alex, the rules were changed to divide roadsters into two classes; stock body and modified bodies, the latter called Lakesters.

Before we built our wheels-enclosed full-bodied car, most of the streamliners were those with P-38 drop-tank bodies, old one-man sprint cars, or one of the older "Modifieds" which had the narrow body but were squared-off behind the driver.

After Bonneville in 1949, the rules committee created a modified roadster class to go along with stock-bodied roadsters, and what had been streamliners with exposed wheels, became Lakesters. It may sound confusing, but the changes made the classes more evenly divided and more fair to competitors.

While the SCTA had only three body classes—Roadster, Lakester, and Streamliner—Russetta Timing Association had been created to provide a means to run coupes and sedans. In typical racing fashion, the NIH (Not Invented Here) syndrome prevailed, and many of the SCTA guys didn't think the Russetta clocks were accurate, or honest, because some of those coupes and sedans were turning times not thought possible.

Don Brown, whose '36 Ford five-window coupe had been running in the low 120s at Russetta, was invited to run at the August 28–29, 1948, SCTA meet. The announcement in the SCTA program said, "The SCTA does not run coupes in its competition, but feels that many fans would enjoy seeing a good fast coupe in action on the straightaway course." Sure. Some probably did, but there were many more hoping Brown would make a fool of himself by turning less speed than he had at the Russetta meets.

When the August 1948 SCTA meet was over, some of the SCTA guys were miffed, most of them were puzzled, and Brown was elated; he had run 121.68mph on Otto Crocker's SCTA clocks which everyone conceded were the best and most accurate. The SCTA members did indeed see "a good fast coupe in action," and they were stunned that a streetable coupe could go that fast.

The ten to fifteen years after WWII were the greatest years of the hot rodding hobby. Although rodding was starting to lose its amateur status to the entrepreneurs, it hadn't quite done it yet. Those were the days when competitors on the dry lakes, at Bonneville, and on the drag strips were running more for the fun and excitement of competition than for money. Sponsorship hadn't taken over, and the atmosphere was more friendly than frantic.

There was an intense rivalry between Chevy and Ford guys, coupe and roadster, four-cylinder and V-8, and club versus club, but it was competition among friends, not enemies. I wish you could have been there. It was great.

USC student Bob McGee built this beautiful '32 roadster, which was on the cover of *Hot Rod* magazine. Dick Scritchfield (shown) later owned it and installed a Chevy small-block V-8. The car's fame continued, and it appeared in movies, TV shows, advertisements, and car shows around the country. *Ralph Poole photo*

Dick Ford's Chevy-bodied roadster (Ford flathead V-8 powered) photographed on a Road Runners Club cruise in 1946 to the jalopy races in San Bernardino. Dick never ran the car at the dry lakes; the body was narrowed and he would have to compete against modified cars because his roadster didn't conform to class rules. *Author photo*

Yam Okamura (he preferred to use Yam Oka) was one of many Japanese-Americans who ran at the dry lakes before and after WWII. This 1947 photo shows his channeled '32 roadster he called *Blue Goose*. As a member of the Glendale Sidewinders Club he ran 118.26. *Peter Eastwood photo, Don Montgomery collection*

Skip Hudson in his '29 A V-8 in an official Riverside, California, Police Department photo taken in 1951 just after he had shown the roadster in a car show, and before "selling" it to keep the police from impounding it for too much illegal street racing. This handsome blue '29 was pictured, along with Jack Morgan's yellow '34 roadster, on the first *Hot Rod* magazine color cover—April 1951. In August 1950, the roadster ran at the Bonneville Speed Trials as the S. Hudson & D. Gurney C Modified Roadster. With a borrowed engine Dan drove the roadster 130.43mph. *Riverside P.D. photo, Skip Hudson collection*

Stan Hartle's '31 Model A roadster with a '32 radiator shell and Kelsey-Hayes 16in wire wheels was one of the best looking roadsters on the street or dry lakes. Stan, who lived in Burbank and ran with the Glendale Sidewinders Club, turned 132.93mph in 1951—and this with a stock bore and stroke Merc (239ci) flathead equipped with Kong ignition, Weber camshaft, Edelbrock heads and Navarro three-carb intake manifold. Stan towed the roadster to El Mirage, and here he's re-attaching the drag link so he can drive the dirt road into the lakebed. Valley Custom built Stan's three-piece aluminum hood and the underbody panels which hide the frame. *Author photo*

CHAPTER 5

The Ford Flathead V-8

*Superb development over two decades
turned an archaic lump of cast iron into the closest
you can come to "poor man's" racing*

My first experience with the Ford flathead V-8 engine was when a Burbank High School classmate, Ed Le Tourneau, brought his brother Armand's Model A roadster to school one day. With only a casual look you'd take it to be a stock 1930 Ford roadster with 16in wire wheels—probably from a '35 Ford because you could buy those wheels from a junkyard for about fifty cents each, compared to seventy-five cents or more for the better-looking Kelsey-Hayes 16-inch wires.

What made this Model A different was that Armand had fitted a Ford V-8 engine under the hood. This wasn't difficult because the V-8 wasn't any longer than the A engine, and Henry Ford and his minions had made almost everything on a Ford—axles, brakes, springs, wheels, shock absorbers, transmissions, even some body parts—interchangeable with his cars from other years. The '32 grille and shell, for example, would fit on a Model A, almost as easily as mounting the stock shell.

This parts interchangeability came in handy because, while the V-8 block wouldn't mate to the Model A transmission, it was a simple matter to use the V-8 transmission and mate the machinery at the driveshaft U-joint.

The engine in Le Tourneau's roadster was stock, as I recall, but if we can believe Ford's advertised horsepower, he had removed a 40hp Model A four-cylinder engine and replaced it with an 85hp V-8 (it was a '35 or '36 engine). That's more than double the power with little more weight, just by swapping engines. And it was so smooth compared to the older four-banger.

After school was out that day, Ed suggested we take the roadster for a spin. We did, but simply driving around town wasn't very rewarding, so Ed decided it would be great fun to get in some track time. A large gate at the edge of our high school athletic field was never locked, so I got out and opened the gate while Ed drove through. I climbed back into the passenger seat, and off we went with Ed playing Barney Oldfield on our high school running track.

With the power to weight ratio we had it was easy to put the roadster into a sideways-past-the-silo stance, and we were having a great time sliding around the curve at each end—hanging the tail out and flinging dirt like it was a real race car, until the school custodian and the athletic coach appeared on a dead run to intercept us at the conclusion of a hot lap. Undaunted, Ed swerved onto the football field and took a short cut to the exit gate where we disappeared into the distance.

Unfortunately, we had been recognized by both men so the next day we were apprehended and punished—and the gate was subsequently locked at all times, requiring a special dispensation to get it unlocked.

This episode took place in 1939, and I'm not suggesting that Le Tourneau was the first to put a V-8 into an A chassis (making what we called an A V-8). He was merely one of many who realized that an inexpensive Ford V-8 engine, probably from a wrecked car, was a quick and simple way to increase the performance of an A roadster to a remarkable degree.

George Riley ohv conversion for the twenty-one-stud Ford V-8 with twin carburetors mounted side-by-side and with hot water outlet to the radiator coming from the center of the heads. *Bob Joehnck*

Opposite page, Harper Dry Lake, 1941. Manuel Ayulo, who worked for Eddie Meyer, and later at the Porter Muffler Shop, was a member of the SCTA Outriders Club and a regular competitor at the dry lakes before the war. His '29 A V-8 had full Meyer equipment—heads, dual intake manifold, and ignition. After WWII Manuel turned pro, first in track roadsters and then midgets and Indy cars. Manuel was one of the first to wear a crash helmet at the dry lakes. *Gus Rollins photo*

Right, George Riley ohv conversion with a home-made manifold with two Chandler-Groves carbs inline, and the water pipes at the front of the heads. *Gene Von Arx photos*

In 1941 Stu Hilborn ran an early Eddie Meyer water-heated dual intake manifold on his '29 A V-8 roadster. He sold the Meyer manifold because Eddie Miller had built this four-carb manifold for Stu's roadster engine. Because the Ford firing order, 1-5-4-8-6-3-7-2, had cylinders two and one firing consecutively, Miller placed a Buick Duplex over those two intake ports and used three Dodge D-7s over the other three pairs of ports. This set-up, with a Scintilla magneto ignition, also ran in Hilborn's streamliner. *Stuart Hilborn collection*

The V-8 Takes Over

Even a hopped-up Model A engine, with one of the overhead valve conversions, couldn't reliably match the power available from a virtually stock flathead V-8. One of the better overhead set-ups for the A, such as the four-port Riley, Fargo, or Rutherford, produced upwards of 100hp on pump gas, but if you raised the power much more than that durability problems set in. The flathead V-8, even in 1939 or '40, could be made to produce as much power with more reliability than you could get from the four-banger.

Over-the-counter speed equipment had been available for the Model T since about 1920, and for the Model A four-cylinder Fords since 1928 (the latter equipment would also fit the Models B and C Ford fours when they came out in 1932 and '33), but very little was available for the V-8 until 1940.

The 1935 Miller-Fords entered at Indianapolis for the annual 500-mile race (there were ten of these front-wheel drive Ford-powered Millers) had three different intake manifolds; a dual, made by the Hexagon Tool Company in Dearborn, Michigan, and two different four-carburetor manifolds made by Miller. All ten Fords had Bosch ignition systems and Bohnalite aluminum cylinder heads.

Of the three manifolds made for the Miller-Fords, only the Hexagon dual was ever made available to com-

The Eddie Miller four-carburetor manifold on Hilborn's engine was replaced by the first Hilborn fuel injection system. Stu designed the injectors while still in the military, and made the prototype soon after his army discharge. Hilborn's engine wasn't built for show, but the neat plumbing, wiring, and fittings indicate his quality workmanship, contributing to his ultimate success as a competitor—and later as a manufacturer of injectors. This was the first hot rod to top 150mph at the dry lakes—driven 150.50mph by Howie Wilson, on July 18, 1948.
Lee Blaisdell photo, Greg Sharp collection

mercial customers, and it didn't work well on the street, so it was never a success. The problem was that a normal Stromberg or Chandler-Groves carburetor installation on a Ford positioned the float chamber at the front so that under acceleration the fuel would be forced into the jets at the back of the chamber. The Hexagon manifold, being made for a front wheel-drive car with the engine turned around in the chassis, placed the float chambers at the back when used on a street car, and the jets were starved for fuel under acceleration.

Wayne Morrison had designed a cast-aluminum dual intake manifold, in 1938, which placed the two carburetors side by side instead of in-line as would become the popular norm. Unfortunately, Morrison's manifold was advertised only in the *SCTA Racing News* so only racers knew about it.

By 1939 Eddie Meyer, Jack Henry, and Tommy Thickstun were offering dual manifolds—with the two carburetors close together so that the standard generator

mount could be used. Pierre "Pete" Bertrand was advertising reground camshafts, Tom Spalding was making dual-coil ignitions (by using the Lincoln-Zephyr coils on a Ford distributor), and Eddie Meyer started casting high-compression aluminum cylinder heads for both the 1932–1936 twenty-one-stud Ford blocks, and the mid-1938–1939 twenty-four-stud engines. The latter would, of course, then fit all Ford flathead blocks through 1948.

Vic Edelbrock built his first dual intake manifold in mid-1939 (the now famous "slingshot" design), and, by 1941, Mal Ord, Dave Burns, and Phil Weiand were making dual intake manifolds, as well. Ted Cannon was offering special camshafts, and Ord was also making dual-coil ignitions, similar to Spalding's, and cylinder heads for the twenty-four-stud block.

When Edelbrock started making manifolds in 1939, he went to the same pattern maker and foundry that Thickstun had used, so with previous experience it was a simple matter to meet Edelbrock's requirements

No. 136: Andy Minnini, RTA, 1952.

No. 206: Bill Faris, Sidewinders,1950.
Author Photo

Lower left, No. 207:
Bill Likes, Sidewinders, 1950.
Author photo

Lower right, typical street '32 with
sunken license plate and '39 teardrops.
Gus Rollins photo

1932 Ford Roadster

Call it a "Deuce," or "High-Boy," or simply "'32," it was and is the epitome of hot-rod-type cars—especially if it also has a flathead V-8 engine (the Model B four-cylinder, which was one of the original equipment options in 1932, was marginally acceptable). The 1932 Ford line of cars, particularly the Roadster, Victoria, or three-window Coupe, were some of the best-looking cars of the 1930s, and that view is supported by the fact that they still look good sixty-plus years later.

If you were a "hot rodder" in the years between 1940 and 1955, the chances are you wanted a '32 roadster. If you didn't own one because you couldn't afford one, we understood that. If you didn't own one because you didn't want one, there was obviously something wrong with your perception of what was right.

The '32 was not only better looking (the form, shape, graceful lines, and marvelous proportions were superb) than the Model A it replaced, but it was a little larger—103.5 and 106in wheelbases—and the '32 had the rear transverse-leaf spring mounted behind the rear axle instead of over it, all of which helped to give it a more comfortable ride.

The '32 Grille and radiator shell were so handsome they became almost a required add-on for the front of a Model A, causing a great deal of confusion among non-Ford people; all of whom seem to think

that anything with a '32 grille was therefore a '32.

In the immediate post-WWII years hot-rodded '32 Fords were everywhere—all around us on the streets of southern California. It was not uncommon to see twenty to thirty of them in a single day while driving in the Los Angeles area. They seemed to come in all colors, but the obvious favorite was black with either red, or natural tan "tucked and rolled" upholstery.

These '32s all had small front tires; 5.00, 5.50, or 6.00x16in, and larger rear tires, usually 6.50 or 7.00x16in. Wheels were sometimes wire, either from a 1935 Ford or the better looking Kelsey-Hayes. But more likely they were disc wheels from a '40, '41, or '42 Ford. These wheels had 4.5in-wide rims making them ideal for the small front tires. The larger rear tires worked better and looked better with wider rims. Fortunately, Ford provided these by making the wheel bolt circle (with the exception of 1936–39, which had a much larger bolt circle) the same for Ford, Mercury, and Lincoln—the latter having wider rims.

The practice of using later Ford wheels on '32s and Model As came from fitting hydraulic brakes, which were usually taken from a 1940–1948 Ford. With the increased horsepower the original Ford mechanical brakes were woefully inadequate, so a change to hydraulics was mandatory for safety.

Even with the bolt circles and bolt-spacing the same, an early wire wheel, when used with the later hydraulic brake drums, required spacers under the wheel so it would sit correctly on the drum. By using wheels which went with the later drums, the spacers could be eliminated.

As a result, a '32 Ford with '40 brakes and wheels and small front and large rear tires became the chosen and accepted norm starting about 1945. It was almost as though Ford had made these cars that way on the assembly line.

The shape, the lines, and the proportions of the '32 Roadster were almost perfect, by any criteria, but we reshaped it to become our car—it wasn't Ford's car any longer. It was the rodder's version of a later Ferrari 250GTO, a 427 Cobra, or a Corvette Gran Sport. With subtle but significant changes we made the '32 Ford Roadster ours.

Right, the 1935 Miller-Ford Indianapolis entries featured a four-carb manifold made by Harry Miller. While the flanges look like they were made for Winfield carburetors, they were fitted with Miller single-throats. The aluminum cylinder heads were made by Bohnalite and had slightly more compression than a stock Ford head. Ten Miller-Fords were made for the 1935 race; several entries used the manifold shown, some had another log-type Miller four-carb manifold, and some had dual manifolds made by the Hexagon Tool Company. *John Lee photo*

Far right, Ford V-8 60 in the So-Cal streamliner had a Winfield 1-A camshaft, Edelbrock heads and dual manifold, and a Kong manual-advance ignition. Bore and stroke were 0.125in oversize for 156ci displacement. At 6200 rpm it produced 110-115hp on straight methanol fuel at Bonneville's 4500ft elevation. In 1950, the car and engine combination set a new class record at 162.950mph —driven alternately by Bill Dailey and Ray Charbonneau. *Greg Sharp collection*

Bottom left, Ford V-8 60s played a big part in post-WWII midget racing. Speed equipment was being made for this engine by Vic Edelbrock, Eddie Meyer, Phil Weiand, Earl Evans, and Clay Smith & Dan Jones. This Smith (no relation to Clay) "Jiggler" had overhead valves on the exhaust only, making it an "F" head. The intake valves were still in their stock location in the block and, on this engine, fed by a Meyer dual manifold. Overhead valve conversions for the Ford flathead overcame poor breathing. There is no evidence of water chambers in these heads, but deep fins on the water return manifolds served as a sort of air-cooling system. *Neal East photo*

Bottom right, Mickey Thompson brought this twin Merc-powered modified coupe to Bonneville in 1952 and established a two-way average of 194.34mph after a one-way qualifying run of 198.07mph. Evans heads are used on both engines, with an Evans three-carb intake manifold on the front engine and an Evans four-carb on the second engine. *Author photo*

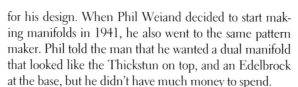

for his design. When Phil Weiand decided to start making manifolds in 1941, he also went to the same pattern maker. Phil told the man that he wanted a dual manifold that looked like the Thickstun on top, and an Edelbrock at the base, but he didn't have much money to spend.

The pattern maker, in a rare lapse of judgment, simply took a mold from the upper part of the Thickstun, and a mold from the lower part of the Edelbrock slingshot, and quickly produced the manifold Weiand wanted. Unfortunately for Weiand, Vic Edelbrock walked unannounced into the pattern shop one day and, seeing the pattern for this new copycat manifold, took a hammer, and broke it into small pieces.

The pattern maker, having committed to Weiand, that he would create a pattern for him for $200, now had, to

make good, so he quickly made a new pattern but didn't take time to align the manifold passages with the ports in the block. If you examine an early Wieand manifold, you'll note that the manifold ports go straight down, to the block, when they should be at an angle matching the ports.

My first hands-on experience with any of this V-8 speed equipment was in 1941 when I bought an Eddie Meyer dual manifold from Stu Hilborn. It cost me $25 but included a second carburetor (to match the one on my '39 Merc), and the fuel line from the pump to the two carburetors. I was never really happy with that manifold. It blocked the exhaust heat risers which made my twin pipes so loud you couldn't carry on a conversation inside the car, and being designed for top speed use, it wasn't smooth on the street.

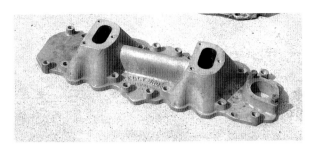

A few months later I traded the Meyer dual to Gene Callahan for an Edelbrock slingshot. We were both happy with the swap; he now had a full Meyer engine for his roadster, and I had a car that would run smoothly on the street. It turned out to be pretty fast, too, for a car that had only a dual manifold and twin pipes.

One day in 1941, with Bill Faris riding shotgun, I stopped for a signal at Olive and Victory in Burbank, headed west on Olive. Lloyd Wade and Cal Evans pulled up alongside in Wade's '36 three-window coupe. It was a slick-looking car; black, with Buick rear fender skirts and whitewall tires, twin foglamps down front, and two spotlights mounted on the windshield posts. It also had what we thought to be a full-house Eddie-Meyer-equipped engine.

This '36 was reputed to be the fastest car in Burbank, circa 1941. "They're gonna wanta race, aren't they?" I said to Bill. "Sure they are," he replied. "Let's do it. So what if they beat us." Easy for him to say. It was me and my car that would suffer the indignity.

When the signal changed to green we both stomped on it, and, to my surprise, we drove off and left

the '36. We stayed on it to the six-way intersection of Olive, Sparks, and Verdugo—about a quarter mile, and then slowed down continuing west on Olive. I don't know if the coupe really didn't have anything but the bolt-on equipment, or if it wasn't running right, or what. I do know that the following week every owner of a supposedly hot car in Burbank wanted to race me. I knew how the gunslingers of the old west felt.

In spite of the unwanted attention, I felt good about beating that '36. It was an unexpected triumph, and the victory was sweeter because I really thought we would look foolish after he had "cleaned our clock," but it didn't work out that way.

The flathead V-8 was slow to be developed into a racing engine, due partly to the lack of speed equipment and partly to the lack of prior knowledge and experience to make the right modifications. The availability of new speed equipment and increasing knowledge of how best to use this equipment grew so fast in the late 1940s and early '50s that the engine had gained its maturity when GM introduced the ohv Cadillac and Olds in 1949.

Above, Bob Meeks balances a connecting rod at Edelbrock's shop in the early 1950s. *Joe Moore photo*

Top, the Kelly Bros. dual, made in San Bernardino, California, was one of the many manifolds available after WWII. The raised section between the carburetors is an equalizer chamber. *John Lee photo*

Lower left, the Wayne Morrison dual manifold, background, handled two Strombergs or Chandler-Groves carburetors side by side. The stock Ford heat risers apparently are incorporated into the manifold design for quick warm-up and flexible street running. The Schnell ("speed" in German) four-carb manifold appears to have a large plenum chamber and also incorporates the stock Ford heat riser. This manifold was made for racing, with mounts for four carbs and no provision for a generator. *John Lee photo*

Mark Cummins heads.
Don Zabel photo

Maxi heads (with Iskenderian valve covers).
Greg Sharp collection

Lower right, Arnold Birner eight-port heads.
John Riley photo

Lower far right, Alexander heads.
Author photo

OHV Conversions for Flathead V-8s

One of the biggest drawbacks to the production Ford flathead V-8 was its breathing ability, both intake and exhaust. The poor exhaust routing also caused engine over-heating because the exhaust passages went through the water jackets.

As a result, a large number of overhead valve conversions were made starting in the mid-1930s. Some were created for commercial use; the E.K. Wood Lumber Co., for example, which had a fleet of Ford trucks, wanted something to give them a little more power and at the same time run

cooler. The Dixon ohv heads were the response to that plea.

The ohv heads (most of which had only the exhaust valves in the head) made pre-WWII were not terribly efficient, and when the racers started using them few went any faster than they had with their old flatheads. The prewar conversions were made mostly by Alexander, Dixon, Maxi, Riley, and Schaeffer and only one, the Dixon, took advantage of the opportunity to fit four exhaust ports in each head. The others usually had three or, in the Alexander, two ports.

All the postwar ohv conversions—Adams-Moller, Ardun, Arnold Birner, Cummins, and the Davis dohc heads—all had four intake and four exhaust ports in each head. These designers were taking advantage of the reasons to equip an engine with overhead valves in the first place.

Good, bad, or indifferent, these conversions demonstrated the inventive and innovative spirit of the hot rodders, and a willingness to try anything that might produce more power.

Riley heads.
Author photo

Dixon heads.
Frederick A. Usher photo

A pre-WWII dual intake manifold on a postwar car. The Davies side-by-side dual was made in the late 1930s, but this photo was taken at El Mirage Dry Lake in April 1946. By the looks of it, the car is probably a spectator vehicle. *Fred Usher photo*

Typical dry lakes set-up—an Edelbrock-equipped Merc which Harold Post ran in his streamliner until he installed a Chrysler hemi. The large tubing is the water return system to a reservoir tank— the car had no radiator. The carburetors have their choke butterflies removed for running straight methanol fuel fed by four neoprene flex lines. The photo, by H. Warren King, was taken at an SCTA meet at El Mirage in 1952.

Like the earlier four-cylinder Ford engines, the flathead hung on, remaining popular with the majority of hot rodders well into the 1950s. However, its fate was sealed even before the appearance of Chevy's V-8 in 1955, which replaced the flathead as the Great American Racing Engine.

Building a Flathead V-8

The flathead Ford/Mercury engines had two major problems which had to be dealt with: Poor breathing, caused by the basic flathead engine design, and over heating caused by the exhaust passages through the water jackets. It took time, but ingenious hot rodders minimized if not completely eliminated both problems. By the time flathead modifications had become commonplace, most engine builders were doing pretty much the same things to their engines—with slight variations.

Some engine builders became legends in their own time, having developed flathead modification to a fine art. One of the most prominent, and arguably the best, is Bob Meeks, who worked for Vic Edelbrock, senior and junior, for more than fifty years.

What Bobby did to these engines is basically the same thing other builders did, but Meeks gave them his own special touch; partly the result of many years of building engines, and partly from endless hours of experimentation on the Edelbrock dynamometer. If any "speed secret" was in these engines, it was one of extreme care in assembly.

The cylinder blocks, usually new ones rather than junkyard remnants, were re-bored by Meeks who paid special attention to perpendicularity between crankshaft axis and cylinder bores. Bob didn't simply rebore the cylinders as they came (which, because of mass production, are not always true), he made certain the new bores were an absolute right-angle to the crankshaft center line. To use more recent parlance, he was "blueprinting" the engine.

Most flathead engine builders enlarge the intake ports with a hand-held portable grinder, which removes metal from the inside of the ports, enlarging them to a guessed-at size. Meeks developed a jig to hold a slightly tapered core-drill which was run into each of the intake ports a pre-determined distance, thus guaranteeing that all eight ports were exactly the same size. Then, a hand-held grinder was used to smooth the ridges at the bottom of the core-drilled holes to blend them into the valve area. After drilling and grinding, the ports were polished with emery paper.

Meeks then removed the stock 1.500in-diameter valves and 1.750in intakes were fitted (the valve seats had to be removed and the valves seated directly on the block) and 1.625in exhaust valves were used with the stock seats enlarged.

Because of the flathead exhaust passage configuration, a core-drill couldn't be used to open up these ports; they were done by hand with a portable grinder. The center cylinders on each side were siamesed into a single port on each side which was located between the center cylinders. To prevent the exhaust pulse from interfering with the adjoining cylinder's exhaust, a metal plate—basically a 0.125in-thick divider—was cut to fit and arc welded in the center of the siamesed port.

Finally, the engine block was "relieved," with metal ground from the block between the valves and the cylinders, increasing the area for fuel mixture flow from valves to the compression chamber. Some engine builders shaped this "relief" to match the head-gasket shape, and others matched the relief to the cylinder head combustion chamber shape. The relief depth was determined by the height of the top compression ring on the piston. The bottom of the relief had to stop short of the top of the top ring.

A stock Ford oil pump had sufficient capacity and pressure (the latter was adjustable to a minor degree) for almost all applications, so there was no need to consider radical modifications (dry sump, for example) to the lubrication system.

Water circulation was a problem, however. The stock Ford system used two pumps, one for each side of the engine, which from 1932 through 1936 were mounted in the front of the cylinder heads, but in 1937 were moved to the front of the block.

In the stock system, a thermostat was fitted at each outlet from the cylinder head to the radiator, but when they got old, they often stuck shut. One of the first things a flathead man did was to throw the thermostats away. Their replacements were two large washers, 1.875in in diameter with a 0.750in hole, which were placed over the outlet from the head and held in place by the water hose. This restricted the water flow but had

no chance of shutting off the flow.

The second thing that was sometimes done was to cut off every other impeller blade from each of the pumps. At high engine speed, or at high engine temperatures, the stock impellers tended to cavitate. The removal of every second blade seemed to cure this.

Serious racers, mainly oval-track types, removed the stock pumps, fitted a flat plate over the holes, then installed a belt-driven marine-type positive displacement pump and ran a pair of outlets into small header pipes plugged into the block below the exhaust ports on each side of the block.

The popular high-compression heads were aluminum castings and came in a variety of shapes, both inside the compression chamber and outside by the number, placement, and size of the fins. The fins seen on most of the racing heads were more for looks and for stiffening the head casting than for any real cooling function.

One outstanding exception I can think of were some heads made in the 1930s by Art Sparks. These twenty-one-stud heads were water-cooled over the valves, and had fins similar to those on a motorcycle cylinder—running transversely instead of lengthwise—over the cylinders. Art explained to me that he wanted a different rate of heat dissipation for the valves and pistons, and this was his way of accomplishing that.

Aside from the different compression chamber shapes, when large valves were used, as Meeks did, it required that the compression chambers be fly-cut around the valve pockets to allow a more even flow of the incoming mixture. Meeks used a "ball cutter" on a drill motor to further finish the chamber shape behind the valves.

Balancing was a part of engine building that got a lot of attention from Edelbrock's builders. Connecting rods were purchased in batches from a Ford dealer, and each one was weighed. They then grouped them by weight, and eight rods were picked for an engine from the same group. The rods were then ground and filed down so each rod would match the weight of the lightest rod of the group. They were then balanced to each other end for end. Total rod weight would be identical, as would the weight of the big-end and the piston-pin end, for all eight.

When balancing the crankshaft, bob-weights were made for each crank throw, the weight of each bob matching the total rod weight plus the weight of another lower end. This was because the revolving weight, as represented by the rod big-end, would have two rods side by side on each crank throw, so the balancing bob-weight then represented that combination. The upper end of each rod was reciprocating weight and didn't play such an important role in crankshaft balance.

Displacement could be increased two ways: bore the cylinders larger, or add to the crankshaft stroke. The

This four-carburetor manifold was hand made of welded steel tubing by Warren Van Sickle. There were no balance tubes or equalizers; Van Sickle felt that each port should be completely separated from the others. This 1939 photo at Muroc Dry Lakes shows the manifold on Kong Jackson's '32. Kong said he tried Stromberg model 48s, 81s, and 97s at various times and that nothing else could match the acceleration of the car, but at top speed fuel spit back out the tops of the carbs and the manifold was never successful for high-speed use.
Mark Dees collection

former was quite simple if one took care not to go too far and end up with paper-thin cylinder walls (a few zealous builders even bored large enough to go into the surrounding water jackets, in which case a sleeve had to be fitted).

Stroking was a bit more difficult. In the early days of the Mercury engine it was discovered by engine builders that the Merc had the same basic dimensions as the Ford V-8, but the crank rod journal was 0.125in larger than the Ford journal. This led to regrinding the Merc crank throws to Ford size but off-center to the outside, which resulted in a stroke increase of 0.125in.

If a longer stroke was desired, the crank journal could be metal-sprayed and reground with an even longer off-set. This system wasn't reliable, as the metal spray was really little more than a muff around the journal and had a tendency to work loose while running.

The Ford Motor Company handed the flathead devotees a real bonus when the 1949 Mercury was introduced; it had the same size rod journals as before, but it also had a 4.000in stroke. That represented a displacement increase of 16.5in (239 to 255.5ci). When this crank was reground to fit Ford rods it could have a 4.125in stroke. One of the best-known flathead configurations was called "3/8 by 3/8." In the sometimes obscure jargon of the hot rodder, this meant that the cylin-

ders were bored to 3-3/8 (an increase of only 0.187in— or 3/16), and the stroke was 4.125, or 3/8in over the old 3-3/4 stroke.

Before Meeks assembled an engine, the rods were polished and bead-blasted to remove any possibility of a sharp edge causing a fracture while under pressure. Sharon Baker, a member of the Russetta Coupes Club, ran a Meeks-built flathead in his '40 two-door sedan for three seasons at the dry lakes with a best time of 132.35 on straight methanol. He then ran it a season in a hydroplane, followed by three seasons in a track roadster, and it never once blew or quit during a race.

One advantage, among many, that the Edelbrock crew had was when they dyno-tested engines they never kidded themselves or their customers. Meeks told me that their engines, when burning straight methanol, put out 240–245hp. We continued to hear stories in the 1950s about fabulous flatheads getting 300 or more horsepower, but, when the race was over, the Edelbrock, engine was often the winner.

One season, I think it was 1949, there were eleven classes of competition at Russetta Timing Association meets, and Edelbrock-built or equipped cars held nine of those records. Both Meeks and Edelbrock claimed there were no "speed secrets" in their engines—at least insofar as special equipment was concerned, but their edge was primarily one of extreme thoroughness and care during engine assembly. They took time to do it right.

Edelbrock tried all the fad "speed secrets" that racers are so fond of discovering—pop-up pistons, 180-degree crankshafts, and anything else they thought might make a difference but always came back to their tried, true, and proven procedures.

The flathead Ford/Mercury engines were not state of the art production engines even at the beginning, and they were a lot more old-fashioned by the late 1940s when the ohv V-8 production engines started coming out. Still, a properly set up flathead was a great racing engine—particularly for the money spent. My complete engine, with every part of it brand new, cost me about $450 in 1947—I assembled it myself, so there was no labor cost involved.

If a flathead was not too radical, (Bob Meeks, Barney Navarro, and others who knew their stuff sel-

dom built a flathead with more than 9.5:1 compression—though Meeks did build the So-Cal Bonneville engine with 10:1) it was a very reliable powerplant.

I ran my '32 roadster on the street for 3-1/2 years, rolling up about 40,000 miles, and ran two seasons—1947 and 1948—at the lakes (eight meets in all) and the engine never once let me down. It had a stock bore and stroke, '47 Merc engine (239ci) with Navarro 9.25:1 heads, Edelbrock Super dual intake manifold, Ord twin-coil ignition, and a Clay Smith 272 camshaft—a grind he had developed for hydroplanes, which brought a lot of derision from my fellow lakes racers. My best time, on methanol, was 126.58 at the September 1948 SCTA meet.

I can't imagine Ford engineers planned it this way, but the company was a great benefactor to the rodder. And with the preponderance of Ford race and street cars, the publicity gained from racing successes undoubtedly helped Ford.

Those were the days my friend, and we thought they'd never end. But they did.

FORD & MERCURY FLATHEAD V-8 ENGINE TYPES

Make BHP	Year	Displ.	Bore x Stroke	Engine Configuration	
Ford	1932	221ci	3.062x3.750	21-stud heads water pumps in heads	65
Ford	1933	221ci	3.062x3.750	21-stud heads water pumps in heads	75
Ford	1934–36	221ci	3.062x3.750	21-stud heads water pumps in heads	85
Ford	1937– early '38	221ci	3.062x3.750	21-stud heads water pumps in block	85
Ford	late '38– 1941	221ci	3.062x3.750	24-stud heads water pumps in block	85
Ford	1942	221ci	3.062x3.750	24-stud heads water pumps in block	90
Ford	1946–48	239ci	3.187x3.750	24-stud heads water pumps in block	100
Ford	1949–51	239ci	3.187x3.750	24-stud heads water pumps in block	100
Ford	1952–53	239ci	3.187x3.750	24-stud heads water pumps in block	110
Ford	1937–40	136ci	2.600x3.200	17-stud heads water pumps in block	60
Merc	1939–41	239ci	3.187x3.750	24-stud heads water pumps in block	95
Merc	1942	239ci	3.187x3.750	24-stud heads water pumps in block	100
Merc	1946–48	239ci	3.187x3.750	24-stud heads water pumps in block	100
Merc	1949–50	255.5ci	3.187x4.000	24-stud heads water pumps in block	110
Merc	1951	255.5ci	3.187x4.000	24-stud heads water pumps in block	112
Merc	1952–53	255.5ci	3.187x4.000	24-stud heads water pumps in block	125

The above chart gives only the stock dimensions and configuration of the flathead V-8 engines, and one of the basic paths to more power is increased displacement. The Ford flathead cylinder blocks could be safely bored to 3-3/8in (3.375in) and if the block was brand new and absolutely perfect from the standpoint of casting (no core shifts or anything that would leave the cylinder wall too thin after boring), it could be taken out to 3-7/16in (3.437in) but that usually led to overheating because of the thinner cylinder walls.

Despite this plea from the So-Cal team, divine intervention was not forthcoming, and the flathead's reign came to an end. *Alex Xydias collection*

The Day the Flathead Died

*"Flatheads Forever" said the bumper stickers;
a forlorn hope for the diehard true-believers*

Actually, the flathead Ford V-8 had been doomed since 1949 when Cadillac and Oldsmobile introduced overhead valve V-8 engines in their production cars. If that development didn't get the flattoppers' attention, then the Chrysler Hemi, which came out in 1951, surely did.

Strangely, well maybe not—no one was making speed equipment for the GM ohv engines at that time—the rodders were slow to utilize these new engines as their powerplants of choice. At Bonneville, for example, and even after the two GM pioneers had been out almost a year, there were none of the new ohv engines running at the Nationals in 1950. There was only one, Bill Edwards' '50 Cadillac-powered '40 Ford Coupe, in the 1951 Nationals.

By the 1952 Bonneville meet things had started to change; there were five Chrysler V-8 entries, four Cadillac V-8s, and two Olds Rocket V-8s. The entry that did-in the flathead Ford was the Chrysler Hemi-powered belly tank lakester entered by Mal Hooper and Ray Brown.

Alex Xydias and Clyde Sturdy had the entry that upheld the honor of the flatheads right to the end. They went to Bonneville with one car and three engines; a V-8 60 to run in Class A, a Merc in class B, and another Merc for Class C. All three engines were flatheads, with Edelbrock heads and manifolds and Kong ignitions (Xydias had taken over the manufacture of Kong ignitions earlier in the year).

Their Class A and Class C engines were built by Bob Meeks, and the B engine was built by Keith Baldwin. By the time the 1952 Bonneville Nationals meet was over, the Xydias-Sturdy team had new records in Classes A and B and had set fastest one-way time in A, B, and C classes. They set a record for C Class on the Friday of that week, only to lose it to the Mal Hooper-Ray Brown Chrysler on Saturday.

One primary reason the flathead-powered tank did so well was the use of nitromethane. Meeks had worked out the carburetion, compression ratio and cam timing to allow the use of 40 percent nitro (60 percent methanol) without burning valves or pistons—usually the first two components to go when things were amiss in a nitro-burning engine.

The So-Cal flathead went down fighting; setting a two-way Class C average of 197.17mph and top time in the class at 198.340. Unfortunately, the Chrysler managed a two-way average of 197.88mph—also boosted by a nitro-methanol mix.

When the 1953 Bonneville program was printed, the future of hot rod engine competition was plain; the listed entries included seventeen Chryslers, seven each Cadillac and Olds, one Lincoln, five DeSotos, one Dodge, and four Studebakers—all ohv V-8s. The Chryslers, Dodge, and DeSotos were, of course, Hemi engines.

There were still some overhead valve conversions on flathead engines; Adams-Moller C-T, Ardun, and the Lee Chapel Tornado-equipped flathead, but as good as these were, they were still stopgaps before the factory overheads took over. It probably isn't a fair comparison to call these conversions "flathead" anyway, even though they were adapted to a flathead block.

Regrinding a camshaft, or making a hotter ignition for the new ohv engines wasn't that difficult, and the usual light flywheels, welded tubing exhaust headers, and carburetors or injectors (Hilborn was starting to make his injectors for other engines) to run alcohol or nitro were practices that carried over from the flathead days.

Most of the dry lakes and Bonneville competitors were capable of making their own intake manifolds, or any other pieces they needed to extract power from these new engines, and they started realizing extra performance almost from the start. Those who had to depend on buying ready-made speed equipment for a given engine simply had to wait until the manufacturers started building equipment for the ohv engines.

Because of the inherent better breathing and cooler running the new engines—they were really quite simple to hop up—they could be bored oversize and stroked (or de-stroked) as easily as could be done on a flathead. Just as Henry Ford had done in 1932 when he brought out the inexpensive V-8, the manufacturers—GM and Chrysler particularly—had just handed the hot rodders much better engines to work with. Rodders, for their part, made the most of the opportunity.

After the Mopar Hemis—Chrysler, DeSoto, and Dodge—the next onslaught to the flathead was the small-block Chevy V-8 which came out in 1955. Due to its light weight, compact dimensions, and performance potential, it was the next "Great American Racing Engine" after the flathead Ford. Because of the exterior dimensions the Chevy V-8 became the engine of choice not only for racers, but as replacements for Ford engines in street rods and customs.

The small-block Ford V-8 (Fairlane) was also a great engine, but because of the ancillary equipment on the front it was about five inches longer than the Chevy. This meant that to fit it into an early Ford engine compartment, either the radiator had to be moved forward, or the firewall had to be re-worked to accommodate the length. It was simply easier to install the small-block Chevy. I've seen license plate frames that said, "Real Fords Have Chevy Engines." Judging from the number of current street rods powered by Chevy small-blocks, that facetious statement may well have come true.

Unfortunately, the era that ushered in the ohv engines from Detroit also brought in strong financial involvement from the same manufacturers and from other related industries; a situation that made racing easier for a select few, and much harder for those not chosen to be part of the act. Racing also wasn't as much fun as it had been.

With the introduction of these new engines, it became a simple matter to buy an off-the-shelf engine which, with very minor alterations, would produce more power than we used to get from a flathead V-8 or a four-banger after weeks, months, or maybe years of experimentation.

By the end of the 1950s one could buy a new car from a dealer that was faster than most of the hot rods we made ourselves a decade earlier. They called it progress and I guess it was, but at the same time it had diminished the feeling of accomplishment we had been able to realize from our hard-won efforts.

And then came the Keith Black development of the Chrysler Hemi. Black was a true gentleman and a brilliant engine developer. His K-B Hemis were the engine to have if one wanted to be a successful drag racer; so much so that most of the Funny Cars (which bear a little resemblance to a Ford, Chevy, Olds, Pontiac or whatever) had K-B Hemis under their hoods.

Hot rodding, in all its forms, would never be the same after 1949. The power extracted from current engines is staggering to those of us who labored mightily to get 200hp from a flathead, but then so is the on-track performance.

Whereas it took us two miles to get our streamliner up to 200mph at Bonneville in 1950, Kenny Bernstein now hits 314mph at the end of a quarter-mile run. It really is progress.

CHAPTER 6

Four-Bangers, Stove Bolts, Straight-Eights and V-16s

It didn't have to be a Ford, or a V-8, to be a racer.

Looking at the Los Angeles area today, it's hard to believe that as recently as WWII there was very little traffic on the streets. And most of that was the go-to-work or the coming-home-from-work crowd. Even with no freeways, it was easy to drive across the city, or to San Diego for the day. This dearth of traffic also made it less risky for guys who were building modified cars because they could test them on the street without bothering too many local citizens.

Anyone who would have been on Lincoln Boulevard, alongside Mines Field (now Los Angeles International) Airport in the early hours of a spring Sunday morning in 1940 would have been treated to a strange sight. A flattened, teardrop-shaped missile with four wheels out at the ends of exposed axles was speeding along Lincoln Boulevard and making enough noise to wake the dead.

Fortunately, there weren't many houses close to the airport, and what few people did live nearby were already inured to aircraft noise.

This odd projectile challenging the airplanes for noise superiority was a home-made race car powered by a 1925 Chevy four-cylinder inline engine, and the owner/driver, Bob Rufi, was testing a new Winfield dual carburetor set-up. Drawn through the carbs was a new fuel mixture of 80 percent methanol, 10 percent benzol, 10 percent gasoline, and a dash of acetone (the latter was supposed to keep the other ingredients from separating).

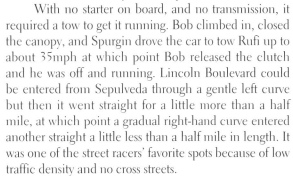

Young Rufi, 23 years old, five years out of Los Angeles High School, and now a contractor (he had completed his apprenticeship as a carpenter) had built this streamlined car the year before but had run it only on gasoline until this day.

It was only a few miles from his home in Culver City to his chosen test site. Accompanied by friends Chuck Spurgin, Ralph Schenck, Bob Giovanine, and sundry hangers-on, the little car, which weighed only 950lb including water, fuel, and driver, was towed from Culver City to the airport.

With no starter on board, and no transmission, it required a tow to get it running. Bob climbed in, closed the canopy, and Spurgin drove the car to tow Rufi up to about 35mph at which point Bob released the clutch and he was off and running. Lincoln Boulevard could be entered from Sepulveda through a gentle left curve but then it went straight for a little more than a half mile, at which point a gradual right-hand curve entered another straight a little less than a half mile in length. It was one of the street racers' favorite spots because of low traffic density and no cross streets.

Bob built up his speed until he was running at well over 100mph when he was spotted by a Los Angeles Police officer going the other direction astride his Harley-Davidson ohv 61 police cycle. Making a quick U-turn, the officer took out after Rufi who didn't know he was being chased and only caught up with the racing car when Rufi stopped at the end of his run.

Tom Davis ran this Olds straight eight two-man modified job at the lakes and on the street before WWII. The chassis was built by Herb Farrington, using two side rails from a Miller Indy car. From there it was basically a shortened '29 Ford body with a long hood to cover the straight eight engine. The grille was made from standard grille work bought from Andrews Hardware in Los Angeles. The Olds engine had a milled head, Winfield camshaft, and a Pierce-Arrow ignition. The car was never a contender for top speed, but it nevertheless offered a bit of variety; at the August 24, 1941 SCTA meet at Muroc, the Olds was one of five non-Ford entries out of a total of 161.

Opposite page, Lee Chapel, his familiar cigar firmly in hand, drove this 1924 Chevy four 111.11mph at Muroc Dry Lake in 1930. The Chevy engine had an Olds 3-Port cylinder head. A fuel pressure pump is mounted on the left side of the cowl within easy reach of the driver. Front springs are leading quarter-elliptic and the tires look like boardtrack racing tires. The odd-looking fixture at the center of the front axle is probably for towing. *Greg Sharp collection*

Jim Woods, of the SCTA Road Runners Club ran this 229ci Ford six-powered roadster in 1948. The 1941 flathead six had a milled and filled stock head, Lyle Knudsen three-carb intake manifold, Clay Smith camshaft, Harman & Collins magneto, and a set of home-made exhaust headers. The tank, a war surplus item used by most dry lakes competitors, beside the driver's seat carried fuel.

After looking the streamliner over, checking Bob's driver license, and delivering the official lecture about speeding, he said, "I should give you a helluva ticket, but I don't know how to describe this car. Promise me you won't run it again on the street, and I'll let you go." Bob was only too happy to promise him that he wouldn't do it again, and they took the car home.

By this time, Bob had learned what he wanted to know; his new carburetor set-up with two sidedraft Winfields mounted directly on the cylinder head without a manifold in between, and his exotic fuel mix, worked. He had planned the carburetion after reading in Harry Ricardo's book, *The High Speed Internal Combustion Engine*, that the most effective carburetion was obtained when the carburetor venturis were as close to the intake port and valve as possible.

The fuel mixture came from a book published in England called *Speed, and How To Obtain It*, which reported a similar mix being used by the 1930s Mercedes-Benz Grand Prix cars.

Left, Ted Cannon with his Marmon V-16 at Muroc Dry Lake, August 24, 1941. Because of the engine displacement (490.8ci), the car ran in the Unlimited Class, which also included cars with supercharged engines. Cannon's friends dubbed the car the "Buckboard," for obvious reasons. Since it ran in the mid-120mph range, it must have been a real thrill for Ted to ride that buckboard down the lake bed.
Gus Rollins photo

Far left, the Chuck Spurgin (pictured) and Bob Giovanine Chevy-four roadster was the high-points car in SCTA competition for 1948, setting an A class roadster record of 123.655mph, a record which stood for two years. The car, a 1925 Chevy roadster body on a '25 Chevy frame and rear axle, had an early Ford I-beam front axle and transverse leaf spring. The '25 Chevy engine had an Olds 3-Port cylinder head, Winfield camshaft, Ford Model C crankshaft destroked to bring displacement down to 182.9ci (just under the 183ci class limit), and a pair of carburetors which featured Winfield float bowls and Duke Hallock throttle-bodies and venturis. In the 1949 season the car clocked 135mph-plus.
Chuck Spurgin collection

Jot Horne brought this Model J Duesenberg-powered (420ci, twin overhead camshafts with four valves per cylinder, rated at 265hp from the factory) roadster to the first Bonneville Speed Trials in 1949. Horne, entered in the "D" roadster class took home a trophy for top qualifying speed, 122.95, and a two-way record average of 127.565mph. The eight short, straight exhaust stacks made wonderful booming sounds across the vast expanse of the salt flats.
Edelbrock collection

Rufi's entire car was the direct result of time spent reading books at the Los Angeles Public Library. He read about the Auto Union GP cars in which the designer, Dr. Ferdinand Porsche, had put the driver in front of the engine, which allowed the driver to sit low in the car because he didn't have to straddle the driveshaft as he would with the engine in front.

Bob also read theories of aerodynamics which said that a teardrop shape was best, and the widest part of that shape should be about 1/3 back from the rounded nose. This all fit his plans perfectly because his engine, the Chevy four, was much narrower than Bob's shoulders, so he designed the car with the driver placed in front of the engine.

Charles Dimmitt's monster was seen first in the 1948 lakes season at El Mirage Dry Lake. Dimmitt, a member of the SCTA Autocrats Club, built his car on a 147in wheelbase and used a 1931 455ci Cadillac V-16 for power. A large expanse of sheet metal joins the 1937 Ford V-8 pickup truck grille and the 1939 Lincoln-Zephyr convertible coupe body, which has its windshield cut off. Drive went through two Cadillac transmissions (one was reversed). The dramatic appearance was not matched by its speed, and the car was never a contender.
Tom Medley collection

John Hartman built this Wayne Chevy roadster in his shop—Hartman Machine—and ran it both at the dry lakes and on the track. His shop was a job shop which did work for the aircraft industry, Twin Coach bus company, and as a sideline made race car components, mainly torsion bar suspensions. The photo was taken at El Mirage Dry Lake, with Bill Spalding, Tom Spalding, and Wayne Horning.
Tom Medley collection

The Eddie Edmunds-equipped flathead LaSalle V-8 in the Fred Vogel-Max Balchowsky '32 Ford they ran in California road races in the early 1950s. The engine had been built by Yam Oka and proved reliable but overweight for road racing; Max replaced it with a Buick V-8.

The light weight was achieved because of the utter simplicity of the car's components. The basic frame was two lengths of 2-3/16-inch-diameter electrical conduit (Rufi had little money to spend on the car so he used whatever material he could get cheap). The Ford I-beam front axle was held to the tubular front cross member by two U-bolts of the type used on rear semi-elliptic springs. To attach the rear axle, Bob drilled two holes in the axle housing into which the frame longerons were inserted and then the pieces were welded together. No springs were used so making the rear axle part of the frame structure wasn't considered a handicap.

Rufi was a well-liked competitor at the lakes because of his honesty and integrity, but, with his chosen equipment, he was known as "one of those Chevy guys," an appellation applied to those who didn't run Ford products. At that time, four-cylinder Fords made up about 97 percent of the entries at Muroc or Harper Dry Lakes. Bob was in rather stellar company as it turned out; Lee Chapel, Chuck Spurgin, Ralph Schenck, and Bob Giovanine, among others, ran very successful Chevy fours.

Things were about to get better for the Chevy crowd. Ernie McAfee held the streamliner record at the lakes with his Winfield-equipped Model-B-Ford-pow-

ered streamliner at 132.89mph—set in 1938—and a best one-way speed of 137mph-plus. Rufi wanted that record, and he would get it in dramatic fashion—and his record would stand for eight years.

May 19 was the first SCTA meet of the 1940 season, at Harper Dry Lake. Rufi was on the lakebed on Saturday to tune and prepare his car for Sunday's time trials. The lakebed looked perfect, and the weather prediction was good. It was also the first time Bob had run a tachometer on his car, and in a warm-up run the tach read 5000rpm, which translated to 140mph. Bob thought there was something wrong with the tach.

The next morning he found that the speed indication wasn't a fluke, and his tach was reading correctly. When Chuck Spurgin towed him to start the car, he let out the clutch at about 35mph, but the engine didn't seem to want to run smoothly. Nursing the car up to about 90mph it suddenly came alive and really stared to haul. Rufi went into the timed quarter mile reading 5000rpm and exited it reading 5300.

While Bob turned the car around to make the return run for his two-way average, he was told the first run had been 143.54mph. Now if he could only equal that speed again. Just as he got underway, someone mistakenly started another car from the starting line. SCTA secretary Art Tilton ran out to the edge of the course to flag Rufi off the course. Bob didn't turn out of the course, but he did back off the throttle.

His time was missed in all the confusion, and later after a lengthy discussion with officials and Chief Timer Otto Crocker, they all agreed that Bob had been easily going 137mph or better, so the officials gave him a two-way average of 140mph. Rufi's tach had been reading 5300 before he backed off, so it's likely that his return

run would have been close if not surpassing his first run, which would have given him a two-way average higher than has been reported since 1940.

Rufi finished the season first in points and would have carried number "1" on his car in 1941 but for an accident at the November 17, 1940, meet. Rain had drenched the lakebed, and, while most of it had dried, parts were still damp. Bob got into the wet stuff just before entering the time traps, and the car spun, dug in, and flipped over, leaving him with a concussion and a broken right arm. After spending three weeks in the hospital and then a couple months with his working arm in a sling, he sold the car and retired from competition.

The Chevy four ranks had lost its top car, but not the man who designed, built, and drove it. Rufi continued to work with Chuck Spurgin, a friend since childhood, Bob Giovanine, Ralph Schenck, and Duane Steele. Spurgin and Giovanine's Chevy four modified roadster was the SCTA top points car in 1948.

Endless Variety

Chevy fours weren't the only non-Ford entries, merely some of the most prominent. Before WWII we also saw Hudson, Oldsmobile, Chrysler, and Buick straight-eights, Cadillac V-8s, Lincoln-Zephyr V-12s, Cadillac and Marmon V-16s, all fitted into various roadster bodies or those special cars that made up the prewar Modified or Unlimited classes.

Then there were the foreign cars Tommy Lee brought to the dry lakes; Talbot-Lago, Bugatti, BMW, and his Offenhauser-powered special.

In the "old days" it was pretty much run-whatcha-brung-and-we'll-find-a-class-for-you. Some of the cars which turned up were pretty wild—from the beautiful to

Above, Tony Capanna drove fellow Albata Club member Jim White's Hudson eight 124.14mph on July 20, 1941, to gain first place in the Modified Class for the meet. We can see four Winfield carburetors and a nice set of exhaust headers. The engine had been run in the Indianapolis 500 before White acquired it to run at the dry lakes. These Hudson racing engines had the intake on the top and exhaust on the side—opposite to the standard Hudson engine of the period.
Creighton Hunter photo,
Don Montgomery collection

Top far left, Bob Rufi built this two-man streamliner—the first built for this new class in 1938—with the help of his friends. Rufi and Chuck Spurgin found a Dodge roadster in the bottom of Decker Canyon, near Santa Monica, California, and after dragging the wreck home, the frame and cowl became the basis for this car. The grille bars are from a 1934 Ford V-8, and the grille shell is made from a Studebaker gas tank. Rufi made the heart-shaped frame around the grille from flat sheet steel. The tail of the car is fabric over a wood and chicken-wire frame, which caused Rufi's friends to dub it the "chicken coop tail." Rufi coaxed 118mph from the Chevy-four-powered car, with a 115mph two-way average.
Chuck Spurgin collection

Top left, under the elongated hood of this '32 Ford roadster is a Buick straight eight. A 3in-diameter straight pipe under the car carries the exhaust to the rear, and Woodlights have been fitted in place of the original Ford headlights. *Frederick A. Usher photo*

Top right, Pasadena Roadster Club (SCTA) members Bob Wright and Don Berg built this Cadillac V-8 powered '27 T roadster. The exhaust ports on the flathead Cad, unlike the Ford flathead, came out through the top of the block. Their exhaust system, while making the doors useless, was beautifully done. Each tailpipe had a muffler inserted near the pipe end. This roadster was built as a street job, so it was essential that mufflers be included. The body is channeled down over the frame, and a '32 Ford grille has been fitted. *Bob Wright photo, Don Montgomery collection*

Bottom left, racer, and book publisher, Don Montgomery tunes the 356ci Buick straight eight in his 1936 Cord sedan. A Howard Johansen "Awful Awful" camshaft, a Scintilla magneto (donated by Ed Iskenderian), a six-carb intake manifold, and J.E. pistons made up the speed equipment on the engine. The exhaust headers were made by Montgomery. In 1952, Don set a new Russetta Timing Association Class B sedan record of 137.509mph. The photo is by Racer Brown who, like Montgomery, was a member of the Glendale Coupe & Roadster Club.

Bottom right, Marvin Lee's B streamliner at El Mirage Dry Lake on July 17, 1949, when the 248ci Chevy-six-powered car set a new class record at 153.545mph. The inline six was equipped with a Wayne 12-Port head and Wayne intake manifold, Bill Spalding camshaft, and Tom Spalding ignition. Left to right in the photo are Bill Spalding, Wayne Horning, Marvin Lee, and Tom Spalding. *Tom Medley collection*

the bizarre. Come to think of it, things didn't change all that much after WWII. Cars raced on the dry lakebeds were still weird and wonderful at the same time.

In the prewar years, these something-other-than-Ford engines were seen typically because the owner happened to have one, and he couldn't afford to buy another engine of any kind. There wasn't any speed equipment available for these "other" engines, so their owners displayed the ultimate in creativity by designing and building their own intake and exhaust manifolds, adapting ignitions from other cars, and spending countless hours in junkyards looking for parts they thought would work better than what they had.

A thorough knowledge of which engine parts might work in your soon-to-be-built masterpiece helped, as did a good background in engine re-building and maintenance. One absolute prerequisite for all this swapping was to know a good machinist; one who was good at his work and undaunted by a challenge could be far more valuable than the cost of his work.

I found a machinist shortly after WWII, who refused to turn some metal off a flywheel for me, saying "the damn car won't run if you lighten the flywheel." He was adamant, and I went elsewhere. He obviously didn't know how many cars with lightened flywheels were on the roads of southern California at the time. The engine wouldn't idle as smoothly as one with a stock flywheel, but who cared? Made it sound more like a real race car, even if it wasn't.

A top-notch machinist was invaluable to the guy who wanted to run an engine which had no racing equipment ready-made for it. In chapter two we noted that Bob Estes had run a Wills Sainte Claire crankshaft in his Model T Ford engine. I don't know who first discovered that this arrangement would work, but you can bet it wasn't a machinist who didn't know you could lighten a car's flywheel.

After WWII quite a few speed equipment manufacturers designed equipment for non-Ford engines. Some of these had a line of Ford equipment and simply added cylinder heads and intake manifolds for other makes to round out their line. Weiand and Edmunds are prime examples.

Others specialized; Lyle Knudsen made a head and intake manifold for the flathead Ford six, and Wayne Horning made a twelve-port "Wayne" head for the Chevrolet six (he brought out a similar head for the GMC six he called the Horning head). "California Bill" Fisher bought the Horning GMC patterns and it became the Horning-Fisher head. Horning's two heads were made of cast iron, the Horning-Fisher head was cast aluminum.

continued on page 115

BELL AUTO PARTS

Featuring the Finest in Racing Equipment

25c

Roy Richter
3633 EAST GAGE AVENUE • BELL, CALIFORNIA

Counter Telephone KImball 5728
Order Telephone JEfferson 5229

CATALOG

MOON

MOON EQUIPMENT COMPANY 10820 SO. NORWALK BLVD.
SANTA FE SPRINGS, CALIF. 90670

OFFICIAL PROGRAM
OF THE 1949
SECOND ANNUAL
HOT ROD EXPOSITION
AND
AUTOMOTIVE EQUIPMENT DISPLAY

LOS ANGELES NATL. GUARD ARMORY—JAN. 21-30, 1949

35 CENTS

THE PERFECT COMBINATION

POWER • EFFICIENCY
ECONOMY • PERFORMANCE

OFFENHAUSER
TURBO-THRUST

360°
POWER
PORT

OFFENHAUSER EQUIPMENT

360° MANIFOLDS

1971 CATALOG
©1971 Offenhauser Sales Corp.

The Greatest Name in Racing

BELL
AUTO PARTS, INC.

the BIG name in Racing Equipment

stock cars
roadsters
dragsters
sports cars
big cars
midgets

3633 EAST GAGE AVENUE, BELL, CALIFORNIA, LUdlow 7-5229

catalog number **32**

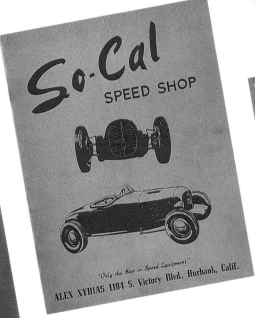

So-Cal
SPEED SHOP

"Only the Best in Speed Equipment"
ALEX XYDIAS 1104 S. Victory Blvd., Burbank, Calif.

Vic Hubbard
Speed & Marine
21032 MEEKLAND AVE., HAYWARD, CALIF.
PHONE ELgin 1-8455 (AREA CODE 415)

INDEX ON BACK COVER
FALL 1964
PRICE $1.00

DISCOUNT CLUB CATALOG

Early speed equipment catalogs. *Author collection*

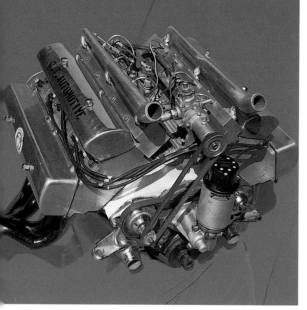

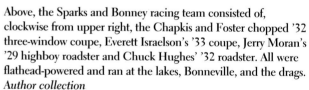

Above, the Sparks and Bonney racing team consisted of, clockwise from upper right, the Chapkis and Foster chopped '32 three-window coupe, Everett Israelson's '33 coupe, Jerry Moran's '29 highboy roadster and Chuck Hughes' '32 roadster. All were flathead-powered and ran at the lakes, Bonneville, and the drags. *Author collection*

Top left, the Adams-Moller ohv Ford/Mercury conversion built by Don Clark and Clem TeBow at CT Automotive. Its 248ci produced 320hp and pulled the Hill-Davis Bob Estes Mercury Special streamliner to a new International Class C record of 229.77mph at Bonneville in 1952.
Jerry Chesebrough photo, author collection

Left, the coupe in the foreground is '32 Ford with a flathead Mercury V-8. It carried no radiator as it was used for drag racing. The white custom is a '47 Ford. Both cars feature the craftsmanship of long-time hot rodder and customizer Gene Windfield (left). *Ralph Poole photo, author collection*

Opposite page, always the innovator, Mickey Thompson arrived at Bonneville in 1952 with two flatheads under the long hood of his Bantam coupe. Nicknamed *Cyrano*, its speed of over 196mph gave Mickey claim to the mythical title of "World's Fastest Coupe." *Author collection*

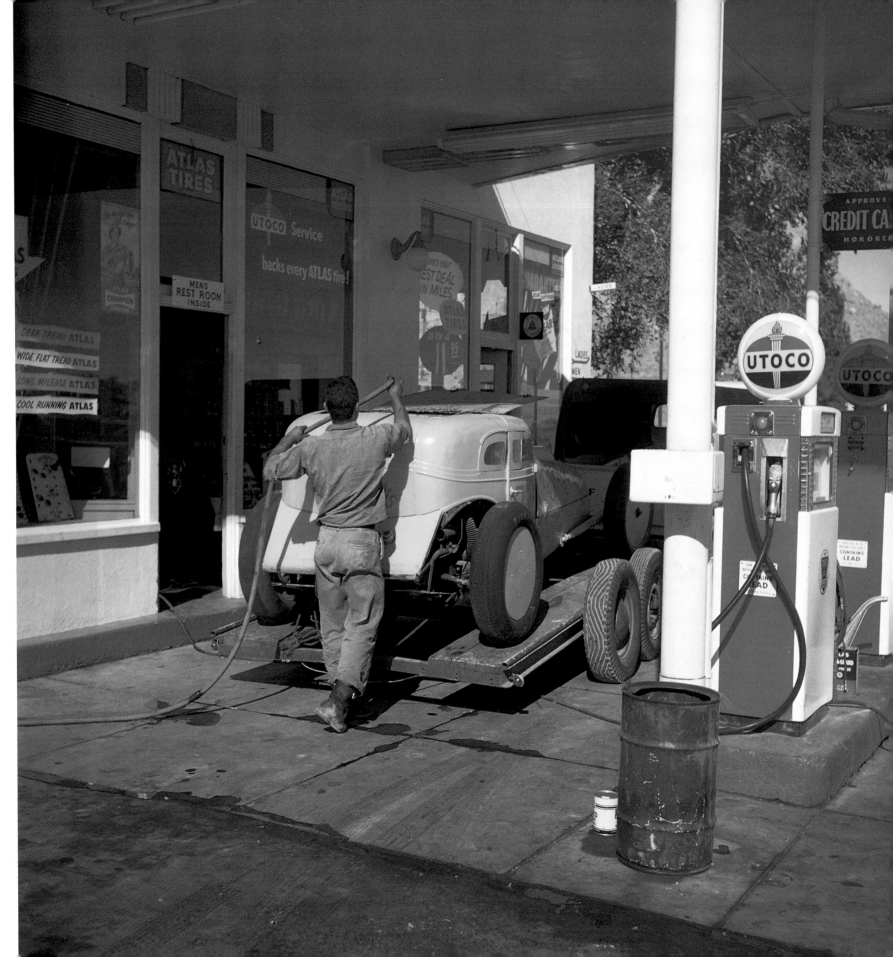

Above, Doug Hartelt's chopped '34 coupe, powered by Chuck Potvin's 364ci Chrysler from the ill-fated Carrillo streamliner, turned over 173mph at El Mirage in the early 1950s. As shown here, it's set up for drag racing where it turned 122 mph. *Author collection*

Above, Denny Larsen's *Streetliner* featured a modified fiberglass Sorrell body, tubular space frame, and Ray Brown-built, injected Chrysler; it turned better than 183mph on gasoline in 1954. The car earned its nickname by being driven the ten miles back and forth between the salt and Wendover. *Author collection*

Top left, Leland Kolb's Chrysler-powered, flamed '32 roadster set a new D/Roadster record of 172.17mph in 1954 clocking better than 173mph one way. Kolb went on to campaign a series of fuel dragsters well into the 1970s. *Author collection*

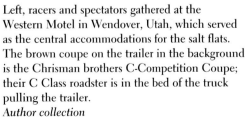

Above, safety took a back seat to the spectacle in the 1950s. This is Paradise Mesa, near San Diego, California. The strip looks wide enough so that a driver shouldn't have trouble staying on the strip, but if something serious goes wrong with the car, he could easily run into the crowd lining the course.
Ralph Poole photo, author collection

Tom Beatty built this famous lakester in 1951 around a tubular truss-type frame and swing-axle rear end built from early Ford parts. It debuted at over 188mph using a supercharged 258ci flathead. By 1955, Beatty had it up to an incredible two-way average of 211.144mph. Beatty had a reputation for destroying engines, and it was not uncommon to see him in front of the Western Motel with a boring bar assembling another engine in the middle of the night.
Author collection

Left, racers and spectators gathered at the Western Motel in Wendover, Utah, which served as the central accommodations for the salt flats. The brown coupe on the trailer in the background is the Chrisman brothers C-Competition Coupe; their C Class roadster is in the bed of the truck pulling the trailer.
Author collection

Club plaques and membership cards. *Author collection*

Above, Fred Lobello's ancient San Diego-based lakester was a familiar sight at Bonneville for decades. Powered by a 212ci four-cylinder Ford with a Riley 4-port head, the tiny car set a record of over 177mph in 1966. *Author collection*

This beautifully constructed streamliner featured a sleek aluminum body formed by Dick Dean. Built by lakes pioneer Bill Burke and powered by a series of Clark Cagle's Chryslers, it was driven by veteran Mel Chastain. *Author collection*

Mallet and Crowe's *Hammer Bird Special* Chevy-powered '29 roadster typified the traditional Bonneville roadster. *Author collection*

The gorgeous Reed Brothers tank. Using an Ardun powerplant, LeRoy Neumayer made a one-way run at 215.58mph and posted a two-way average of 205.71mph in 1954. Neumayer went sprint car racing the next year, and his replacement, John Donaldson, became the Bonneville Nationals first fatality when the tank overturned. Head-high roll bars were immediately legislated. Some lessons were learned the hard way.
Author collection

Bonneville and dry lakes programs, pit passes, result tags, and timing tags. *Author collection*

Above, hot rodding pioneer Ak Miller cruised through the traps at Bonneville at over 189mph in one of his many Devin sports cars. This one was powered by a 427 Ford. Ak had at least one entry in every Bonneville meet for nearly three decades.
Dave Friedman photo

Jot Horne and Norm Taylor of Bell Auto Parts definitely had something different in mind when they built their '27 T on '32 rails. Powered by a 441ci six-cylinder Ranger aircraft engine the unique roadster reached 105mph at the drags and better than 132mph at the dry lakes in the early 1950s.
Author collection

Above, the B & N Automotive A/Modified Roadster driven by Noel Black of Sacramento, California, clocked an outstanding time of 264.90mph in 1966. Using a blown 392ci Chrysler, it upped the record to 256.685mph.
Dave Friedman photo

Above, the beautiful Ruddy and Weinstein modified roadster was a product of Chuck Porter's Hollywood custom shop. In 1956, using a rear-mounted Ardun-Merc for power, Tom Ruddy squeaked into the 200 MPH Club with a two-way average of 200.009mph. On his return record run, Tom misread the course markers and shut off early resulting in his "just barely" time. For thirty years he held the dubious distinction of being the "slowest" Club member. *Author collection*

When new flathead classes were established for hard-core Bonneville racers in the mid-1960s, Bob Westbrook was among the first in the record book. His sleek little streamlined '27 T modified roadster turned an over-157mph average using a 296ci '48 Ford. *Dave Friedman photo*

Above, the Bennet and Rochlitzer team gave a whole new slant to belly tank lakester construction. Using a smaller diameter F86 jet tank rather than the WWII variety, they moved the driver behind the rear axle much like the slingshot dragster configuration. Using an unblown Chevy V-8 they upped the record in the E/Lakester class by more than 8mph to a 221.819mph average in 1966. *Author collection*

The Dana Fuller streamliner—a former Chet Herbert "Beast" car—featured a GMC 671 diesel. It set international records in 1953. *Author collection*

Left, Bob McGrath at the wheel of the Hammon-McGrath-Whipp "Redhead" streamliner set Top Speed of the 1966 Bonneville Nationals at over 331mph using a single blown-Chrysler. *Dave Friedman photo*

Bottom, Nolan White's modified sports car from San Diego, California, set an E/Modified Sports record early in the 1966 Bonneville meet at 184.284mph using a small-displacement, blown Chevy. Later, using a bigger engine, he flipped the car in the timing traps at about 240mph! As a testament to Bonneville safety regulations, Nolan suffered only stretched neck ligaments in the crash. *Author collection*

Using a variety of engines ranging from flatheads to Chryslers, the beautiful Chrisman Brothers Model A coupe held records in several classes in the early 1950s, eventually reaching a top speed of 196mph in 1955. Chrisman restored the coupe for car show promoter Bob Larivee in 1985.
Author collection

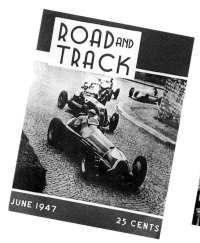

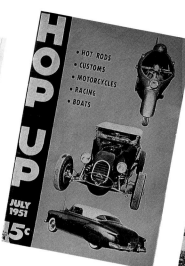

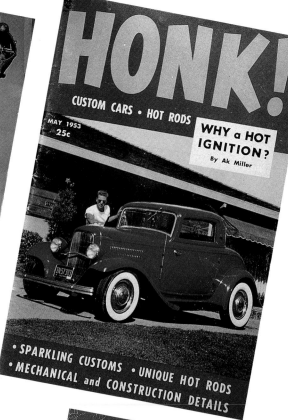

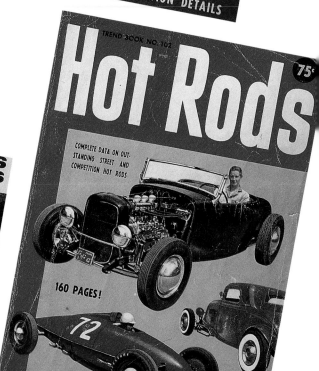

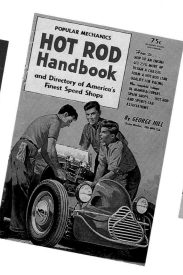

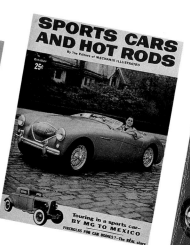

Early hot rodding publications. *Author collection*

This page, Norm Taylor and Jot Horne worked at Roy Richter's Bell Auto Parts and built this "Airoadster" in 1951. The 1927 T roadster body with 1932 Ford frame and running gear (with a Halibrand quick-change center section in the rear axle) were pretty straightforward, but the inverted and reversed Ranger aircraft engine was a departure from anything seen on the drag strip or dry lakes. The 441ci (4-1/8x5-1/2in bore and stroke) sohc air-cooled six-cylinder engine weighed 370lb, and the entire car tipped the scales at only 1,600lb. The engine was left virtually stock, except for an intake manifold which carried five Stromberg model 48 carburetors and had a 17qt capacity dry-sump lubrication system with an oil radiator to aid cooling. A Ford flywheel was mated to the crankshaft output end (where the propeller would mount on the aircraft) and then to a 1939 Ford transmission with Lincoln-Zephyr gears. The *Airoadster* was featured in the October 1951 *Hop Up* and again in February 1952 *Hop Up* when it was on the cover. The second feature said the roadster had run 105.26mph at the Santa Ana Drag Strip. The owners spent eight months and $800 to build the red roadster, and after the magazine features, a race car nose was added.

continued from page 96

Both the Wayne Chevy-six head (designed to be used with the 235 Hi-Torque block) and the Horning GMC heads were cross-flow, twelve-port designs with six intakes on one side and six exhausts on the other. The Wayne Chevy head was subsequently sold to one-time Horning partner Harry Warner, who then added a GMC head, carrying the Wayne name, to his line, but it was a "plank" type head which had no combustion chamber built into the head itself. Howard Johansen also made a plank head for GMC engines.

Nicson (the name derived from Nick Glaviano, and his son) made an aluminum Chevy six head with intake and exhaust ports on the same side. Joe Jagersberger made a cast-iron Chevy six head with the intake and exhaust on the same side, but it had three siamesed intake ports, and four exhaust ports. Like his Model T heads, he called these Rajo heads.

Specially-designed cylinder heads for the inline sixes were few and far between, but many manufacturers made intake manifolds for single, twin, and triple carburetor application; Nicson, Edelbrock, Tatersfield, Edmunds, McGurk, Weiand, and Sharp come to mind. Johansen made a five-carb intake for the GMC, but it was only for racing. Ignitions could be obtained from Spalding or Mallory, or serious racers could get magnetos from Joe Hunt (Scintilla) or Barker (Wico).

Popular carburetors for the inline sixes were Stromberg twin-throat downdraft, or Riley single-throat side draft. The full-bore competitor probably bought a Hilborn injector for this inline six, and Cook Machine made adaptors to mate a Chevy or GMC six to a Ford transmission.

It wasn't difficult for a cam grinder to create a camshaft for "other" engines; most cam grinding equipment would hold any length camshaft made for an automobile (some marine or aircraft camshafts might present a problem) engine, so it became only a problem of finding a suitable cam-lobe profile. I suspect that reground camshafts for the inline flathead eights—Chrysler, Studebaker, Hudson, Oldsmobile, and others—had lobes that looked a lot like those ground for a flathead Ford Model A or B.

Because of porting, rocker-arm ratios, and valve size limitations, a reground camshaft for overhead valve engines needed an individual solution for each engine type. Pistons also required a special type for each engine, but the piston makers soon worked it out, and it really wasn't difficult to find equipment for the less pop-

ular racing engines; there just wasn't a variety available.

Lincoln-Zephyr V-12 engines were tried, without much success, and both Cadillac and Marmon V-16s were seen on the lakebeds before and after WWII. Clint Seccombe set a new SCTA roadster record in 1940, at 125.52mph, but, because he set it with a Cadillac V-16-powered roadster, they made a new Unlimited Class for 1941 and moved Seccombe and his record into that new class. This record stood until 1945.

Don Blair broke the Unlimited record in 1945 with his Roots-blown Ford flathead V-8 by posting a two-way average of 130.27. That record was in turn broken by another V-16 when Tony Capanna's Marmon ran a two-way average at 137.24, with a one-way run of 145.39.

The last appearances of Marmon V-16 engines were Howard Johansen's entries, combining the largest engine (490ci) in the smallest sedan body (Crosley). These racers should have made some of the highest speeds in the D Modified Sedan class. They did indeed go fast—in the 160s—but in the end Chrysler and Chevy-powered sedans won out.

Some of the most successful, or at least, potentially so, inline engined non-Ford cars were Marvin Lee's. On July 17, 1949. Lee's Wayne-Chevy six streamliner set a new SCTA B Class record at 153.545mph at El Mirage Dry Lake. In 1950, the type of streamliner Lee ran (streamlined body but with exposed wheels) was renamed Lakester. By this time Lee had built a new aerodynamic wheels-enclosed car to run a Horning GMC six.

On a Bonneville record run in August 1950, at an estimated speed of 230mph, the rear wheels of Lee's Lakester lost traction and the car spun and flipped. The driver, Puffy Puffer, escaped with minor injuries due to the excellent construction, but the car was a write-off, and Lee gave up on streamlined cars.

The Wayne Chevy six and the Horning GMC six worked particularly well in track roadsters and sprint cars. John Hartman and the Spalding brothers built Wayne Chevys that were extremely fast and very reliable, making a better racing reputation on the track than they did in straightaway competition.

As a Ford man, I viewed these inline-engined cars with more interest than envy, but they added a great deal to the competition scene, and some of them were awfully fast. I think if guys like Wayne Horning, Bill Fisher, Frank McGurk, Howard Johansen, and Nick Glaviano had started a few years earlier, they could have made competition even tougher than they did for Ford entries.

Above, Tony Capanna's Marmon V-16, which was bored 1/16in over stock to 3-3/16 in (making 515ci), had specially made crowned pistons and variously a Winfield or Harman & Collins camshaft and four Stromberg 48 carburetors. The chassis had been built by Johnny Junkin to hold his Pierce-Arrow straight eight. Tony drove the Marmon 145.39mph to qualify for a record run and fellow Albata Club member Babe Ouse drove it to a two-way record of 137.24mph in July 1946, the last year of the SCTA Unlimited Class. Tony, in the passenger's seat, and driver Babe Ouse are looking at Bill Burke's first belly-tank streamliner, a front-engined Ford flathead V-8, as it arrives on a trailer to compete for the first time.
Author photo

Opposite page, the Kelly-Junkin GMC-powered C Modified roadster clocked 155.54 at the 1952 Bonneville Nationals, good for only fifth in class. The 292ci inline six had a Howard five-carburetor manifold, and Scintilla magneto.

CHAPTER 7

Clubs and Associations

*Individual accomplishments by hot rodders
have been highly praised, but it was the clubs and associations
which made it possible for them to achieve.*

In any discussion of hot rodding history, some names are repeatedly brought up as being "The ones who made it happen." Okay. They deserve praise and recognition for their accomplishments, but stopping there ignores a larger contribution, namely the organizations that made it possible for the individual to excel by giving him a venue in which to display his skills.

In the first six years (1932–1937) of dry lakes competition there was little evidence of real organization. The meets were planned by members of the Muroc Racing Association and did include timing the cars and awarding trophies, but it was every man for himself as there were no clubs to join and no organized association to oversee everything.

Car clubs (they weren't hot rod clubs then, as the designation hadn't yet been used) began to form in the mid-1930s. Although several clubs would band together to put on weekend lakes meets, the clubs weren't tied together in any official manner. It was a mutual but unofficial cooperation.

On November 7, 1937, after the last meet of the year (sponsored by seven clubs: Desert Goats, Night Flyers, 90 MPH Club, Ramblers, Road Runners, Sidewinders, and Throttlers), members of the Hollywood Throttlers and the Glendale Sidewinders proposed a merger of all Los Angeles area car clubs. A meeting was held on November 29, 1937, and the result was the birth of the Southern California Timing Association (SCTA), a non-profit California Corporation.

Charter member SCTA clubs were: Idlers, Ramblers, 90 MPH Club, Road Runners, Sidewinders, Knight Riders, and Throttlers. By the time the second meeting was held, thirteen more clubs had joined the fledgling association, and by mid-1938 there were twenty-three clubs in the SCTA. Ten years later, according to a tally compiled by Don Montgomery, there were thirty-eight SCTA member clubs.

Of all the hot rod racing organizations, the SCTA is arguably the catalyst that really got things going. It was, as much as a volunteer organization can be, run under strict rules of order, and a technical committee elected from the membership made running changes to update competition classes.

In 1938, the first year of official SCTA meets, seven classes were listed in the race programs: 90–100mph, 100–110mph, 110mph and over cars with stock roadster bodies; 90–100mph, 100–110mph, 110–120mph, and 120-plus with modified roadster bodies. Side-by-side races were still held between cars in each class.

These side-by-side contests were abandoned, for safety reasons, in 1939 and another body class, Streamliner, was added. The time trials were now strictly that—timed runs to see whose car was fastest. If you wanted to race another entrant, you had to arrange it yourself and do it somewhere else. The SCTA, to its credit, had become safety conscious.

The Outriders Club hangout was The Triangle, at the intersection of Fletcher Drive, Verdugo Road, and Eagle Rock Boulevard in north Los Angeles.

Opposite page, in 1947, the Road Runners Club took a weekend cruise to look for a new dry lakebed to replace El Mirage, which was getting chopped up from so much use by SCTA and Russetta meets. Here we're stopped on Foothill Boulevard near Euclid in Ontario to wait for some stragglers.

The Road Runners Club makes a breakfast stop at Harrison's Summit Cafe at the top of Cajon Pass during a weekend cruise. This photo was taken on old Route 66. *Author photo*

I don't know who took this and the chapter inset photo, but they seem to have become Outriders Club members' general property—Don Montgomery (in *Hot Rods As They Were*) got his copies from Bud Van Maanen, and I got mine from Gus Rollins. All three roadsters are '29 A V-8s—one of the most popular combinations of the 1940s and '50s.

The Streamliner class amounted to a catch-all for cars that didn't fit in Roadster or Modified classes. These were sometimes an ex-sprint car or something similar, and usually had pointed tails, unlike the Modifieds which were squared-off behind the driver. The first two real streamliners, that is, cars with fully enclosed wheels, appeared in 1939. One was built by Jack Harvey and the other by the Spalding brothers (photos in chapter one).

In mid-1941, the SCTA added a fourth class, Unlimited, after Clint Seccombe set a new roadster record with a Cadillac V-16-powered roadster. The association simply moved Seccombe's car and his record into this new class, leaving the Roadster record to Vic Edelbrock who had previously held the record.

The SCTA Throttlers Club was one of the most active in the SCTA, being both a racing and a social club. On this Sunday in 1947 the club members and their friends met at the Porter Ranch in the San Fernando Valley to picnic and do a little impromptu racing on the movie-set horse track.
Mal Meredith collection

The four body-class divisions—Roadster, Modified, Streamliner, and Unlimited—remained through 1946, and engine size entered the picture for the 1947 season: 150–250ci ran in Class B and 250–350ci ran in Class C. By this time, though, there were only two body classes, roadster and streamliner. At the July 6, 1947, meet (which had been moved from El Mirage to Harper Dry Lake for safety reasons) two engine classes were added: A, 0–150ci, and D, 350ci and over.

In 1949 the Roadster Class was divided into two groups, stock-body and altered (channeled bodies, Model T-bodied cars, and those with streamlining ahead of the firewall) and were called Lakesters. After three fully-enclosed-body streamliners appeared in 1949 (Lee Chapel, Howard Johansen, and the So-Cal Special), a further change was made for 1950 which put the old exposed-wheel streamliners (belly tanks and sprint car types) into the Lakester class. Altered roadsters became Modified Roadsters.

Russetta Timing Association was formed in 1948 to provide timing for sedans and coupes, body styles the SCTA had never allowed except on invitation. It was an immediate success. Entries at Russetta meets were not only these "other" body styles, but SCTA members who joined a Russetta club so they could run their cars more often. Russetta also accepted roadsters, modified roadsters, and streamliners.

Timing at Russetta meets was done by Ray Ingram, who had run some pre-WWII meets simply by making it known that he and his timing equipment would be there and all were welcome. When the new racing association was formed, the group took the Russetta name and appointed Ray Ingram as their official timer.

Speeds posted by Russetta members met a great deal of skepticism from some of the long-time SCTA members; they didn't think it possible that a coupe or sedan could go as fast as a roadster, and some of the Russetta cars were going faster than similar SCTA cars. Open hostility continued until the SCTA invited Don Brown to run his '36 Ford coupe at the August 29, 1948, SCTA meet.

When Brown ran his street-legal coupe at 121.68mph through Otto Crocker's SCTA clocks, it served to stop some of the bitterness displayed by a few of the SCTA members and probably did a lot to bring the two groups closer together. What these doubting SCTA members had overlooked was that quite a few SCTA members had also joined Russetta, and these dual-Association members turned almost identical speeds in each Association.

A Throttlers Club member gets in a little track time at their Porter Ranch picnic. The Throttlers picnic became an annual affair which is still going—the first Sunday in October—but there is no more racing as the picnic is held in a Burbank public park. *Bill Yates photo, Don Montgomery collection*

Russetta's first official meet was held at El Mirage Dry Lake May 2, 1948, and by year's end there had been seven Russetta meets while the SCTA had held six. In 1949, Russetta and SCTA each held seven meets, although the August SCTA meet was at Bonneville and was a week long rather than the two-day meets held at the dry lakes.

Even though both associations strived to outdo each other in total membership and in creating general benefits for their members, they both also made every attempt to make the lakes meets safe for competitors and spectators. It was a common goal to police themselves and thereby protect their activities from scrutiny and possible censure from law enforcement or from government regulations.

In spite of competition safety requirements, and strict self-imposed regulations governing their racing activities at the lakes, there were accidents. Despite this, local law enforcement and the San Bernardino County Coroner's Office took a "we don't care if you hurt yourselves, just don't hurt any spectators or get into trouble going to or from the dry lakes" attitude about the whole thing.

The Birth of the NHRA

The year 1951 was a pivotal one for hot rodders, and became a milestone in the history of this unique activity. Wally Parks, who was then editor of *Hot Rod*, conceived the idea that a national organization was needed. To get his project going, Parks asked the company's general manager, Lee O. Ryan, to write a "letter to the editor" of *Hot Rod*, signing a fictitious reader's name to it, suggesting the formation of a national organization.

As the editor, Parks responded to this "reader letter" by announcing the formation of the National Hot Rod Association and inviting everyone to join. The idea had the blessing of *Hot Rod's* copublishers, "Pete" Petersen and Bob Lindsay, and for the next twelve years Parks acted as president of NHRA while fulfilling his obligations at Petersen Publishing Company. Even though he had been promoted to editorial director of the Petersen Automotive Group (*Hot Rod, Car Craft, Motor Trend, Motor Life, Rod and Custom* and *Sports Car Graphic*) he left Petersen's employ in 1963 to work full time for the NHRA.

The success of NHRA can be demonstrated in part by comparing its membership in 1994 of more than 80,000 to SCTA and Russetta Timing Associations, neither of which ever topped 1,000 members.

Realistically, there was no reason why SCTA or Russetta should get any larger than they were. The percentage of each membership that participated in the racing activities kept dry lakes entries to a manageable number, and those who didn't run their cars could contribute by helping to run the meets: This activity wasn't as exciting as running a car, but it was a very necessary part of running a successful and safe meet.

NHRA, on the other hand, by its very nature was geared to enlist as many members as possible. In addition to the usual membership cards, lapel buttons, and car decals—typical items supplied by clubs and associations world wide—there was soon a weekly tabloid paper called *National Dragster*. The paper kept members informed of both event coverage and results, and of NHRA activities.

NHRA sanctioned races at more than 130 strips in the U.S., and an unexpected benefit of this vast mem-

Wally Parks

An editor's job isn't always slaving over a hot manuscript. Wally Parks took time away from his *Hot Rod* magazine job in 1957 to run this Plymouth HRM Special at Daytona Beach, turning 166mph one way with a two-way average (record) at 161 mph.

It's difficult to imagine hot rodding or dry lakes racing before Wally Parks became involved in this activity, and there wasn't much going on before he became part of the picture. Parks was a spectator at Muroc Dry Lake in 1932, and ran a car, a 1927 Chevy-four fenderless convertible coupe, to 82.19mph in 1933. Parks was a member of the Road Runners Club when the SCTA was formed on November 29,1937, and by 1938 was editor of the *SCTA Racing News,* a monthly association newsletter. It was Parks who first used the term "drag race," in the March 1, 1939, *Racing News*

Returning from WWII military service (754 Tank Battalion, stationed on Bouganville), Parks became the first paid SCTA employee, with the title secretary and general manager, in 1947. He was working in that position when Pete Petersen and Bob Lindsay brought out *Hot Rod* magazine, in January 1948. Wally was the magazine's contact with the racers, and in 1949 he was named editor of *Hot Rod,* ending his two years as SCTA secretary.

In 1951, after being editor of *Hot Rod* for two years, Parks conceived the idea for the National Hot Rod Association and, with the blessing of his employers, formed this group and became its first president. Parks was promoted by Petersen to editorial director for the five Petersen automotive publications; *Hot Rod, Car Craft, Motor Trend, Motor Life,* and *Rod & Custom,* but left Petersen's employ in 1963 to devote his full time to the NHRA.

Parks admits that countless NHRA members contributed to the group's success—more than 80,000 members and 2500-plus events per year at 130-plus drag strips year—but Wally Parks was the moving force behind the association's huge expansion, and the NHRA bears his personal stamp.

bership came about in 1957 when Ak Miller took his *Caballo II* to Italy to run in the 1957 Mille Miglia race. NHRA members who were in the U.S. armed forces stationed in Europe were called on for all kinds of help, and it gave Miller a huge "pit crew" if he needed it.

As could be expected in an organization this numerically and geographically large, controversy surrounded much of what was done. The Association officials, led by Wally Parks, did what they thought best for the members and the sport while some racers, egged on by Doris Herbert's *Drag News* publication, fought almost everything done by NHRA officials. Most of the

disagreements revolved around fuel—gas, or methanol, or nitromethane—and prize money.

The racers, spearheaded by Don Garlits, a vocal, long-time opponent of the NHRA, thought they should be paid to race, and the NHRA was slow to respond to their demands. After years of bickering, the issue finally resolved itself when enormous amounts of sponsorship, prize money, and television time came into the picture.

Regardless of one's feelings about the NHRA (even its detractors grudgingly admit the sport wouldn't be what it is today without the organization), it has to be considered the major factor in excitement, competition, and long-term stability of hot rodding.

Speed enthusiasts around the world eagerly await the results of the major NHRA weekend races. When Kenny Bernstein recorded 314mph in the quarter mile (Pomona, 1994), it was just as exciting to enthusiasts in England, France, Germany, and the Scandinavian countries as it was here in America. Without the NHRA this worldwide enthusiasm would not be.

Other Organizations

A fourth major association, which isn't even known to some hot rodders but is every bit as important, is SEMA. Started in 1963 as the Speed Equipment Manufacturers Association, the acronym has stayed the same but the designation changed in 1967 to Specialty Equipment Manufacturers Association. It changed again in 1979 to Specialty Equipment Market Association.

The changes were made because a large number of potential members didn't actually make speed equipment, but they made items that were closely associated with the cars that were running hopped-up engines. Twelve years after changing from Speed to Specialty, Manufacturing was dropped for Market because even more potential members didn't make anything, but they sold and distributed millions of dollars worth of products each year made by someone else.

Today SEMA represents a combined group of manufacturers, distributors, wholesalers, and retailers that do several billion dollars a year in sales, and SEMA membership has passed the 2,000 mark—a long way from its March 26, 1963, founding with thirty-six members.

SEMA's activities include establishment of safety and performance standards for all products manufactured by members; monitoring and involvement, through the SEMA attorney in government actions in both Washington, D.C. and Sacramento, California; a member commitment to produce products that fall within the requirements of safety and emission regulations; consulting and cooperation with the major automobile manufacturers and the automotive press; and the production of the Association's annual trade show in Las Vegas, Nevada.

Actually, the list of activities goes much farther, but space is limited here. I find it a pity that the Las Vegas trade show is open only to SEMA members and the press, and I think it would be a great idea to reserve a weekend for public viewing of these new products. It should easily convince hot rodders that SEMA is probably the most important organization affecting their hobby. SEMA goes so much further than strictly racing organizations can, but is largely unknown and unappreciated by the car-buying public.

One of the oldest, and possibly least known clubs outside hot rod circles, is the Bonneville 200 MPH Club. The club's origin dates to 1953 when Lou Kimzey, Ralph Poole, and I were having lunch in the Copper Skillet in Glendale. We were *Hop Up* magazine staffers, and Ralph had just returned from the Indy 500.

While telling us about May in Indianapolis Ralph mentioned the Champion 100 MPH Club—membership requiring a race average of 100mph or better. Almost at the same time, all three of us thought there should be something like that for hot rodders. But what?

Before we finished lunch we had planned the 200 MPH Club and took the proposal back to the office to our publisher, Bill Quinn, who agreed to sponsor it. The first two years were the *Hop Up* Magazine 200 MPH Club, then it became the Grant Piston Ring 200 MPH Club, and since then it has been sponsored by Ed Iskenderian and Dean Moon, among others.

Qualifications for membership were simple; you had to surpass 200mph for a two-way average over a measured mile at Bonneville (rules have since been amended to include any two-way run over a measured mile if timing is done by the FIA or FIM). Honorary membership was extended to Maj. Goldie Gardner, Bernd Rosemeyer, and Rudolf Caracciola even though they hadn't achieved that speed at Bonneville. The first hot rodders who qualified were George Hill, Willie Young, Otto Ryssman, Art Chrisman, and LeRoy Holmes.

By establishing the rules the way we did, we inadvertently excluded Ray Charbonneau and Bill Dailey, who drove our So-Cal Special in 1950. Both had gone well over the 200mph mark several times, but neither had done it two ways on a record run. The "Two Club" started with five members, but by the 25th anniversary of the Nationals and the 20th anniversary of the club, membership had grown to well over 100 and is still climbing.

Collectively these clubs and associations have made it possible for the individual to be recognized for his efforts. Without them, he might as well run in a vacuum.

The Pasadena Roadster Club
on a reliability run in 1949.
Greg Sharp collection

A 1961 gathering of hot rods at Tiny
Naylors drive-in in Hollywood.
Greg Sharp collection

CHAPTER 8

Road Racing Specials

East and west and both sides of the law.

While many of us tend to think that road racing in America started at Watkins Glen, Bridgehampton, Elkhart Lake, Pebble Beach, Torrey Pines, and Golden Gate Park, *real* road racing was already underway in the southeastern part of the U.S. It was done on public roads in the hills of the South, mainly North and South Carolina, Tennessee, Kentucky, Georgia, and Arkansas. These are the southern Appalachian hills, and if most of us thought the western, midwestern and northeastern lot in life was tough during the depression, this area made other parts of the country look like Shangri-La.

The land was not kind to these mountain folk, and it made no difference whether they tried to raise livestock or crops, they were generally unsuccessful. It became a necessity to look for other means of earning a living, yet there were no jobs to be had in these areas.

The answer turned out to be very simple, but not one that was universally acceptable. The product they made was whiskey, also known as "moonshine," "white lightning," or "mountain dew."

To sell this invigorating liquid, they had to move it from their back-country stills to a ready market .

The more you could produce, deliver, and sell, the more money you made. With self delivery, for which there was no shipping charge (unless you got caught, in which case you not only did time, but the law confiscated your car), your profit was directly related to how much you delivered and got paid for.

Unfortunately for those enterprising souls, the law not only didn't condone their activity, the law did everything it could to stop it. It became a game, albeit a very serious game, and one that often had dire consequences when a chase got ugly.

The moonshiners developed faster and faster cars, initially 1939 and 1940 Ford coupes with stiffer springs and shock absorbers (so a load of whiskey wouldn't put the frame down on the axles and to help the car's handling) and, as time went on, highly modified engines.

Many of the first engines built by these 'shiners had racing equipment purchased from manufacturers or speed shops. Then they discovered that they could order a complete engine in a crate, ready for installation, from Vic Edelbrock, Howard Johansen, Ray Brown, or Lou Senter at Ansen Engineering.

Once the law in the south discovered this out-of-state racing engine supply they, too, started ordering engines from the same sources which furnished them to the moonshiners.

The mountain whiskey makers, while often short on schooling, were savvy entrepreneurs and kept up with the automotive state of the art. After WWII they bought newer Fords; '49, '50 and so on, because of their better suspension, better brakes, and larger hauling capacity. But when the OHV V-8s started to appear in the late 1940s, suddenly liquor was being hauled in Olds 88s or Fords with Cadillac engines. After introduction of the Mopar Hemi engine in 1951, Chryslers, Dodges,

When Ak Miller decided to build a car for the 1953 Carrera Panamericana, he relied on his hot rod roots to create the machine he dubbed *Caballo de Hierro*, or *Iron Horse*, in Spanish. Based on a 1950 Ford frame, narrowed to fit the 1927 Ford Model T roadster body, he retained the front independent suspension, but fitted a transverse leaf at the rear to replace the semi-elliptics used on the '50 Ford. The wheelbase was shortened to 100in. Chrysler 13in brakes were adapted to the Ford hubs, and Houdaille 50/50 shocks were used. Power came from a 1951 Olds V-8 with milled '52 Olds heads, 1/8in oversize valves, Howard F6 camshaft, and a Nicson four-carb (Stromberg 97s) manifold. Drive went through a '53 Olds clutch; '37 Cadillac floor-shift, three-speed transmission; and a Nash overdrive; the overall ratio being 2.73:1. Miller, with Doug Harrison as riding partner, finished the 1953 race eighth in class and fourteenth overall; then drove the car home to Whittier. The pair finished the 1954 race fifth in class and seventh overall, with a 94.1mph average for the 1,921 miles.

Opposite page, a later version of the Sterling Edwards special shown on page 126. This body was built for it by Phil Remington and Jack Hagemann in 1952. This was a lighter, pure race-car body with no pretense at dual race/street usage. By this time the car had also acquired an Ardun ohv conversion for its Ford V-8 60, and power was about 120 on pump gas. This shot is an Official U.S. Navy Photo.

Above, one of the first (1948) hot rod/sports car specials was built by Willis Baldwin for Phil Payne. It was based on a 1932 Ford frame with the wheelbase shortened to 103in. A 268.4ci Merc flathead with an Iskenderian track-grind cam, Evans 9:1 heads, and triple-carb intake manifold— mounted 15in behind the stock location— furnished the power. Drive went through a 10in Merc clutch and three-speed Ford transmission with a home-built remote shift linkage to a 3.78:1 rear axle. Payne took the special home with him when he moved back to England.
Strother MacMinn photo

The Sterling Edwards special, built in 1949, looks like a sports car but the engine and driveline are pure hot rod. Norman Timbs engineered the Edwards, and Emil Diedt, Lujie Lesovsky, and Phil Remington built it. Phil Remington, who worked for Eddie Meyer at the time, built the Ford V-8 60 which had Meyer heads, ignition, and dual intake manifold. Suspension was fully independent—coil springs in front, torsion bars at the rear, and the wheelbase was 100in. In this form, it finished first in class, in 1950, at Palm Springs, Buchanan Field, and the Santa Ana Blimp Base races. In 1950, it was third overall and first in its class at Reno.
Joe Denker photo

and DeSotos became the cars of choice.

The cars were only a part of the competition between police and "runners." Driving skills were developed to a degree not seen on the highway before or since, and many of these moonshiners became the nucleus of early NASCAR racing.

The driving skills developed by both the runners and the chasers would have made many would-be SCCA road racers in the rest of the country green with envy. The famous handbrake U-turn came from the 'shiners—a maneuver that ditched many a following police car (and can you imagine doing that with 500–1000lb of sloshing liquor on board?).

These chases were almost always done at night on, at best, two-lane blacktop roads through the mountains. Quite often, if the law was getting too close, the 'shiners would take off onto familiar dirt roads, and then things really got hairy. A favorite ploy was for the whiskey haulers to run a familiar dirt back-road without lights.

Not incidentally, moonshiners didn't have a large tank built into the back of their coupes as we've seen in movies. The term "tanker" probably emanated from the movie "Thunder Road," starring Robert Mitchum but, in actual fact, the liquor was typically carried in gallon or half-gallon fruit jars—glass until plastic was available. Plastic jars were quicker to load and unload, and with their lighter weight more liquor could be carried.

It doesn't take too much imagination to understand the degree of skill and bravery required to make these late-night runs while carrying anything from 500 to 1,000lb of hooch in glass jars. The game wasn't played for fun, although competitors on both sides of

the law were happy when they won. If you were the runner, it meant escaping capture and delivering your load. If you were the law, it meant making the bust and adding another fast car to your office car pool.

More often than they liked to think about it, a 'shiner might be chased by an officer driving a car the 'shiner had built. By the time the law finally got cars that were somewhat equal to those they were chasing, it became a real test of driving skills and overall cunning.

In Alex Gabbard's book *Return to Thunder Road*, he quotes ex-moonshiner Thurmond Brown talking about future stock-car driver Junior Johnson: "I had the liquor and the customer in Winston, and Junior had the car, a '50 Oldsmobile, a souped-up coupe. I told Junior 'I got the liquor and the customer, why don't we haul this liquor to Winston. You furnish the car and drive, and we'll split the profit. He said OK. We got there and set the liquor off, 132 gallons, twenty-two cases, and comin' down back through Winston Junior was runnin' about wide open. I looked over at him and said, 'Junior you need to slow down. You might get the law after us.' He reached over and patted me on the knee and said, 'If we can't outrun 'em empty, what was we doin' down there loaded?' I knowed we could outrun 'em, loaded or empty, I was dreadin' that ride."

One final note on Junior. Gabbard interviewed Joe Carter, an agent of the Alcohol, Tobacco and Firearms Division of the U.S. Treasury. Quote Joe Carter: "The height of my career, I often tell people, is that I'm the only Federal Agent to catch the great Junior Johnson, the famous race driver. . . I have to be honest and say I caught him on foot, not in an automobile. There's never

been an officer that could catch Junior Johnson in a car."

Observant readers will note that we have no photos of these early moonshiners or their cars, and for good reason. Those enterprising souls weren't interested in self-congratulation and were not on ego trips, so they didn't waste time having their pictures taken or in taking others' pictures. In fact, they did everything they could to remain anonymous and not bring attention to themselves.

Early Road Racing

Some organized road racing was done in the U.S. before WWII, mostly by members of the ARCA (Automobile Racing Club of America), in upstate New York and in Connecticut. It wasn't until after WWII that road racing, mostly in sports cars, really hit its stride in this country, particularly when the Sports Car Club of America was formed. Later some western renegades started the California Sports Car Club.

Unlike the southern races between moonshiners and police, the SCCA and CSCC encouraged spectator attendance—gate receipts helped pay racing expenses incurred by the clubs. There was no prize money. A trophy, and recognition by one's peers and assorted race enthusiasts was all a winner could hope for.

The majority of participants raced an MG, Singer, Jowett Jupiter, Triumph, Austin-Healey, Jaguar, Porsche, or Allard. The richer ones probably raced an Aston Martin, OSCA, Ferrari, Mercedes-Benz, or Maserati.

You will note that there are no American car names in that listing. Simply, there were no American sports cars being built in the late 1940s and early '50s. Would-be competitors unable to afford one of the above-named cars built their own. These were called "specials."

Competitors who build their own race cars generally fall into one of two categories: those who really can't afford to buy a ready-made race car, and those who think they can do better than the "factory-built" cars. Sometimes these two factors overlapped, but more

Chuck Manning's Merc V-8 was of the "fast counts, looks don't matter" school of car design. A stress engineer at Douglas Aircraft, Manning designed his own tubular frame: two 2.75in-diameter tubes on each side, one above the other, with tubular cross members. Axles and springs (with every other leaf removed) were from a 1939 Ford, as were the wheels and hydraulic brakes. A 259ci 59A Merc block had Weiand heads and dual intake manifold, an Iskenderian track-grind camshaft, and Manning-built exhaust headers. The 100in wheelbase car weighed about 1,700lb. Manning won the March 1952 Palm Springs road race and generally placed in the top three at other circuits. *Jerry Chesebrough photo, author collection*

This looks like a roadster straight off the dry lakes or Carrell Speedway, but is, in fact, built specifically to road race. Frank "Duffy" Livingstone, a partner with Roy Desbrow in Duff & Roy's Muffler shop in Pasadena, was the prime mover in getting the car built. A '25 Model T Ford roadster body, with a race-car-type hood and nose, is set on channel frame rails. The running gear is almost totally Ford— 1932 front spring, 1937 V-8 60 tubular front axle, 1934 rear end with 3.78:1 gears, 1940 rear brakes, and Bendix aircraft front brakes inside Lincoln drums. The engine, set back in the frame, was a '42 Merc bored to 3-3/8 with a '52 Merc crank stroked to 4-1/4 inches, giving 304.17ci. A Potvin "Eliminator" camshaft, Evans heads and four-carb manifold, and Potvin ignition were used by engine builder Tim Timmerman. In 1955, the flathead was replaced with a '55 Chevy V-8 and performance vastly improved, the car winning first or second in its class in five races.
Chesebrough photo, author collection

This clone of Chuck Manning's special was built for Jacques Bellisiles by Sparks and Bonney Automotive. The frame and body were acquired from Manning, and the car was assembled, race-prepped, and tuned by Tom Sparks. The S & B-built engine was a Ford flathead V-8 with Edelbrock heads and manifold, Harman & Collins camshaft, Spalding dual ignition, and what rodders called a "3/8 x 3/8," meaning the bore was 3.375in and the stroke was 4.125in, resulting in 296ci.
Tom Sparks collection

Ak Miller

Akton Möller, born in Arhus, Denmark, in 1920, came to the U.S. with his family in the early 1920s, settling in Whittier, California. Ak's introduction to dry lakes racing was in 1935 when he and his brother Siegfried "Zeke" Miller (the family had Americanized their name) took their four-cylinder Chevy roadster to Muroc Dry Lake. Fifteen year-old Ak drove the Chevy, which had a Tornado head, to 94mph.

The Miller brothers, Ak, Zeke, and Larry, joined the SCTA Road Runners Club and, much to the consternation of his siblings who were "Ford guys," Ak ran a '32 roadster with a Buick straight-eight engine, then a flathead Cadillac V-8. In 1949, Ak retired the '32 and built a mid-engined '27 T roadster with Ford V-8 power. Once again, his brothers would speak to him.

Ak prepared a 1952 Olds for Whittier dealer Clint Harris for the Carrera Panamericana. Miller wasn't scheduled to drive the Olds, but when Harris fired his driver, Ak, with Doug Harrison as co-driver, started the race. The car dropped out with a transmission bearing failure, but the seed had been planted.

Miller and friends built a hot rod, the *Caballo de Hierro* (iron horse) to run the Carrera in 1953. It had a '50 Ford frame, '27 T Ford roadster body, and a '51 Olds engine. Ak and Harrison finished eighth in class and fourteenth overall and drove the car back to Whittier. In 1954, the same team and car were fifth in their class and seventh overall, at a speed of 94.1mph.

Starting in 1958 Miller entered the Pikes Peak Hill Climb twenty times, won his class eight times, and dnf'ed once when his Lotus 19-Ford lost an oil pump. Miller has, for years, been producing propane conversions and turbocharger installations, in his "hobby shop" as he calls it. He has eight employees and doesn't want to get any bigger. He's happy the way things are.

Ak Miller with *Caballo de Hierro* at Oaxaca, the first stop during the 1953 Carrerra Panamericana road race. *Greg Sharp collection*

often they didn't. A third part of the equation, at least in road racing, was a chauvinistic attitude, that is, those Ferraris, Porsches, Jaguars, Maseratis, etc. really go, but *I want to race an American car!*

Many of these specials were modified MGs or Jaguars, but some were scratch-built, using only proprietary engines and running gear; and many of this group were Ford based. The availability, adaptability, and low cost of early Ford V-8 components appealed to the home builder who wanted to road race just as it did to the hot rodder who went to the dry lakes.

The degree to which these specials succeeded said everything about the knowledge and ability of the designers/builders. Given a modicum of talent (welding skills were a real bonus), it wasn't a major chore to assemble a special. Hot rodders did it all the time—even before magazines such as *Hot Rod* came about to show them how to do it.

Building a road racing special was very similar to building a rod for the street or dry lakes. The ultimate purpose was, of course, different (which affected the overall design), but the choice and assembly of compo-

Above, the Cannon MK I was built by Ted Cannon, mostly from old parts found in his garage or at his Cannon Engineering shop. The frame is from a 1930s Dodge. The independent front suspension was retained, but Cannon added a Ford rear axle with its transverse leaf spring. He boxed the frame for stiffness and shortened the wheelbase to 100in. Cannon reground the camshaft in the early flathead Ford V-8, milled the heads, ported and relieved the block, and ran only a single Stromberg carburetor at the start. He bought a used Lincoln Zephyr to get the three-speed close-ratio transmission, and used the sheet metal from the top to make the special's hood and cowl. The Zephyr's trunk lid became the special's rear. The car was finished barely two weeks before the first Pebble Beach road race, November 5, 1950. Jim Seeley drove that race, finishing third behind Phil Hill and Don Parkinson in Jaguar XK-120s.

Top right, Chuck Tatum, who had raced stock cars, sprint cars, and track roadsters, teamed up with Doug Trotter, who had road raced a GMC-powered Aston Martin, to build this unique special. Tatum designed the tubular frame and Jack Hagemann built the aluminum body. The 301.6ci "Jimmy" had three Carter side draft carburetors, a Mallory ignition, and Howard camshaft. Suspension was a combination of various year Fords, and the transmission was a three-speed Ford with Lincoln Zephyr first and second gears until replaced by a Jaguar four-speed. Tatum won two novice races in 1953, then finished ninth at Santa Barbara. *Author photo*

Dick Troutman and Tom Barnes worked for Kurtis Kraft in the mid-1950s, and the pair built this sports racer at home in their spare time. A truss-type tubular steel frame, with 87in wheelbase, had independent front suspension and a Ford live rear axle. Several engines powered the T-B Special during its six-year racing history; first, the traditional flathead Merc, Edelbrock equipped with aluminum cylinder heads and three-carb intake manifold, then a 347ci Ford T-Bird engine, and finally a small-block Chevy V-8. Ken Miles drove the T-B in 1954 while he finished his own R-2 MG special, and then Chuck Daigh took over the driving before going to work for the Scarab team. Miles is shown in the car at Santa Barbara in 1954.
Jerry Chesebrough photo author collection

Opposite page bottom, this channeled '32 Ford roadster was owned by Fred Vogel but prepared, maintained, and driven by Max Balchowsky. The LaSalle V-8 engine was built by Yam Oka, a Nisei from Glendale, California, and had the usual hot rod treatment of higher compression ratio, ported and relieved block, hotter camshaft and ignition, and welded tubular steel exhaust headers. Fred and Max were just learning about road racing when they started in 1952. The transverse-leaf springs were retained, but Max replaced them with similar units from a Ford V-8 60, which were lighter. Dodge steering was added, the Ford hydraulic brakes were replaced with Bendix self-servo brakes from a Lincoln Zephyr, and, finally, 1949–51 Lincoln brakes. Max also tried Olds, Chrysler, Cadillac, and DeSoto ohv V-8s, finally settling on Buick.
Author photo

nents was very much the same for both. A few cars seen on road racing circuits in the 1950s were actually hot rods with modifications to make them somewhat suitable as sports racers.

Most of those who built road racing specials somehow knew that a low center of gravity and near 50/50 fore-and-aft weight distribution were desirable, if not absolutely essential factors. Both were easy enough to accomplish. In fact, it was often easier to achieve those goals in a road racer than it was a dry lakes car because both SCTA and Russetta Timing Associations had strict rules in all their various classes about what could or couldn't be done to the car.

The would-be road racer simply moved the engine and transmission, and cockpit, rearward and placed them as low in the chassis as possible. A road race special builder had other rules and regulations he had to meet, but engine and driveline placement were up to him.

Both the Sports Car Club of America and the California Sports Car Club, which, between them, put on the vast majority of sports car road races (the Four Cylinder Club or the Long Beach MG Club put on a few races), required that the race car be fully street legal. This meant the inclusion of headlights, taillights, spare tire, doors for entrance and exit, driver and passenger seat (one on either side of the car's center line), fenders, horn, and some sort of transmission which included reverse gear; and all had to be in working order.

The old line sporty car crowd tended to look down its collective noses at home-built specials—they didn't carry a badge of distinction, with nameplates like Ferrari, Jaguar, or Aston Martin. The situation wasn't helped by the fact that some of these specials were fast enough to outrun some of the exotic machinery, much of which cost two or three times as much to put on the track. And the specials builders didn't show deference to the owners and drivers of exotic makes.

One result of all this was an us-versus-them attitude. Both racers and spectators played the game. On one side were the rich, or nearly so, types who favored exotics from overseas. On the other side were the specials builders—hot rodders mostly.

The foreign engines were usually of less displacement than those found in American cars, but made up for their smaller size by having single or double overhead camshaft valve operation. These engines also revved higher to get their horsepower.

The howling screech of a many-cylindered, small-displacement engine running at 8000-plus rpm was a

The Kurtis 500S, which was developed from the Kurtis 500K Indianapolis car, may be a marginal "home-built," but Bill Stroppe did buy the car in kit form, assembled it, prepared it for racing, and drove it—to the 1953 season championship. The Kurtis 500S was normally built with 94in or 98in wheelbase, but Stroppe wanted a shorter, more maneuverable car so he ordered his car with 88in wheelbase. A chrome-moly tubular front axle and Ford rear with a Halibrand quick-change were used with transverse torsion bars and tubular shock absorbers. Channel frame rails had tubular extensions front and rear to provide mounting for the torsion bars and radius rods. A flathead Merc engine with Edelbrock heads and three-carb manifold, Potvin "Eliminator" camshaft, Scintilla Vertex magneto, and W-type headers made up the primary speed equipment. Displacement was 282ci (3 5/16x4 1/8in). Even with a marine, positive-displacement water pump, Stroppe ran the car with the hood sides removed to help keep it cool. *Author photo*

Willis Baldwin, the "father" of road racing specials, built this car in 1949. Baldwin started with a '46 Ford frame, shortened 14in to provide a 100in wheelbase. The flathead 59A Mercury engine was set back 22.5in in the chassis. Suspension was virtually stock Ford with the front transverse springs ahead of the axle, the rear spring behind the axle. The 284.4ci V-8 (3.312-x4.125in) flathead drove through a Merc clutch assembly with the centrifugal weights sawed off the pressure plate to facilitate shifting at high rpm. A '46 Ford three-speed transmission had a remote shift mechanism designed by Baldwin. The body was made from pieces from a Plymouth hood and Chrysler fenders; the grille was made from a refrigerator shelf. In April, 1950, the Baldwin Special had fast qualifying time at the Palm Springs road races, seven seconds faster than the next qualifier. *Author photo at Pebble Beach*

wonderful contrast to the huffing and chuffing of a big American V-8 which, more often than not, produced its power below 5000rpm. Remember, this was before the small-block Chevy and Ford V-8s. We're talking Ford flathead, and ohv Cadillac, Olds, and Chrysler.

It was David and Goliath any way one looked at it;

limited money versus big bucks, or home-grown cubic inches versus imported small-bore sophistication. This was one of the great crowd-pleasing facets of early 1950s road racing, and it really gave everyone somebody to root for.

Some of these early homebuilts were very successful and some weren't, but then not all those who bought Ferraris were successful either. I think this is typical of any vehicular competition, be it cars, boats, motorcycles, or aircraft.

One major problem with many of these ambitious builders who wanted to go road racing was that they knew a lot more about engines than they did about how to make a car handle on a road course. The result was that they invariably started out with familiar equipment, which makes sense; usually a Ford flathead V-8 engine, early Ford solid axle suspension with transverse-leaf springs, mediocre Ford brakes, and, more often than not, the wrong tires for road racing.

Unfortunately, the familiarity of these components didn't offset the fact that they weren't the best that could be had. Some of these hot rod racers did better than others, by watching what their competitors did,

Dick Morgensen was never a hot rodder in the sense that we think of them today—drag racing or running at the dry lakes and at Bonneville—but the car he put together in 1953 was typical of what hot rodders did. Using mostly parts acquired from junkyards and scrap heaps, he brought this homely mess into the sports car racing arena. Powered by an in-line, six-cylinder Plymouth flathead engine with three Stromberg carburetors on a home-made manifold, and covered by a sheet metal body with no compound curves (the rear fenders were from a pick-up truck, the front fenders were aftermarket trailer fenders), the special was relatively successful in club racing. Its real claim to fame is that Morgensen sold it, in 1955, to Max Balchowsky and, with a Buick V-8, it became the first *Ol' Yeller*. *Jerry Chesebrough photos*

and by asking a lot of questions. Some, of course, had that innate natural knowledge and ability that was learned over many years of experimentation.

One of the more cerebral of the home builders was Chuck Manning, an engineer at Douglas Aircraft who designed the frame for his road racing special, wrote a two-part feature for *Road & Track* magazine about how and why he arrived at the end result, and then offered chassis blueprints for $2.00 to anyone who wanted to duplicate it. Several did, although they designed a different body for their cars.

With only a few exceptions—Pebble Beach, Golden Gate Park, Torrey Pines, Elkhart Lake, Watkins Glen, and Bridgehampton—road race courses in the 1950s were on airport runways. This was particularly true after General Curtis LeMay allowed the use of Strategic Air Command (SAC) bases, starting in 1952. It would seem, then, that these flat and relatively smooth surfaces would not require sophisticated suspension. This is true, but the courses also favored cars with great acceleration and top speed. Unfortunately, too many homebuilts, particularly those with flathead Ford power, were too heavy, placing undue strain on engine, clutch, and brakes.

Road racing, fortunately, was new to all the competitors at that time, so they all started somewhat equally. There were no racing drivers schools as there are today, so early road racers drove with whatever natural ability they had and developed that skill any way they could.

Ak Miller, one of the foremost and most success-

Max Balchowsky driving *Ol Yeller* at Riverside in 1958. The car was an amazing amalgam of parts powered first by an ohv Buick and later by a Chevy. In eight years of competition, culminating in 1960, *Ol Yeller* beat some of the best including drivers Carroll Shelby, Richie Ginther, and Phil Hill, and cars from Ferrari and Maserati. *Greg Sharp collection*

ful hot rodders of all time (dry lakes, Bonneville, Pikes Peak Hill Climb, and the Carrera Panamericana) admits to learning his road racing skills on back roads around his home town of Whittier, California. It would seem logical that other drivers did the same in their own areas.

Road racing was great sport for both competitors and spectators and provided a competitive arena which offered something other than a straight line speed run. And it was a great time for those who wanted to build their own race cars—maybe the last time this will ever be possible.

Before *Ol Yeller*, Balchowsky road raced this 1932 roadster. It was originally powered by a flathead Cadillac V-8, which was swapped for the ohv Buick shown in this picture. *Greg Sharp collection*

Bottom right, Dick Siefried built this flathead Merc-powered special to go road racing after he decided against building a track roadster. A welded steel tubing ladder-type frame was built to use Ford axles and transverse leaf springs. Typically, the Merc engine had the full hot rod treatment—ported and relieved block, aluminum heads and three-carb intake manifold, hot ignition, welded steel tubing headers—driving through a Ford three-speed transmission with column shift and Zephyr first and second gears. Seifried deviated from the norm at the rear by using a Hudson rear axle with safety hubs. Dick Seifried, Sr., built the aluminum body and fenders. The car was completed in 1951 and raced, mostly on the West Coast, for several years; in 1951 it won the Carrell Speedway road races and was fifth at Palm Springs. *Bob Canaan photo*

Bottom left, Ed Ingalls, then living in Lafayette, California, built a hot rod sports racer in 1953 that was considered unorthodox by both hot rodders and sports car fans. Starting with a frame from a DeSoto Airflow, he mounted a 1930 Ford roadster body which was dropped over the frame rails (channeled body, as custom car guys call it). Suspension was Ford all the way: a Model A front axle with late spindle and 1939 hydraulic brake set-up, a Ford rear axle, and transverse leaf springs at each end. Under the hood was a 1941 260ci Chrysler six-cylinder Spitfire engine with three Stromberg dual carburetors, a high-compression head, and special ignition. A Ford three-speed transmission was fitted to the Chrysler engine. Gemmer steering from a 1936 Chrysler provided the quicker ratio needed for road racing. Bobbed Model A fenders were used at the rear, while the front fenders were cycle type made from Ford spare tire covers. *Bob Canaan photo*

CHAPTER 9

Superchargers and Super Fuels

Power from a blower or power from a can,
both paths offer tremendous performance improvement,
and both can spell disaster if not correctly applied.

Superchargers, and even turbochargers, for automotive applications are not new. The 1908 Chadwick race cars, made in Pottstown, Pennsylvania, were the first cars known to have been supercharged. Chadwicks used a centrifugal-type supercharger driven by a flat friction-belt from the 18in-diameter flywheel and then a shaft to the supercharger itself which was mounted alongside the in-line six-cylinder engine.

In 1908, Chadwick added two more impellers (all contained in one case) making it a three-stage supercharger. Air was picked up behind the radiator through a short length of tubing to the center of the impellers, which blew the pressurized air through the carburetor to the engine. Very little information was published about these supercharged behemoths so we don't know how successful they were.

The most successful pre-WWII supercharger applications were on the German Auto Union and Mercedes-Benz Grand Prix cars of the 1930s. For the Grand Prix formula starting in 1934, the A.I.A.C.R. (Association International des Automobile Clubs Reconnus; forerunner of the Federation Internationale de l' Automobile) decreed that a GP car couldn't weight more than 750kg (1650lb) less driver, fuel, water, and tires. The idea was that the designers wouldn't be able to get a big, powerful engine into a car this light. Typically, they underestimated race-car builders.

By 1937, the fourth year of the formula, the Mercedes-Benz W-125, a twin-cam straight eight displacing 345.2ci, put out 580–610hp at 5800rpm—depending on the state of tune for the particular racing circuit—and 465lb-ft of torque at 3000rpm. The sohc V-16 Auto Union had 366ci and produced 545hp at 5000rpm, but it made 629.3lb-ft torque at 2500rpm. Each design utilized a single-stage Roots blower, and it's obvious that these engine designers knew what they were doing.

Just after WWII, the Alfa Romeo Type 159, a 91ci twin-cam straight eight, achieved nearly 440horsepower—aided by a two-stage Roots blower set-up. It's possible that the hot rodders weren't aware of the Alfa as it didn't get much publicity here in the U.S., but I think they did know about the German cars, particularly after Auto Union's participation in the 1937 Vanderbilt Cup Race on Long Island.

We know Bob Rufi knew about these cars because he ran almost the same fuel mixture in his Chevy four streamliner in 1940 that Mercedes-Benz had run in their GP cars.

In 1941, Ray Besasie, of Milwaukee, Wisconsin, built an exhaust-driven supercharger (he didn't call it a turbo, but that's what it was) complete with new intake and exhaust manifolds that bolted directly to a 1941 Chevrolet six engine.

Besasie was about thirty years ahead of his time. Unfortunately, he drew on experience with centrifugal superchargers as used on production Auburn, Cord, Duesenberg, and Graham engines, so his impeller was far too

John Beverage designed and built this Roots blower seen on the Bob Wright-Don Berg flathead-Cadillac-powered '27 T roadster. Beverage has chosen to drive the blower with four V-belts. A unique feature of this set-up is the cable-operated throttle mechanism. *Bob DeBisschop photo, Don Montgomery collection*

Opposite page, the Quincy Automotive, Brissette Bros. & Eichenhofer Lakester had a Gilmer-belt-driven 6-71 GMC unit on top of the engine (with a Hilborn injector on top).

Right and far right, the Spalding brothers, Bill and Tom, built this V-8 Modified in 1941. Two Stromberg carburetors sit on a Roots blower from a Mercedes-Benz. A Riley overhead valve conversion for the twenty-one-stud Ford V-8 engine, and a Lincoln-Zephyr twin-coil ignition made by Tom Spalding can also be seen. The car, usually driven by Bill, consistently ran in the mid- to high-120s. The Spaldings were members of the SCTA Walkers Club. *Don Blair photo*

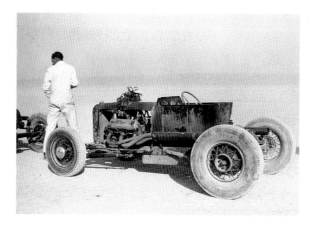

July 11, 1937—O. R. Peterson's Whippet-powered sprint car at Crossbay Speedway, Brooklyn, New York. A Winfield carburetor, which looks like one made from Model M and Model S parts, with a barrel throttle, sits atop a Graham shaft-driven supercharger. While impressive to look at, this type of supercharger isn't a practical application for track racing. *S.H. Oliver photo*

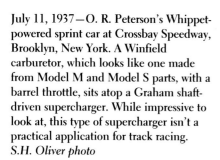

large to be effective when exhaust driven. I rode in a '41 Chevy coupe, during WWII, equipped with the Besasie set-up, and the car had a pretty good top end, but didn't accelerate much faster than the stock version. The supercharger sounded like a siren because of its high rpm.

The hot rodders got into superchargers fairly early, some because they were certain more horsepower could be obtained, some because it was the thing to do (if the great cars—Auburn, Cord, Duesenberg, Mercedes-Benz—had superchargers, it must be right), and some simply because it was "different."

The rodders' use of superchargers sometimes, but not always, proved beneficial. Like every part of a high-performance car, the installation of a supercharger re-

quired planning, preparation, and very careful assembly of all the components. The Spalding brothers, Tom and Bill, ran a Roots blower from a Mercedes-Benz on a Ford-powered modified as early as 1941. The car ran consistently in the 120s, showing a best time of 128-plus, but the engine also had Riley overhead valves. Was it the overhead conversion or the blower that made it faster? Given the performance of other Riley conversions, I'd bet on the blower.

Frank Morimoto brought a Cragar Model A-powered roadster to the dry lakes also with a Mercedes Roots blower (it could have been the same blower, as these things had a way of making the rounds of the true believers). Morimoto's roadster was fast, but not exceptionally so.

Super Charged. McDowell.
4.7 M.P.H. 7/3/38

Left, Ted Cannon's ohv McDowell-Model-A-powered Modified has a Graham centrifugal supercharger. On May 18, 1938, Ted drove the car 111.87mph at a Muroc Timing meet, but on July 3, with the cover over the carburetor and supercharger, he could get only 94.7 out of it. Such were the problems of early dry lakes racing. *Edelbrock collection*

Top far left, possibly the first, exhaust-driven supercharger for an automobile engine was built by Ray Besasie of Milwaukee, Wisconsin, for a 1941 Chevy six. It is seen here on a four-cylinder engine of some sort in a '32 Ford roadster. Unlike current turbochargers, the impeller of this unit was so large that the inertia kept it from spooling-up fast enough to be a practical street application, but it should have been good for top speed runs at the dry lakes. The photo was taken in 1941 or '42 by Vince Cimino.

Bottom, the Morimoto brothers' Cragar-equipped Model B engine in a '29 roadster ran a Roots blower from a Mercedes-Benz. The camshaft was stock, but the ignition was a Bosch unit. On September 21, 1947, the car clocked 115.83, and on October 19, it managed to run 116.73mph. The brothers ran with the SCTA Mobilers Club. *Author photo*

McCullochs and other centrifugal superchargers (most of them being Auburn or Graham units converted to use on some other engine) were quite common. McCulloch made a unit specifically for the flathead Ford V-8, and because it included everything needed, it was a fairly simple installation. Most of the centrifugal superchargers produced only about three pounds pressure so they didn't make a great deal of improvement.

Judging from the photos accompanying this chap-ter, there was no shortage of ideas for the use of super-chargers, whether centrifugal or positive-displacement units like the Roots. Their success was spotty, but we don't know if the supercharger was used correctly, nor do we know if everything else in the engine was done properly.

If a supercharged rod was fast, we knew that every-thing was done right, or at least done well. But, if the car didn't perform well, we never knew whether to blame the supercharger installation or something else

Right, a stock McCulloch supercharger application, complete with a single Chandler-Groves carburetor, as made for the Ford flathead V-8 engine. The installation required the addition of four-sheave pulleys on each water pump to match the supercharger drive pulley. Hot water is picked up from the outlet from the right cylinder head and routed through the intake between supercharger and manifold and then to the radiator. This type of supercharger, which produced only about 3lb pressure, was ineffective and seldom provided a noticeable power increase.
Mark Dees collection

Top far right, Jim Berger's T roadster pickup has a McCulloch with an adapter to mount two Stromberg or Chandler-Groves carburetors. Notice that the hot water inlet to the incoming mixture is blocked off—the water routed directly from the head to the radiator. This probably worked a great deal better than the stock installation with one carburetor and water-heated intake mixture.
Jim Berger photo, Don Montgomery collection

Bottom right, the Frenzel centrifugal supercharger was designed with the impeller vertical instead of horizontal as seen on most centrifugal set-ups. The mechanism between the three-sheave pulley and the impeller chamber is a case for the step-up gearing (centrifugal superchargers typically run from five to seven times faster than engine crank speed). There are two carburetor flanges (one visible) on the impeller intake side, designed to carry Stromberg or Chandler-Groves twin-throat carburetors.
John Lee photo, Neal East collection

Bottom far right, Tony Capanna, co-owner (with Red Wilson) of Wil-Cap Automotive, pours fuel into the tank of Glendale Sidewinders Club member Frank DeMarco's '32 roadster. Wil-Cap was primarily a machine shop, but they installed an engine dynamometer which they rented out to racers for engine tuning. The shop also became a distributor of racing fuel, primarily methanol, and later nitromethane.
Author photo

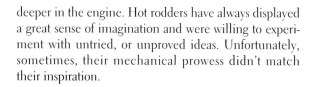

deeper in the engine. Hot rodders have always displayed a great sense of imagination and were willing to experiment with untried, or unproved ideas. Unfortunately, sometimes, their mechanical prowess didn't match their inspiration.

Liquid Power

It was inevitable that hot rodders would discover fuel that was more powerful than gasoline. Aviation gasoline, which had higher octane ratings than the gasoline bought in a normal gas station, was tried, again, with mixed success. Some, whether by luck or knowledge, realized significant improvements in power by using Av-Gas, and others might as well have not bothered.

As discussed previously, Bob Rufi had been experimenting with exotic fuel blends in 1940 when his Chevy four streamliner set the 140mph two-way average on May 19 at Harper Dry Lake.

At that same Harper Dry Lake meet, Bud Meyer ran straight methanol in his rear-engined '29 roadster (the first rear-engined roadster to run at the dry lakes) and turned fast time of the day for his class at 121.94mph. It was also the fastest roadster speed ever at the time.

Prewar, there wasn't much activity with alcohol or other so-called exotic fuel blends, partly because not many of the competitors had thought of it, and those who did were not sure how it could be used properly. And, as always, there was cost to consider. Straight methanol was usually about two to three times the cost of gasoline, and even though the country was pretty well out of the depression by the late 1930s and early

'40s, most hot rodders still didn't have much money, many being high school or junior college students.

Postwar methyl alcohol, or methanol as we called it, came into common use because the manufacturers and some speed shops had dynamometers which made experimentation easier. The manufacturers passed along what they had learned to their favored customers who then, if they wanted, shared it with their buddies. One way or another the word got around.

The engine itself didn't require major change to run alcohol in place of gasoline, but the carburetors did require reworking. Most rodders kept two sets of carburetors, particularly if the car was also street-driven—one set for gasoline and one set for methanol. When running alcohol, the volume of fuel required for proper mixture was double that needed for gasoline. We even ran larger fuel lines when using methanol.

The carburetors themselves, usually Stromberg Model 48s, which had slightly larger ventures than did the 97, were reworked by enlarging the jets, needle seats, dump tubes, and idle tubes. Some serious racers

Tom Sparks works on a flathead-Ford-powered drag racer, equipped with an Italmeccanica Roots-type positive displacement blower. The blower is Gilmer-belt driven from the crankshaft, and the huge fuel lines and choke-less Stromberg carburetors indicate the fuel is something other than straight gasoline. No radiator is fitted, and the engine runs with what water is contained in the block and heads. This engine went into Tony Nancy's 22 *Jr.* roadster when Sparks and Bonney stopped racing the Willys coupe. *Tom Sparks collection*

Walt Rose, of the SCTA Road Runners (the photo was taken at a Road Runners picnic at Santa Anita Park in January 1948) drove an 812 Cord V-8 powered '27 T roadster. The 1937 Cord carried a centrifugal supercharger as stock equipment. Like the Cadillac V-8, exhaust came out the top of the block. Rose's engine had to be mounted backward in the chassis because it had rear drive, unlike the front-wheel drive of the Cord for which it was designed. *Lee Blaisdell photo*, Hot Rod *magazine*

removed the choke butterflies from the carburetors to lessen airflow restrictions. As we found after our first use of methanol, it required a complete cleaning of the carburetors within a few days after use, or the alcohol left in the float bowls and jets would gum up to the point where it virtually solidified.

The use of nitromethane sort of crept in through the back door, and I make no claim to knowing who used it first, or when, but in 1949 Vic Edlebrock and Bob Meeks became intrigued with those small, single-cylinder engines made by the Dooling brothers for model airplanes and model race cars. The Dooling's shop was near Edelbrock's, so the pair paid a visit to the Doolings to find out more about the super fuel used to power the tiny engines.

They learned the source for the fuel, bought some, then began a series of dynamometer tests to learn more. Edelbrock, at that time, ran a pair of midgets, one Offy powered and one V-8-60 powered—the Offy driven by Perry Grimm and the V-8 by Rodger Ward. The two drivers occasionally traded rides, but on one epic night at Gilmore Stadium in Hollywood, the value of nitromethane as a fuel was demonstrated superbly.

Edelbrock usually ran his midgets at different circuits, but the night of August 10, 1950, both cars were on the program at Gilmore Stadium. His two drivers qualified first and second and sat in the two-lap Trophy Dash. The V-8 60, driven by Ward, won the Dash, and then Rodger went on to win the main event. The crowd in the stands was on its feet for the entire race because no one had ever seen a V-8 60 go that fast, and particularly that fast for that distance.

The secret, of course, was that Meeks and Edelbrock had found the right ratio of alcohol and ni-

Above, the crank-driven 4-71 GMC Roots blower was a popular method of supercharging in the 1950s.
Alex Xydias collection

Barney Navarro, builder of Navarro racing equipment, ran this '27 T Modified roadster as a member of the SCTA Glendale Stokers Club. The engine was a 1937–38 twenty-one-stud flathead with the stroke shortened to 3in which resulted in a displacement of 176ci. When Navarro added a GMC 3-71 Roots blower it put the car in B Class. With this set-up, his best clocking was 146.8mph. The hood, radiator shell, and cast-aluminum grille were made by Art Ingels.
Ralph Poole photo, author collection

tromethane. That ratio was of utmost importance; too little nitro and the sought-for power wouldn't materialize; too much nitro and you were likely to destroy the engine.

Once upon a time we generally worked with air-to-gasoline ratios between twelve and fifteen to one. If the ratio was off just a bit it didn't matter that much because a slight increase or decrease in spark advance could compensate. It didn't even seem to matter that much when we ran straight methanol. I can remember coming back from a run at El Mirage in my roadster and finding frost on the intake manifold—which I was told was an indication of a good air/fuel mixture.

All those traditional values went out the window when it was discovered that nitromethane could be used. Being an oxygen-bearing fuel, the criteria were now how much pressure your engine can stand and for how long. Whereas the racers started out with, maybe, five percent nitro to ninety-five percent alcohol, a straight 100 percent nitromethane "mixture" is now fairly common, particularly in drag racing.

Drag racers and Bonneville racers have to solve many common problems, but one that isn't common is that a drag race engine runs at peak power for about five seconds at a time, while the Bonneville engine may run flat-out for several minutes. The Bonneville engine isn't putting out the horsepower that a drag race engine produces, but it has to do it for a far greater length of time. In each case, it is critical that absolutely everything in the engine be right.

At one time a racing mechanic had only to be that; a good mechanic. Now, if he's to be competitive, he almost has to be a chemist as well. Or, barring that, he needs someone on his crew who is. There is no longer any margin for error if the engine is to last the race.

The vast improvements in the technology of chassis, tires, suspension, and engines took racing away from the drivers and gave it to the engineers. Super fuels have added the chemist (or maybe the alchemist) to the team.

Some racers might want to take a step backward (saving money in both the cost of racing and the cost of replacement of broken engines), but spectators and sponsors won't permit it. They've had a taste of super

speed from superchargers and super fuels, and they won't relinquish that spectacle.

A 100mph race on a track, if a closely-fought contest, can be as exciting as a 200mph parade on the same track, but drag racing and, to some extent Bonneville racing, isn't like that. Speed (and the more of it the better) is the spectacle and that's what people go to see.

The Herda-Hartelt streamliner engine has a blower mounted down low and driven off the front of the crankshaft. Two runners, one to feed each cylinder head, come from a plenum chamber at the outlet side of the blower, but there are two equalizer crosstubes connecting the main induction pipes just to make sure no cylinder will be starved of its mixture. *Author photos*

CHAPTER 10

Bonneville Speed Trials

"The road to Wendover [Utah] is the only road
in the world that's uphill both directions."
—Anonymous Bonneville competitor

Our anonymous sage may have been joking, but those who have made this trip tend to agree with him. After a full year of planning for this week-long meet, there still seems to be a million things to do at the last minute, and the midnight oil burns in shops and garages all over the country as racers prepare for their once-a-year speed fest.

They are bone-tired and emotionally wrung out, trying to solve last minute problems with the car, the trailer, the tools, the crew, and their spouses or girlfriends who may or may not agree that this week is the most important of their men's lives. Then after a week of tuning, running, tuning, running, and all too often repairing something that broke—a repair that could be done in a few minutes or an hour if they were home in their own shops or garages, but takes hours or days to fix on the salt or in Wendover—they are worn out.

Then comes the trip home. If there's a trophy or two in the home-going load, it's a nice drive. If the car broke and couldn't be fixed, it doesn't matter much if it's a two-dollar part or a complete engine that needs to be replaced. It really does seem like an uphill battle, or drive, both ways. Not all the excitement of the week is on the salt, either. The journey to and from can be every bit as trying as the week of competition.

In 1952, Mal Meredith and Jack Reilly were entered at the Nationals in B and C Lakester Class, running Mal's B engine and Jack's C engine—both flat-head Merc V-8s. The belly tank was trailered behind the tow car, Reilly's A V-8 roadster pickup.

From their homes in North Hollywood, they had two route choices to Wendover and the salt flats: Highway 14 to 395, and then at Bishop take the right fork on Route 6 over Montgomery Pass and then through Tonapah, and Ely, Nevada, to Wendover; or they could go east via San Bernardino, Victorville, Barstow, and Las Vegas with a left at Glendale, then north through Pioche and Caliente to Ely and on into Wendover.

They opted for the Las Vegas route because it had fewer high-mountain passes to negotiate. Their first drama came when they went through Baker as fast as the tow car would go to get a running start at the infamous Baker Grade—a straight stretch twenty miles long that is almost a six percent grade. This one climb probably destroyed more automotive cooling systems than any other grade in California.

It was August, and it was hot, and their pickup had been boiling before they got to Baker, so the running start was considered a necessity. Unfortunately, a California Highway Patrol officer saw them go through Baker and stopped them about three miles up the grade. Aside from the indignity of the citation, they now had to get the tow car and trailer moving up this hill from a standing start. Before they reached the crest, one was sitting on a front fender pouring water into the radiator as the other drove.

Then, between Pioche and Caliente, where the going was easier, they spotted an overturned car beside the road. When they investigated they found a badly in-

Members of the "Two Club" (200mph Club) Art Chrisman, Otto Rysmann, George Hill and Willie Young acknowledge new member LeRoy Holmes. Driving Charles Scott's Ardun V-8 B Lakester Holmes averaged 201.015mph at the 1953 Bonneville Nationals. Scott, you may recall, was the boy who was lured to the dry lakes in the first chapter. Membership in the 200mph Club requires a driver to post a two-way average over 200mph. *Ralph Poole photo, author collection*

Opposite page, the Jim Lindsley-A.J. Michele twin-Chrysler roadster (see text) at Bonneville in 1953. A year later it became the first roadster to set a two-way average over 200mph. Jim Lindsley qualified for the 200mph Club by averaging 202mph. The blue and white roadster looked as good inside as it did outside. Friends of Jim's were towing the trailered roadster home from Bonneville when the driver went to sleep demolishing both the tow car and the roadster in the ensuing accident. Fortunately, both occupants of the tow car were shaken up but okay.
Author photo

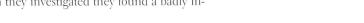

jured woman lying beside the upside-down car. They quickly unhooked the trailer and while Meredith stayed with the woman, Reilly went to find help. While Reilly was gone, Mal rejected the offers of several drivers who stopped and wanted to take the woman to the hospital. Meredith wisely felt she shouldn't be moved until the ambulance got there.

After Reilly had returned with the sheriff and an ambulance, one of the women bystanders offered the boys lunch, which they happily accepted. Upon returning to the spot where they had left the Lakester, they found no car and no trailer. They knew it hadn't come south on the highway because they were at a ranch just off the road, so driving north they found their race car beside a gas station. Inquiring about the arrival of their car the station attendant told them the Sheriff had had it towed there because he had been so impressed with their efforts to help the injured woman.

Three years earlier, Alex Xydias and I had worked day and night for weeks to get our streamliner ready for the first Bonneville meet and we were bushed. We left

Above, Bill Kenz brought his "Odd Rod" twin flathead Mercury-powered truck to the first Bonneville Nationals in 1949. Laughter and derision faded when Kenz drove the truck to a two way average of 140.95mph. Both front and rear Edelbrock-equipped engines drove the rear wheels. After his successful runs, Kenz vowed to bring a twin-engined streamliner to Bonneville in 1950.
Tim Timmerman photo,
Don Montgomery collection

Wednesday, Bonneville week 1949. The So-Cal streamliner's V-8 60 had stripped the fiber timing gear and was replaced after a new one was sent out from Salt Lake City by Greyhound bus. Keith Baldwin is at the left (in pith helmet), Bill Dailey and Alex Xydias are on trailer leaning over, and Bob Meeks is in foreground. The streamliner hood seems to have spent a great deal of time on the top of my '39 Ford. The hoist is part of a tow truck at the Texaco gas station next to the Western Motel where we stayed.

Above, this Kurtis sports car had a Merc flathead built by Bob Meeks and was sent to Bonneville to top the 132mph record set by a Jaguar XK-120 in Belgium earlier in the year. Wally Parks was to drive the Kurtis, but when the car was ready for its first run, Parks was elsewhere on SCTA business, so Meeks asked the author to drive the car—admonishing me to keep it under 5000rpm because "it's a fresh engine." I drove the car through the traps but was unable to get the engine over 3000 indicated. Returning to the starting area, Meeks was livid, having heard the car screaming all the way through the traps. Investigation told us that the Sun electric tachometer was wired wrong, and the engine had been turning 6000, not 3000. The engine lived through the ordeal, and Parks later drove the Kurtis to a 142.15mph two-way average (after switching to methanol).
Tim Timmerman photo,
Don Montgomery collection

Top, Riverside, California, August 20, 1950. The Skip Hudson (at right with white cap), and Dan Gurney (wearing a "Snuffy Smith" hat, a grubby T-shirt, and waving to the photographer) Bonneville entry: a '29 A V-8 entered in C Modified Roadster class. Their entourage was about ready to start the tiring trek from Riverside to Wendover, Utah, about 700 miles north of home. They had worked nearly round the clock to get the car ready, and there would be little relaxation the rest of the week, as they would discover that running Bonneville, while exhilarating, is an endurance contest.
Riverside Police Deptartment photo,
Dan Gurney collection

Bottom, Dan and Skip arrived at the salt with three engines, but the one that started in the car (borrowed from a friend) stayed in it the entire week. Gurney is at the wheel of the '29 roadster awaiting the starter's signal to go. His best run of the week was 130.43.
Skip Hudson collection

LeRoy Neumayer at the wheel of the Neumayer-Reed brothers "C" Lakester, Bonneville 1954. The tank body was from one of the 165gal tanks as used on P-51 and P-47 aircraft. The tank's smaller size wouldn't cover the width of the Ardun ohv cylinder heads as it would have one of the 315gal P-38 tanks as used by most competitors. The Lakester set a record of 205.71mph average so the protruding valve covers didn't slow it down much. *Ralph Poole photo, author collection*

Many had tried to make an Ardun overhead valve conversion live up to its potential, but no one had succeeded until Don Clark (in car) and Clem TeBow (at right) brought their Ardun-powered '32 to Bonneville in 1951. In spite of a chassis that didn't handle all that well (Clark spun it once at about 160mph) the pair set a new C Roadster Class two-way average of 162.459mph. *Duane Allen/Hop Up magazine photo, author collection.*

Valley Custom Shop in Burbank with the streamliner on a trailer towed by my '39 Ford convertible coupe and another trailer with our tools, luggage, and a Merc engine, towed by Bill Dailey's '41 Ford convertible coupe.

Aside from being my tow car, I also had more towing experience at that time, having towed the 'liner to El Mirage Dry Lake on four occasions (a total of about 800 miles), so I drove when we left Burbank. After stop-ping for breakfast in Tonapah, our group decided I was too tired to continue driving, so Alex and Keith Baldwin took over the towing chores with my convert while I tried to sleep in the back seat of Dailey's car.

Before we had gone very far, Alex and Keith were out of sight because my Ford was pulling a slightly lighter load and it could run faster than Bill's car. A few miles south of Ely, Nevada, we came over a rise and started

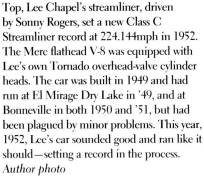

Top, Lee Chapel's streamliner, driven by Sonny Rogers, set a new Class C Streamliner record at 224.144mph in 1952. The Merc flathead V-8 was equipped with Lee's own Tornado overhead-valve cylinder heads. The car was built in 1949 and had run at El Mirage Dry Lake in '49, and at Bonneville in both 1950 and '51, but had been plagued by minor problems. This year, 1952, Lee's car sounded good and ran like it should—setting a record in the process. *Author photo*

Bottom far left, Willie Young at the wheel of Bill Kenz's Floyd Clymer Motorbook Special in 1952. The high-gear-only twin-engined streamliner needed a push to get it going, and what better push car than a hot '32 roadster? The car ran first, in 1950, as the Kenz Twin-Ford Special, averaging 206.5048mph to set a D Streamliner record. In 1951, it was again the Kenz Twin-Ford, and raised its record to 221.479mph. In 1952, it ran as the Floyd Clymer Motorbook Special and boosted its own record up to 244.66mph; all driving done by Willie Young. *Author photo*

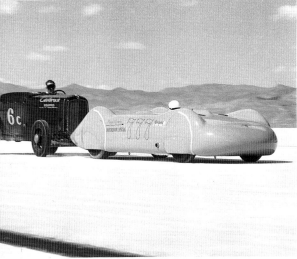

Left, SCTA and Bonneville Chief Timer J. Otto Crocker, facing camera, relaxes while the author listens to comments from the starting line. LeRoy Neumayer is an interested onlooker. Crocker always sat in the stands at the start of the measured mile. Trap timing lights were at the end of the quarter mile distance (for qualifying runs) and at then at the end of the first, second, and third miles. When the photoelectric beam at the start was broken it started the timing process, and when the car tripped the light at the end of the measured distance, it was recorded on a printer in front of Crocker. *Ralph Poole photo, author collection*

down a long hill and immediately spotted my Ford and the streamliner in the ditch on the wrong side of the road.

Our trailer was difficult to tow because the load wasn't balanced correctly (not enough weight on the trailer tongue). When it started to weave back and forth it got away from Alex, and the tow car and trailer jack-knifed and spun 180 degrees. Fortunately the 'liner stayed on the trailer but the left front of the streamliner body hit the left

rear fender of my Ford and dented both rather severely.

We stopped at a body repair shop in Ely to get help, and the man took one look at the streamliner, threw up his hands and said, "I'm going to lunch, you can use my tools." We hammered the body out the best we could, but the streamliner ran at Bonneville with masking tape covering the bare aluminum in front of the left front wheel.

Fran Hernandez works on the engine in the Fernandez & Likes C Roadster while Bob Meeks supervises from a seat in Vic Edelbrock's Ford sedan. Bill Likes ran his own B Class engine in the car but loaned it to Hernandez so he could run his C engine—both were Edelbrock-equipped flathead Mercs. In 1951, when this photo was taken, Likes got the B Roadster record at 144.241mph, but Hernandez was running against the C-T Automotive Ardun-powered roadster and couldn't quite equal the speed of that record setter. Salt is caked onto the cowl of the '29 A roadster body. *Author photo*

The World's Biggest Race Course

The Great Salt Lake Desert of Utah, encompassing the salt lake and the Bonneville Salt Flats are phenomena of nature that many observers find hard to believe and impossible to understand. The creation of this area started more than 50,000 years ago when a brackish salt lake covered an area of some 45,000 square miles in what is now western Utah.

In the 1930s, the Great Salt Lake, on the west edge of Salt Lake City, was one of the most unusual and most popular vacation destinations in the western U.S. Visitors reveled in the water that had such a heavy concentration of salt (about 25 percent) that the human body couldn't sink in the water. Coming from a dip in that lake left one's body thoroughly caked in salt, and too long in the sun and one could imagine himself a salt-layered prime rib just removed from the oven.

Farther west, on higher ground, a vast area turned into a flat, crusty, but smooth surface. The area was named for an American Army Captain of French descent, Benjamin Bonneville, and has been known as the Bonneville Salt Flats since the 1870s.

When the Western Pacific Railroad completed its roadbed south of the Great Salt Lake and then west across the salt flats in 1907, the town of Wendover was born on the Utah-Nevada border as a water stop for the steam locomotives which provided motivation for the transcontinental trains.

On July 28, 1914, the last connection in the coast-to-coast telephone line was made in Wendover, and when the line went into service the following year, Alexander Graham Bell spoke the memorialized words to his assistant, "Mr. Watson, come here, I want you" from his telephone in New York City. Thomas Watson, who was in San Francisco, replied, "Sorry, Mr. Bell, I can't. I am too far away."

Potash, a necessary ingredient in making fertilizer, began to be mined from the salt during WWI, an activity that seemed harmless at the time but which, as we shall see, was to ruin the salt flats as we knew (know) them.

U.S. Highway 40 (which became U.S. 50 and finally I-80) was finally completed across the salt flats, paralleling the railroad from Salt Lake City west, and Wendover became a tourist stop, although primarily for food and water, and a possible overnight rest. By 1937 Nevada had legalized gambling, and this split Wendover into two factious town areas. On the Nevada side one could roll dice twenty-four hours a day and order any drink known to man, but on the Utah side you could only get three-two beer. Wendover, Utah, be-

The Buddy Fox-Alex Xydias So-Cal Speed Shop C-Competition Coupe is in the Western Motel "garage" for some midweek work. The concrete sidewalk in front of our rooms made a good, solid base for the portable A-frame and chain fall. The engine is a B-Class flathead with Ardun overhead valves and a GMC Roots blower which moves it up into Class C. This coupe ran Bonneville the year before as the Fox & Cobbs C-Competition Coupe and D-Competition Coupe (a C engine with a GMC Roots blower). *Ralph Poole photo, author collection*

came the "bedroom" while Wendover, Nevada, became a cross-country-stop gambling haven.

WWII brought the U.S. Army Air Corps (later U.S. Air Force) into town when a base was built for bomber training crews. This was to be the location where the B-29 crews which dropped the atomic bombs on Hiroshima and Nagasaki were trained. The base was closed in 1952 and reopened as a jet-training base in 1954.

It's not clear when the actual first run (speed or joy-riding) was made on the salt by a wheeled vehicle, but Wendover resident Ferg Johnson took his Packard onto the salt in 1909. Ab Jenkins followed a year later aboard a Yale motorcycle, and in the mid-1930s he set so many speed and endurance automobile records (25km to 10,000km) that it's difficult to list them all. Jenkins set many of these records driving solo, but occasionally Babe Stapp or Cliff Bergere shared driving—particularly on the really lengthy runs.

In 1935, Sir Malcolm Campbell (he had been knighted in 1931 after setting the first speed record of more than four miles per minute) had managed a two-way average at Daytona Beach of 276.82 miles per hour but had come to the conclusion that he couldn't go any faster there. On September 3, 1935, he posted a two-way average at Bonneville of 301.129 with no changes to his *Bluebird* after the Daytona run.

Hot rodders' participation began in 1949 after R.E. Petersen, Wally Parks, and Petersen's company manager Lee Ryan flew to Salt Lake City to meet with the Chamber of Commerce. There they found a friend in the person of Robert D. "Gus" Backman who headed the Bonneville Speedway Association part of the Salt Lake Chamber of Commerce.

The meeting resulted in permission to stage a "test" meet sometime in 1949, and the date finally selected (based on known weather patterns) was Monday August 22 through Saturday August 27. Forty seven entries were listed in the program; all but two (Bill Kenz from Denver and Virgil Gardner from Salt Lake City) were from southern California. This wasn't surprising as the final dates weren't known until just a few weeks before the meet, and there was no quick or easy way to notify possible entrants from other parts of the country.

A few entrants listed on the program didn't show, and some post-program entries were accepted, so there isn't an accurate tally on just how many cars participated in the first meet.

As would be expected, speeds rose at a tremendous rate over the years, although increases were greater in some classes than in others.

During the first ten years of the Bonneville Nationals, classes started at the small displacement level. Class A included engines up to 180ci, Class B allowed engines between 181 and 260ci, Class C was for engines between 261 and 350ci, and Class D was for engines over 351ci. A supercharger moved the car up one class.

Class	1949	1958
B Roadster	132.075	168.797
C Roadster	129.690	174.133
B Modified Roadster	132.730	198.567
C Modified Roadster	151.900	200.009
B Streamliner	no record	236.842
C Streamliner	189.745	248.260

In 1959, the class designations were reversed to conform to the FIA (Federation International de l'Automobile). Consequently, the small class for 1959 was Class G, 0–60ci; F, 61–90ci; E, 91–122ci; D,

Some spectators, these were on the salt in 1954, came to the salt as well prepared as any competitor—height, for visibility, shade and seat for comfort, a cooler with refreshing liquid of some sort, and something to eat when the urge strikes. *Ralph Poole photo, author collection*

Buddy Fox and Tom Cobbs borrowed the '34 Competition Coupe from Alex Xydias with the provision that they run it as the So-Cal Speed Shop Team car—it was good publicity for Alex's speed shop with Fox & Cobbs' carrying number one for the previous season's championship. When the 1953 Bonneville meet was over, the team held the new Class C-Competition Coupe record at 172.749-mph. The chopped and channeled coupe was not only fast, it was one of the better looking cars to run on the salt. *Author photo*

Opposite page, a ritual, daily for some competitors, and at the end of the week for others, was washing to rid the cars of salt—this scene at one of the local gas stations. In the foreground is the Ford-powered Chrisman & Duncan C Class Roadster, and behind it the DeSoto-powered Chrisman brothers C-Competition Coupe, which set two class records—180.08mph in class C, and 180.87mph in Class B, with a Dodge Hemi V-8. The roadster went one way at 174.16mph but didn't go home with the record.

As entrants and spectators leave I-80 to enter the road leading to the pit area they pass a tribute to John Cobb (fastest land mile—403.35mph) and Ab Jenkins (100 miles—196.35mph) with an artist's depiction of John Cobb's Napier Railton Special, sponsored by Mobilgas and Mobiloil. This was 1953, and the entrance to the lake has changed since then.
Ralph Poole photo, author collection

The Bonneville Nationals was visited by two historic racing luminaries in 1954; Ab Jenkins and Capt. George Eyston (with LeRoy Neumayer in front of Chet Herbert's *Beast No. 5*, a twin-Dodge streamliner). Eyston's Thunderbolt held the World Land Speed Record in 1937 at 312.00mph, and twice in 1938 at 345.50; then three weeks later at 357.50, before surrendering it to John Cobb at 369.70. No strangers to speed, both men were enthused about the hot rodders' performance on the salt.
Ralph Poole photo, author collection

123–180ci; C, 181–305ci; B, 306–488ci; and A, all engines over 489ci. As before, a supercharger moved the car up one class, except when running for an International Record which made no differentiation for superchargers.

The reason for the seemingly odd numbers is that the SCTA stayed with cubic inches but matched the International Class metric displacements, namely 1000cc=61ci, 1500cc=90ci, 2000cc=122ci, 3000cc=183ci, 5000cc=305ci, and 8000cc=488ci

The racers, particularly those who had run on any of the dry lakes, became absolutely infatuated with Bonneville. With its enormous area (in the best years we had courses as long as thirteen miles), hard, dust-free surface, unlimited visibility, and, except for a wind that came out of the mountains north of the course and crossed it in the measured miles, it was an ideal place to go fast with great safety.

Cars did turn over, and drivers did get hurt—a few lost their lives—but considering the speeds obtained, the safety record is exceptionally good. We never learned exactly where the crossover point was reached, but it seemed that if a car spun out while going less than 200mph, it would simply spin. But if the car was going faster, the chances are that no matter what body

style; roadster, coupe, modified, lakester, or streamliner, it was going to get upside down.

Rigid safety rules concerning car construction saved many driver's lives. Cars have flipped at well past the 200mph mark, and the driver not only lived, but was barely scratched due to safety harnesses, roll-over

Joe Walden's '57 T-Bird, which he used for daily transportation with a 406 drag racing Ford engine, ran at the 1964 Bonneville Speed Trails with a 427 Mercury Marauder NASCAR engine built by his father-in-law Vern Houle. His best run was 200.78mph.
Don Cummins photo

Bill Waddill's Crosley-bodied C-Competition Coupe from Flint, Michigan, was 1949 Cadillac powered. Why have a hinged hood to work on the engine when you can, with the help of several friends, lift the body off? The car was entered as *The Speed Shop Special* for the 1952 meet. Waddill was the first class winner from east of the Mississippi.
Ralph Poole photo, author collection

Never one to follow someone else's lead, John Vesco, of the San Diego Roadster Club, turned a belly tank backward (to run point first) and reworked the body, so the driver could be completely enclosed and look out through a small windshield. At the 1953 Bonneville Nationals the 4-Port Riley-powered (displacement reduced to 180ci to fit Class A) Lakester was first in its class with a run of 161.00mph and set a record with a two-way average of 156.956mph.
C.W. Scott photo

bars, Snell Foundation-approved helmets, and generally excellent chassis construction. As cars got faster, safety rules mandated fire-proof driving suits, parachutes for quicker stopping, and dictated engine placement and wheelbase minimums.

It has always been easy to spot a newcomer to the salt. He'll look around to see if anyone is watching, and then when he thinks he's free from scrutiny he'll rub his fingers across the salt and lick them to see if it really is salty. It is. You can also spot a newcomer to the salt at the end of his first day because he'll have worn a hat of some kind and will have slathered suntan lotion over his face and arms, but he will have forgotten (or never thought to do it) to apply lotion under his nose and chin—not realizing that the reflection off the salt is as bad as the direct sun.

As long as a contestant isn't fighting some really puzzling problem, running on the salt during speed week is some of the most relaxing and pleasurable racing you can find anywhere. Even competitors help each other; sometimes the help is offered altruistically, and sometimes it could be given with the realization that the giver might want help later. Whatever the reason, tires are swapped, tools are loaned; hands-on help to change a clutch or a complete engine is always there.

In 1952, Jim Lindsley blew the Chrysler engine in his D Class non-fendered coupe, and A.J. Michele, a spectator from Louisiana who had driven onto the salt to

A combined effort from Don Clark and Clem TeBow (left) of CT Automotive who put together the Adams-Moller ohv conversion to the flathead Merc block which, with 248ci produced a bit more than 320hp, and George Hill, in cockpit, and Bill Davis, at right, brought this Bob Estes sponsored streamliner to the salt in 1952. George set a new Bonneville Nationals Class B Streamliner record, and then two weeks later they returned to the salt to run under AAA sanction and set a new International Class C record of 229.77mph. The body was designed by the author. *Author photo*

Opposite page bottom, in 1953, Mal Hooper's Shadoff Special set a new International C Streamliner record at 236.36mph (sanctioned by AAA/FIA) for the measured mile. He also set slightly slower records from one kilometer to ten miles. His crew is, left to right, chassis builder Carl Fleischman; sponsor Bill Shadoff; Ray Brown, whose shop built the Chrysler engine; Bob Taylor; Mal Hooper in car; and Herb Fisher. The car body was designed by the author and is very much like the Hill car from the year before except that Mal's engine is behind him while George's was in front. The same car, with Bob Bowen driving and a larger Chrysler V-8 engine set International B Class records at 272mph-plus, making it the fastest unblown single-engined car in the world. *Author photo*

find out what was going on, offered his engine to use. Going back to Wendover they pulled the engine from the man's Chrysler convertible and, after fitting Lindsley's camshaft, heads, magneto, Hilborn injectors and the exhaust headers, Jim set a class record at 138.57mph.

After his record run they met again in the parking lot of the Western Motel and re-installed the engine in the man's car so he could drive home to Louisiana. In 1953, Lindsley and his benefactor teamed up before the meet and brought a twin-Chrysler-engined roadster to Bonneville. The first year for the car wasn't outstanding, but in 1954 it became the first roadster to average better than 200mph when Lindsley drove it to a 202.00mph record in E Modified Roadster Class.

As this is being written, the salt flat is in grave danger of disappearing. The lake has been mined so heavily for so many years that the once thick and extremely hard surface is now very thin. The surface is not only poor, but the area has diminished to the point where finding available space to lay out a long course is almost impossible.

Several groups are working to save the salt, but it has apparently come to the point where money, or the lack of money, is both the problem and the cure. Both the mining company and the racers have legal right to use the salt, but unfortunately their goals differ. The mining company would consider measures that would rejuvenate the lakebed, but it costs money the company isn't willing to spend, and the racers don't have it.

If a solution isn't worked out, Bonneville racing will come to an end in the near future.

CHAPTER 11

Early Drag Racing

*If you think your car is so hot,
drag it out and we'll see what you've got.*

A drag race, as we know it today (1994) is a far different beast from what it was when this activity first started. In fact, when it first started it wasn't called a drag race because the term hadn't yet been invented.

The first use of the term that I've been able to find was in the March 1, 1939, edition of the *SCTA Racing News*, a semimonthly newsletter for SCTA members. At that time it was a six-page mimeographed affair which kept members informed about the activities of their association.

On page five of that March 1 edition (Volume 1, Number 7) editor Wally Parks makes note of the fact that "a drag race scheduled by the 90 M.P.H. club was interrupted by the law. They left, with no questions asked, when J.J. (Johnny Junkin) told them it was an 'economy run and we weren't exceeding 35 miles per hour.'" Yeah, sure. Hot rodders were inventive even when it came to non-mechanical things.

For some reason (and in a recent conversation with Wally Parks, he couldn't shed any light on the matter either), the term didn't catch on. He used it again himself in the April 1, 1939, edition, writing, "Lyle Knudsen, unattached, has been challenged to a drag race with a plenty hot T Ford owned by Monte, who holds the old T record. The race will be from 40 m.p.h. up or faster."

It is very likely that the Monte's T referred to is the Modified that eventually became the Jack Harvey/George Harvey/Jack Lehman/Doug Caruthers/LeRoy Neumayer/Art Chrisman number 25 dragster. The first owner is known to have run a Rajo T engine in that car although it never set a wheel on a real drag strip until after WWII.

When the cars we now call hot rods ran at Muroc Dry Lake in the early 1930s, the procedure was to time each car through the measured quarter mile traps and then match them by classes; 80–90mph, 90–100, 100–110, 110–120. Then the racing began. The cars in each class, up to five at a time, would take off from a slow rolling start, and the car that reached the finish line first was the winner in each class.

It was a dangerous way to race. The driver in front could see where he was going, but those behind him were running in dust that sometimes got so thick they couldn't see ahead. It's a miracle that these races didn't turn into disasters, but somehow they didn't, and these acceleration races continued until 1939 when the newly-formed Southern California Timing Association eliminated them from their lakes meets.

Street racing, which was a way of life in southern California at that time, was also a disaster waiting to happen. Typically, guys raced in impromptu races from one stoplight to the next, but some were well organized (if illegal) and were staged by pre-arrangement at one of the favorite streets in the area.

Sepulveda Boulevard south of San Fernando Road beside the Van Norman reservoir was a popular rendezvous, as was Glenoaks Boulevard just west of the

Paradise Mesa, 1953—Ralph Lynde takes off in his Yo-Yo Engineering Special which was named for the aluminum frame's propensity to flex and bounce up and down as he went through the quarter mile. Author photo

Opposite page, the starter's art was never better than in the mid-1950s. This is Bakersfield in 1954, and the athletic flag waver (he did this for every run) is waving off two modified roadsters. Ralph Poole photo, author collection

In the early 1950s, the police in Los Angeles, the L.A. section of the National Safety Council, and the Hearst newspapers were trying to get hot rods banned from the streets, thinking from their garbled perspective that it would end street racing. The street racers did, for one event anyway, do it off the streets. Unfortunately they picked the concrete-paved L.A. Riverbed in downtown Los Angeles. That's the Fourth Street Bridge in the background. The authorities weren't any happier about this venue than they had been about doing it on the streets. There isn't a hot rod in sight that we can see in this photo, but the *Examiner* story was headlined "police round up hot rodders in L.A. Riverbed." *Hearst Newspaper Collection, University of Southern California Library*

Burbank city limits. On the east side they ran on Foothill Boulevard in Arcadia near the Santa Anita horse racing track, or on Peck Road in El Monte. The racers in the South Bay area used Lincoln Boulevard beside Mines Field.

These strips were relatively safe, if the racers waited for traffic to clear, because there weren't any cross streets. Even so, the car builders paid a lot more attention to making the car go than they did to making it stop. Although most builders had converted the brakes to hydraulic, a 100mph-plus coupe, roadster, or sedan still took a long distance to get stopped. A careful eye for traffic of any kind was essential if the drag racers wanted to survive.

An off-road strip with some organization behind the racing was the way it should go, and it did, to a degree, in 1949. The Santa Barbara Acceleration Association (SBAA) began holding events at the Goleta, Cali-

fornia, airport, a field that had been a Marine base during WWII and would later play host to California Sports Car Club road racing events.

The SBAA ran some of the loosest races ever seen. There were no entry fees, no car inspection, no timing equipment, and no ambulance. They passed the hat to help support the meets. The cars, two at a time, ran from a rolling start on a straight section of a two-lane perimeter road on the airport.

In spite of the casual approach and a rather short run-off area, the meets were popular and drew a good crowd of both competitors and spectators—possibly because it was the first venue for off-street drag racing. It was almost like running on the street in that you probably didn't know who you were running against, but at least there was no fear of cross traffic or police raids.

The first organized drag strip in the country was

Ernie McAfee photo,
Pete Henderson collection.

Horse vs. Hot Rod

In early 1945, pioneer southern California hot rodder Ak Miller was approached by a stranger who wanted to bet on a race between his horse and Miller's roadster, a 1932 Ford with a LaSalle V-8. The stranger's proposal was a drag race on the highway from one telephone pole to another, a distance of sixty yards.

Miller discussed the proposal with Connie Weidell, owner of a '27 T with a Cadillac V-8 engine. They discovered that the most famous race horse of the day, Seabiscuit, could run sixty yards from a standing start in 4.2 seconds.

Miller and Weidell raced each other from pole to pole and neither could cover the distance in 4.2 seconds. But a friend, Pete Henderson, had a '32 roadster powered by a flathead Ford V-8 which they found could accelerate sixty yards in 4.0 seconds.

So it would be Henderson's Deuce versus the stranger's horse. Word of the match spread, and a considerable number of spectators was on hand for the event, which was held on California State Highway 39. Apart from the bet between the stranger and the hot rodders, there were a lot of side bets among the spectators.

The roadster was to run on the pavement, while the horse and rider would be in the dirt alongside. The race would begin when the starter dropped his hat.

But when the starter lifted his hat from his head, the horse took off. Henderson, caught off-guard immediately punched the accelerator. His roadster caught the horse and passed it just before reaching the second telephone pole.

Henderson and his hot rod had won a greater victory than Miller, Weidell, and Henderson realized at the time. The stranger had been traveling around the country with what turned out to be a quarter horse, which reached maximum speed in about three strides and, over a short distance like the sixty yards, was even quicker than a thoroughbred like Seabiscuit.

—*John Lawlor*

at the Santa Ana Airport (later Orange County Airport and now John Wayne International Airport) which had been a primary training base for Air Force pilots. C. J. Hart, Frank Stilwell, and Creighton Hunter organized their first drag meet there which occurred on an abandoned taxiway on July 2, 1950. Unlike the Goleta strip, this one had timing equipment and an ambulance. They didn't pay prize money, but winners could sell their trophies back to Hart for the wholesale cost—$7.00. Some cynics commented that after his first few purchases of new trophies, Hart never went back to the original source because he got all the trophies he needed by reclaiming the ones he had just given out.

Prior to the Santa Ana debut, *Hot Rod* magazine had published a feature written by editor Wally Parks called "Controlled Drag-Racing" in its April 1950 issue. The photos show races with five cars going at one time in one photo, and six cars taking off in another photo. Parks' story didn't say that what was pictured was right; he was saying how it should be done.

Nowhere in the story is a location named, but it had to be a WWII airfield in Los Alamitos, California,

Top right, Don Montgomery's GMC-powered 810 Cord Sedan was an amalgamation of many cars: Cord body, GMC engine, Dodge front axle, Pontiac rear axle, and Buick transmission. The 298ci engine had a Howard 12-Port aluminum head, a fabricated six-carb manifold, Howard F-6 camshaft, Venolia pistons, and a Scintilla magneto. The car ran 107.14 at Pomona, and 135.338 at Russetta Timing at El Mirage Dry Lake, setting a B sedan record. *Ralph Poole photo, Santa Ana, June 27, 1953*

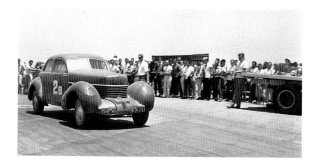

Top far right and middle, the Sparks & Bonney Willys coupe ran with an Italmeccanica-blown flathead Merc (the engine is pictured in chapter 9). The engine was destroked to reduce displacement to 258ci, and the fuel was 15 percent methanol, 15 percent benzol, and 70 percent nitromethane. When Sparks & Bonney quit racing this car, the engine was installed in Tony Nancy's 22 Jr. and, running in the X-Fuel Roadster class, Tony held both the ET and Top Speed class records, the latter at 136.42mph. *Tom Sparks collection*

Right, Paradise Mesa drag strip in 1953 was host to many of the racers who would later become legends. Shown here is the Drifters' '35 Ford coupe, Ed Stewart's '32 roadster, the Bean Bandits' dragster, and Lloyd Krant (holding a trophy and being kissed by the race queen) on Chet Herbert's Harley-Davidson—one of the many "Beasts" built by Herbert. *Ralph Poole photo*

Bottom far right, Bakersfield, 1954. Jarvis Earl's straight-eight Buick displayed not only one of the wildest looks—eight straight pipes and six Strombergs sitting on a log manifold— but it was the noisiest engine at the strip. Went pretty well, too. *Ralph Poole photo, author collection*

called "Mile Square." The paved runway was certainly wide enough for six cars abreast, but Editor Parks wisely commented that "Mass takeoffs, as above (in the photo), are not the recommended method for these events."

Almost a month after the opening of the Santa Ana strip, the Southern California Timing Association and the American Motorcycle Association held a joint meet on July 16, 1950, at the Santa Ana Blimp Base. If we can judge by the photos published in *Hot Rod*, the Morton & Rubio Modified Roadster, Larry Shinoda's "Chopsticks Special" Modified Roadster, Jim Woods' Ford Six roadster, and the Wally O'Brien '32 street roadster came out on top—winning their races against the bikes.

As these drag strips became more popular, more strips were opened—located all over California and soon spreading to Oregon, Washington, Arizona, and then eastward as stories appeared in *Hot Rod*. The eastern, midwestern, and southern hot rodders may have lagged their California counterparts at the beginning, but that wouldn't last. This activity was something young men identified with no matter where they lived.

The interest even spread overseas, where a former U.S.A.F. base at Podington became the first drag strip in England. Using a runway where B-17s once took off in the early morning for missions to Germany, a pair of dragsters might sit, their two engines producing more horsepower than the four engines of the B-17. As a tribute to American drag racing, the British enthusiasts called their strip Santa Pod—Santa as an honor to Santa Ana, and Pod for the strip's location in Podington. [By coincidence, Podington is the field the author flew from with the 92nd Bomb Group of the Eighth Air Force.]

Early drag racing was not very scientific, and there was no precedent for how such a specialized car should be built. Most of the cars participating were either straight off the street, or were dry lakes specials which, while good for their originally created purpose, weren't quite right for acceleration from a standing start.

Unless the owner could afford a quick-change rear axle center section, the dry lakes cars were geared wrong for quick acceleration. Of course the owner could change the ring and pinion gears in the stock rear axle, (and some did) but that was a laborious and time-consuming chore. Most competitors didn't bother with these measures because drag racing hadn't yet become really competitive.

Those dry lakes racers who virtually abandoned the dry lakes and became drag racers had to rebuild their cars, going well beyond a mere change of axle gearing. Weight was the enemy, and where lightening the car to run at the lakes was something that everyone did, a drag racer turned lightness into a moral obligation.

The Santa Ana strip started out with top speed timing at the end of the quarter mile because most rodders were accustomed to seeking the highest speed. It soon became obvious that the car which recorded the highest top speed wasn't necessarily the first car to reach the end of the quarter mile. This was a hard lesson for many would-be drag racers to learn, but the successful ones got the point very quickly, and the ones who didn't lost races.

When drag racing really came into its own, the serious racers stopped running former dry lakes cars and started building cars specifically for drag racing. This meant longer wheelbases for stability, engines moved back in the chassis for better traction, absolute minimal weight, and finally, the driver in a seat mounted so far to the rear they called it a "slingshot."

There is some argument about Mickey Thompson being the first to narrow the rear track but regardless of who did it first, Mickey made it work—and combined it with the slingshot seating. Narrowing the distance between the rear wheels may well have done more for dragster stability than did the longer wheelbase.

Basically, the rear axle can act as a lever, and when one rear wheel is getting a good bite but the other one is about to spin, the wheel that's grabbing the pavement can actually head the car off-course no matter what the driver is doing with his steering. The longer the axle the more leverage that biting tire has and the quicker it rear-end-steers the car off its straight line. The

Above, Winternationals at Pomona, 1965. The *Pulsator* was built by Nye Frank and driven by Bob Muravez. The twin Chevy V-8s achieved a top trap time at 186, but when the rather heavy streamlined body was removed, the car was quicker. (Bob Beazer is in the Indian costume. He would perform an "anti-rain" dance when conditions seemed to require it.) *Ralph Poole photo, author collection*

The Winternationals Pomona, 1965. Don Garlits' *Wynn's Jammer* is lined up for an elimination with Zane Shubert. This is one of many cars Don called *Swamp Rat*, although his name for the car is written small at the tail while the sponsor's name claims the most visible spot on the rather small body. The car is Dodge powered featuring heads by Mondello. In addition to being fast, Garlits' later cars were well turned out and good looking. It won more often than not, and looked good while doing it. *Ralph Poole photo, author collection*

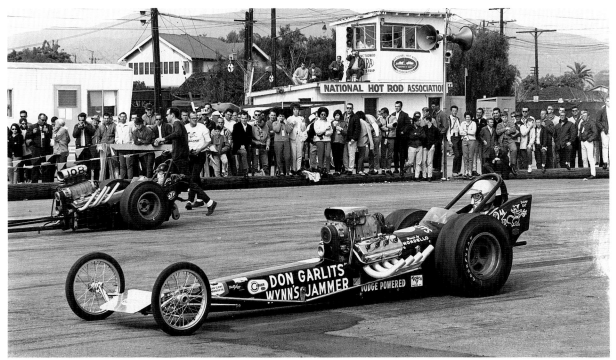

narrowed track doesn't have that leverage, and the car will tend to run straight regardless of tire bite.

Some racers, and most spectators, tend to think in terms of power, more power, and yet more power. It's an obvious if slightly erroneous solution to faster times and shorter ETs, but power has never been the real problem. From the time drag racing began, there has always been more power than the car could put to the track. The problem was how to get that power applied to the traction needed to move the car at the fastest possible speed.

Chassis builders played with wheelbases, usually getting longer, and with engine placement, and wings—over the rear axle, over the engine, over the front axle. Experimenting was nonstop. The use and placement of components was largely trial and error, as no one had really determined the absolute ideal set-up by mathematical or engineering expertise.

Scotty Fenn, Nye Frank, Dragmaster (Jim Nelson and Dode Martin), Kent Fuller, Lefty Mudersbach, Woody Gilmore, and Connie Swingle were all renowned chassis builders. They were, to a man, innovative and successful. Like Indianapolis, where racers bought chassis from Eddie Kuzma, A.J. Watson, Lujie Lesovsky, or Frank Kurtis, depending on last year's success, the drag racers skipped back and forth between Fenn, Frank, Fuller, or Dragmaster depending on current wins. Some racers might run two or three different chassis in one season, hoping the new combination would be the one.

Aside from the chassis design and redesign, I think the real progress was made in two other areas (obviously everything on the car has to work to make it successful): clutches and tires. When Paul Schiefer worked with Keith Black to create a "slider clutch" wherein the power wasn't instantly grabbed by the clutch, ETs improved considerably. The idea that made the difference was a three-disc clutch, with two floaters in between, in which Schiefer programmed the springs and counterweights to engage gradually instead of instantly; thus allowing the rear tires to bite without simply spinning on the pavement.

As we know today, clutches and even transmissions have been developed to such a degree that traction, even with nearly 5,000hp, is no longer the problem it once was—at least as far as the tires are concerned. But this new technology could be a subject for another book. We're concentrating on the early days.

While clutches were being developed, Goodyear was simultaneously developing better and better tires. To do this the company embarked on a testing program and hired Tony Nancy, Don Prudhomme, Don Garlits, Connie Kalitta, and others, at times, to do actual track testing during the week. If a tire worked well in testing, Goodyear made it available to all the racers. If a new design didn't work out, it quietly slipped into obscurity.

Dragster development progressed in a fairly straightforward manner, but a new idea hit the strips in 1964. After being hurt in a dragster accident, Jack Chrisman received a Factory Experimental class 1964 Mercury Comet equipped with a fiberglass front end and powered by a 427ci V-8 backed by a four-speed transmission. Never a fan of shifting gears, Jack decided to mate the Comet with a fuel dragster thus creating the first "funny car" (al-

Shirley Shahan, the "Drag-On-Lady," won titles at Pomona, Bakersfield, Long Beach, and other tracks and proved that the ladies were as fast as the men if they had the right equipment to drive. This is at LIONS in Long Beach in February 1966. *Ralph Poole photo, author collection*

Probably one of the crudest-looking, yet most significant of Mickey Thompson's cars was this dragster which combined slingshot seating and narrowed rear track. It worked, to everyone's surprise except Thompson's, and became the norm for future dragsters—until they went to rear engines. Even then, they kept the narrow rear wheel spacing. *Hearst Newspaper Collection Special Collections, University of Southern California Library*

Far right, the 1964 *Ramcharger* (shown at Pomona at the '64 Winternationals) displays notice that it won the 1963 Top Eliminator title, but these Chrysler Corporation race cars would change dramatically in 1965. The rear axle would be moved forward as much as 6in, and the front axles would be moved forward 2 or 3in, all to get better weight distribution. The body wheel well arches would be moved with the wheels so the cars looked as stock as possible, and they were the start of what we know today as Funny Cars. *Ralph Poole photo, author collection*

though it wasn't called that at the time). Bill Stroppe added a well-braced roll bar, a lightweight aluminum seat, hefty traction bars, and a parachute mount.

Jack added a 6-71 GMC Roots blower, Hilborn injection, direct drive, and long, individual headers under the body. The car easily smoked its huge slicks the length of the quarter mile, and the crowds went crazy. The NHRA didn't much like what Chrisman had done, so the car was forced to run in the C Fuel dragster class, but the fans reaction led to establishment of one of the most popular classes in drag racing.

The Funny Car name seems to have been first applied to the Chrysler Corporation Dodges and Plymouths in which the Chrysler engineers moved the rear axle forward to get more car weight on the driving wheels. These cars ran in the Factory Experimental Class on gasoline, but later injectors were fitted and fuel replaced gasoline as the power supplier.

An entire book could be written, in fact several have, about drag racing, and we've only hit some of the highlights here. It is a part of racing that has become uniquely American, and the performance seen today is, unbelievable—even when witnessed first hand.

CHAPTER 12

Speed Shops and Speed Equipment

*First there was George Wight,
then Lee Chapel, then Karl Orr,
and then everyone got into the act.*

As I've mentioned several times already in this book, in the early days of racing equipment manufacture (they didn't call it speed equipment then) the racers' source was the manufacturer, who sold his equipment directly to the customer and mainly for dirt track racing. There were no shops selling a variety of racing parts.

The manufacturer promoted what he made in race programs, trade magazines, and by word of mouth. A few automobile sales agencies (Ford dealers were early players) were quick to add this equipment to their parts inventory, which made it easy for the non-racing car owners to put a bit of zip into their Model Ts. The *Ford Dealer News* carried ads for this equipment.

Rajo, Frontenac, and Roof all made variations of their Model T cylinder heads to fit a given purpose—actual dirt-track racing or street set-ups which would have a single carburetor in place of the racing duals, lower compression ratio heads, and very likely a milder (or stock) camshaft grind.

In 1923, forty-six-year-old George Wight opened an automobile junkyard, calling it Bell Auto Parts, at 3633 Gage Avenue in Bell, California. Inasmuch as Ford had made about 7 million Model Ts by that time, there was always a great selection of Model T Fords in Wight's yard. He noted that some of these cars had unusual cylinder heads, intake manifolds, ignitions, water pumps, or other non-stock components.

His next step was to remove the special equipment from any Model T that came into his junkyard and place that equipment on shelves in his little office/store. Would-be racers now had a single source for parts to hop-up their engines.

Wight built a small brick building on the street in front of his junkyard, and Bell Auto Parts acquired the look that it would have for more than sixty years. Additions were made to the building, but the original brick facade was retained.

After the Model A Ford came out in 1928, Harry Miller and George Schofield formed a company (Schofield) to manufacture an overhead valve conversion—designed by Leo Goossen—for the Model A engine. Within two years Miller-Schofield was bankrupt, a victim of the depression, and its assets were purchased by a new company called Cragar, named for Crane Gartz, an heir to the Crane Plumbing fortune who put up the money, and with ex-race driver Harlan Fengler as manager.

Cragar was hit also by the depression blues, and when it was set to fold in 1932, George Wight spent his saving to acquire the patterns, fixtures, and left-over parts along with the all-important Cragar name.

Bell Auto Parts and Cragar became synonymous, a mutual benefit that would last for sixty-plus years.

George Wight had turned his full-time junkyard and part-time parts business into the first known speed shop in America, and likely the world, and was organizing races called the Gilmore Oil Company Speed Trails at Muroc Dry Lake.

Howard Johansen was not only a top competitor at the dry lakes and in track racing, but was one of the great innovators in engine and race-car building. He's shown here while testing a Cadillac V-8 which has four Stromberg carburetors mounted on a manifold designed for two four-barrel carbs. Howard produced camshafts marketed under the Howard's Cams name, built two twin-boom (catamaran) stream-liners for Bonneville, built the Packard engines for the Carrera Panamericana, and ran Marmon engines in a variety of dry lakes and Bonneville cars. He also built a Four-Port Riley track roadster. *Tom Medley collection*

Opposite page, the granddaddy of all speed shops is this one built by George Wight at 3633 Gage Avenue in Bell, California. This photo was taken in the 1950s when Roy Richter owned the shop. The cars are typical of what one would see on the street in southern California at that time; a channeled '32 roadster, an MG TC with 16in wire wheels, and Wally Parks' '29 A V-8. The large rear tires on the MG suggest that it had something other than an MG engine under the hood. *Art Bagnall collection*

The Eddie Meyer exhaust-heated dual manifold (here with two Chandler Groves carburetors) was made after WWII primarily for street use. Having the carburetors close together like this, enabled the stock generator mount and location to be used, making installation on the engine quick and easy.
Mark Dees collection

In 1932, Lee Chapel started doing pretty much the same thing Wight had done, using the office of a junkyard at 3263 San Fernando Road in north Los Angeles to sell racing equipment salvaged from wrecked or used cars. By 1933, Chapel had moved his operation to 4557 Alhambra Avenue in Los Angeles where he would be until 1937 when he closed the shop to spend two years touring the country with a midget race car. That trip over, he returned to California, this time settling in Oakland where he opened his last shop at 1143 East 14th Street.

Both Wight and Chapel were examples of the early racer-turned-businessman, as both realized that as the number of would-be racers grew—and they were certain it would—parts to modify their cars would be needed.

Both began to make racing equipment (Chapel, using the name "Tornado," made a three-port head for the Chevy four and later an ohv conversion for the Ford flathead V-8). After George Wight died, Roy Richter took over Bell Auto Parts in 1945 and continued the manufacture of Cragar equipment but added sideplates for the A and B engines, four-cylinder intake manifolds, and finally Cragar alloy road wheels and Bell helmets. Both shops also acted as sales outlets for other manufacturers, which made them full-line speed equipment stores.

All through the 1930s advertisements had ap-peared in racing programs for special equipment and/or engine building, but it was mostly backyard work with no pretense of being genuine retail sales outlets. Many of these shops were operated by racers who dabbled in engine building for customers when they weren't racing.

It's likely that Karl Orr had the first post-WWII Speed Shop, at 11140 Washington Place, Culver City, California. Like those to follow, his was a one-stop store where you could buy any needed equipment to make your car faster. During WWII when many SCTA members were overseas, Karl's wife Veda, produced the *SCTA Racing News*. This mimeographed, usually four-to-six page newsletter kept the dry lakes racers informed about what was going on at home and acted as a clearinghouse for SCTA members to get in touch with each other.

A rub-off benefit for the Orrs was that a great many of the returning servicemen headed for Orr's Speed Shop at the first opportunity after coming home. No one objected to this publicity benefit to Orr's shop; the men were thankful and appreciative of the effort made by Veda to publish the newsletter.

Don Blair opened Blair's Auto Parts at 826 Arroyo Parkway in Pasadena in 1945 to sell new and used speed equipment and to build engines for customers. He didn't call it a speed shop but that's what it was. Unlike most speed shops at that time, Blair's became known for its excellent supply of used speed equipment. In addition to running his shop, Blair ran his Roots-blown flathead V-8 Modified at the dry lakes, and a 1948 advertisement in *Hot Rod* magazine claimed it to be "Holder of the Fastest V-8 time at SCTA." Blair called his car the "Goat," but it most certainly wasn't.

Alex Xydias was one of the returning veterans who jumped on the speed shop bandwagon. He opened the So-Cal Speed Shop on West Olive Avenue in Burbank the same day he was discharged from the Air Force: March 3, 1946. A year later, when his lease expired, he moved to his more famous location at 1104 South Victory Boulevard in Burbank.

Jack Andrews and Lou Senter started Ansen Automotive Engineering in 1947 to make parts for race cars, but the business soon became a speed shop with a full line of speed equipment sold both over the counter and by mail order. Like Bell Auto Parts and So-Cal, Ansen produced a large catalog to promote the line of equipment carried, and Ansen was one of the sources for full-race, crated engines sold to the moonshiners in the southeastern United States (Vic Edelbrock and Ray Brown also did this, and they all sold engines to the law enforcement officers, too).

Co-owner Lou Senter came to the business with hands-on race car experience, having raced on Cali-

Bonneville, 1954. Alex Xydias, in white t-shirt, is discussing some technical point with officials (L to R), Dean Batchelor, Jim Lindsley, and Jim Frostrom, back to camera, while Wally Parks, then editor of *Hot Rod* magazine, looks on.

Alex Xydias

Alex was born March 22, 1922, in Los Angeles, California. He attended schools in Los Angeles, graduating from Fairfax High School in 1940. His first car, a '29 Ford roadster, was paid for with earnings from part-time work while in high school, and by the time he went into the Army Air Corps in 1942 he had owned a '34 coupe and a beautifully customized '34 Ford Cabriolet—which he found in the lower basement garage at the Ambassador Hotel in Los Angeles.

He opened the first So-Cal Speed Shop, on Olive Avenue in Burbank, on the day of his discharge from the Air Corps—March 3, 1946. When his one-year lease was up, he moved the shop to 1104 South Victory in Burbank on a lot where he had placed a Sears-Roebuck prefab two-car garage.

In 1955, Alex started filming races; Sebring, Pebble Beach, Daytona, Bonneville, Indianapolis 500, and the first four NHRA Nationals. The films he had put together were occupying so much time he closed the speed shop in 1962, and in 1964 went to work for Petersen Publishing as editor of *Car Craft,* which led to a stint as editor of *Hot Rod Industry News* and then associate publisher of *Hot Rod.*

Alex was instrumental in producing the first SEMA shows (Speed Equipment Manufacturers Association), but in 1977 he left Petersen's employ to join Mickey Thompson to produce the SCORE Off-Road show. Even though Mickey and Alex were partners, Alex and his wife, Helen, produced the shows. They sold the show to Harcourt Brace Javonovich in 1987; Mickey kept his own business going but Alex retired.

Xydias's racing exploits can be found throughout this book.

fornia dirt tracks in the 1930s and wrote features for *Throttle* magazine in 1941. The racing connection continued through both Ansen entries or Ansen sponsorship of cars.

Going back almost seventy years it's difficult to say with assurance just which shop was started first, or second, or third, and I'm not sure it makes a great deal of difference anyway. Speed shops sprung up like mushrooms after a spring rain in the immediate postwar years, and they all served a useful purpose. Fortunately they weren't too close together, instead being spread throughout southern California, giving potential buyers a chance to patronize a local business.

The manufacturers, eager to help these shops do well (it was to their benefit to have as many outlets for their product as possible), stopped selling directly to the customer, and most of their advertisements said "See your dealer." The speed shops ran the gamut from hole-in-the-wall stalls with a minimum of stock (quite often these places specialized in equipment for one make of car, or for only flathead Fords, or six-cylinder Chevys), to large facilities with a complete line of speed equipment sometimes augmented by mufflers, wheel discs, and chrome-plated "doll-up" accessories.

The shops with the "general store" approach were most often patronized by neophyte car builders, ones

Mal Ord made log-type intake manifolds for the flathead Ford before the war with flanges to mount Winfield carburetors—two Winfield Model S carbs shown here. Ord made adapters to put Strombergs or Chandler-Groves carbs on this early manifold, but after WWII he cast the three-bolt flanges into the manifold so twin-choke carbs could be used without adapters. The low fins on the cylinder heads are for strength, not cooling. Early Ord manifolds didn't run well on the street because any raw fuel from the carbs puddled in the log and, because a Ford engine was mounted at a slight angle, the fuel puddle went to the rear which flooded the rear cylinders while starving the front ones. His later manifolds had a low dam in the center of the log to keep the fuel from running to the rear.
Mark Dees collection

who didn't have a connection with a club, or have a friend who could steer them to a quality shop, which was too bad because the racing connection continued through both Ansen entries or Ansen sponsorship of cars.

There wasn't a shortage of quality speed shops—hey just weren't on every street corner. San Fernando Valley rodders probably went to C-T Automotive in North Hollywood or So-Cal in Burbank. West-siders could shop at Lewie Shell's in West Los Angeles, the Pasadena area was the bailiwick of Don Blair's shop, and Dean Moon held forth in Santa Fe Springs.

Before January 1948 when *Hot Rod* magazine came out, and well before the magazine published how-to-do-it features, the would-be rodders' only source of information might be the speed shop. At least there he could ask serious questions of the owner, and quite often he could elicit information from other customers.

I changed the brakes on my '32 roadster from mechanical to hydraulic and built a full-race '47 Merc V-8 for the car before *Hot Rod* had published anything on either subject by asking questions of those who had done it themselves. My benefactors were found at the So-Cal Speed Shop or were fellow members of the Road Runners Club. Engine information came mostly from Randy Shinn.

I bought most of the equipment for my roadster from So-Cal because I had developed a friendship with Xydias, and because the shop was handy to my home in Burbank, but I did buy the Ord ignition directly from Mal Ord, and I bought a Clay Smith cam at the Smith & Jones shop in Long Beach. I took a lot of ribbing from my racing buddies for the Smith "speedboat" cam as they called it.

It was a Smith 272 which Clay had developed for the 266 hydroplane class V-8 engines, but why not install it in a roadster engine? A hydroplane was doing exactly what I wanted to do: go like hell in a straight line. A 266 hydroplane ran on a course that was two long straightaways with a sharp turn at each end, and I was going to run for top speed only at El Mirage Dry Lake. It worked great, and I never regretted the choice.

It would be almost impossible to list every maker of speed equipment, even if the list was broken down to prewar and postwar or by make of car. Suffice it to

Earl Evans, who was one of the real gentlemen of this hobby, worked in the foundry that cast more than 90 percent of the racing cylinder heads—Riley, Cragar, McDowell, etc.—made in southern California, so when he started making his own speed equipment after WWII he built a small foundry in back of his shop at 545 South Greenleaf in Whittier. Here he's installing one of his four-carburetor manifolds on a flathead block. The relief, between the valves and the cylinder bores, can be clearly seen. *Mark Dees collection*

say that an activity that started by furnishing components for racers using hopped-up production engines—mainly Ford Model T, Chevys, Dodges, and Stars (all four cylinder engines)—grew into a multimillion dollar industry by the late 1960s and today has gross revenues in the billions.

Hopping-up production cars isn't uniquely American; the Germans, Italians, French, and English were doing it about the same time it started here in the U.S. Sometimes the European approach was for racing; more often it was to beat the high tax levied on cars by engine displacement. A hopped up 1500cc engine

This engine Bob Joehnck built for his roadster in 1949 displays the typical look of the day—Navarro 9.25:1 heads, Navarro triple intake manifold with three Stromberg 97s topped by chrome-plated air cleaners, and a Scintilla Vertex magneto which Bob brought home from Germany after WW II. Rajah spark plug wire terminals complete the picture if one overlooks the flex-tubing headers which were an economical expedient for a not-so-wealthy ex-GI. As a precursor of Joehnck engines to come, this one was a race winner, bringing Bob numerous trophies at Goleta and subsequent drag strips in California. *Photo Joehnck collection*

Bottom, Vic Edelbrock with a pair of his midget racers outside his Highland Avenue shop in the late 1940s. *Greg Sharp Collection*

could propel a small car as fast as a stock 3.0-liter engine could move a bigger car, but the small car owner paid about half the tax of that assigned to the larger car.

Because Ford had a good marketing program in Europe, German, French, and English enthusiasts often used a Ford as the basis for their racing machines. Sometimes they used racing equipment made in the U.S., but often they made their own. The basics of engine modification were known to all car-culture countries.

However, hot rodding as we know it here was unique to the U.S. When the Europeans hopped-up their cars, they still looked like standard production cars. When the young American hopped up his car he usually removed fenders, bumpers, and other extraneous pieces; and fit small front tires and large rear tires, all to give his car the "race car look."

Also, and probably more important, the American rodder was blessed with so much available speed equip-

Don Blair in his booth at the first SCTA hot rod show held in the Los Angeles National Guard Armory, January 29-30 1948. The Roots-blown flathead V-8 out of his Modified was on display. That car was the fastest V-8 at the dry lakes at the time, so the engine was a popular attraction to his booth. Blair's shop, at 826 Arroyo Parkway in Pasadena, had been open for almost three years at this time and, being both a mechanic and a racer, he was in a good position to help his customers sort out their problems. *Tom Medley collection*

ment at a reasonable price that the development of this type of car outpaced any other part of the world. In the immediate postwar years, California outpaced the rest of the U.S., but eventually eastern and midwestern rodders caught on and caught up, and it was no longer strictly a West Coast thing.

If a potential rodder lived in a rural area with no speed shops nearby he could still acquire all the needed pieces by reading *Hot Rod* magazine to see which manufacturers or speed shops had a mail order department. Sending off for a catalog (the price was usually deducted from your first purchase) was like having Christmas early.

This same rural resident could get instructions for the installation of the equipment from the manufacturer or speed shop owner. The installation of an intake manifold or cylinder heads for the flathead V-8 was a pretty straightforward task and didn't require much help beyond, possibly, the torque reading for the nuts holding the aluminum cylinder heads.

Piston clearances and camshaft timing and clearances could be a problem to one who had never installed these items before or had never done it for a high-performance engine. The answers to these questions were easily obtained by making a few phone calls, and the smarter rod builders relied on this information

One of the earliest dual manifolds made for the flathead Ford V-8 was this Davies set-up which carries two Stromberg carburetors on what look to be adapters from the square four-bolt flanges designed for Winfield carburetors. The engine is an early twenty-one-stud V-8 with Federal Mogul copper cylinder heads. *Don Blair photo*

Top far right, cross section of Ardun ohv conversion for flathead V-8 Ford/Mercury engines shows the lifters and pushrods operating from the stock Ford camshaft location. The valves are inclined, at 75 degrees included angle, in hemispherical combustion chambers. The old ports and valve seats are covered by the new heads and the intake manifold/cam valley cover. An oil return tube on each side allowed excess oil in the cylinder head to drain back into the sump. An Ardun ohv converted V-8 was about 12in wider and 100lb heavier than a similar engine with aluminum finned flatheads, but the Ardun also produced probably 25 to 50 percent more power, depending on carburetion and tuning.

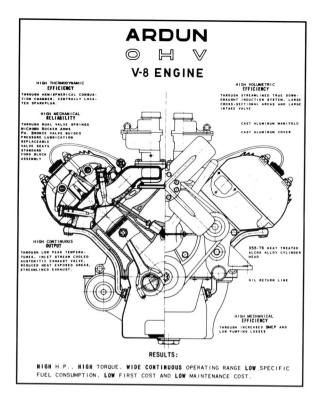

rather than go it alone and possibly do something stupid to their new engines.

The peak of this activity was in the 1950s. The U.S. economy was good, everyone who wanted to was working, the interest in rodding was high, and the availability of both parts and the knowledge to assemble them was there. It was no longer, as it had been in the 1920s, '30s, and most of the '40s, a mysterious pastime—a black-art so to speak. Hot rodding was maturing and the rodders were ready for it.

Right, the So-Cal Speed Shop after it was expanded from the single, small building shown earlier. This photo was taken for a feature article that appeared in *Hot Rod* in 1950. The streamliner had run 210mph at Bonneville that year, posting the fastest time of the event.
Greg Sharp collection

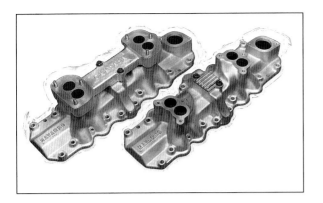

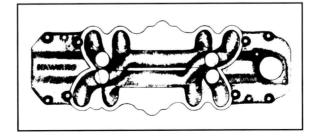

Top left and middle, two versions of the Ardun conversion for the Flathead Ford V-8 block: the standard single carburetor set-up as designed by Zora Arkus-Duntov, and a racing version with Hilborn Fuel Injection on Charles Scott's belly-tank lakester. The hemi-head design with short intake rockers and long exhaust rocker arms was similar to the 1951 Chrysler hemi, but preceded it by four years as the Ardun was in production by 1947. Scotty's B-Class lakester was the first open wheeled car to top 200mph. LeRoy Holmes, driving the Scott lakester averaged 201.015 in 1953. Two years earlier, Don Clark and Clem TeBow built an Ardun Ford V-8 powered 1932 stock-body roadster which posted a two way average of 162.459mph. *Stock engine photo, author; racing version from Charles W. Scott collection*

Top far left, racing intake manifolds were what were called "cold" manifolds; the mixture going to the intake valve with no pre-heating while a street manifold was usually heated by water from the cooling system or by exhaust passages around the intake runners. Barney Navarro tried to cover both bases by making a manifold that could be run hot or cold. At right, the exhaust passage is blocked by a small cover plate hence this set-up would be used for racing. At left, the auxiliary exhaust heat carrier is in place, to pick up exhaust from the center heat risers and carry it around the carburetor bases. *Navarro Engineering photo*

Bottom, drawing made by Barney Navarro for his speed equipment catalog illustrates the 180-degree firing order of the manifold porting. Navarro used the same sequence that the Ford factory used for its manifolds. Most of Navarro's speed equipment competitors also had 180-degree porting, but reversed the sequence. One side of each carburetor fed four cylinders; two directly and two indirectly. The 180-degree firing order was important, particularly for cylinders one and two (right front on the Ford flathead) which fired consecutively—number one starting the sequence, number two finishing it. In this arrangement, cylinder one draws from the right side of the carburetor, and cylinder two draws form the left side. *Navarro Engineering drawing*

National Speedway Weekly

[The Finest and Most Complete Publication on Automobile Racing]

10c

July 11, 1934

CHAPTER 13

The Publications

*Hot Rod magazine wasn't the first,
but with good timing, hard work,
and the right stuff for its time,
it became king of the mountain*

The last SCTA dry lake meet in 1947, on October 19, sticks in my mind for several reasons. Alex Xydias and I had driven up to El Mirage in my '32 roadster, and it would be the first run with my new Merc flathead engine. We drove up on Saturday to make it easier to get ready for Sunday's time trials.

While walking around the pit area a young guy neither of us knew collared Alex to show him the layout for a new magazine he said he was going to publish. He didn't say, "I'm thinking of publishing it," he said, "I'm going to publish it." He discussed the magazine's proposed coverage with Alex, how it would be circulated, and other things related to the publication's format, and then he asked Alex if he would advertise his speed shop in it. Alex put him off by suggesting he call or come by his speed shop during the week.

After he left, Alex turned to me and asked, "What do you think? Will it work?" My reply was, "I think it'll sell great in southern California, but I can't see much success in other parts of the country." Right. I've eaten those words many times since 1947. The young man was Bob "Pete" Petersen who, with Bob Lindsay, started *Hot Rod* magazine, the circulation of which has since topped 1 million copies per month.

Saturday was used as a tune-up and preparation for Sunday's timed runs, and Bert Letner fired up his modified roadster ('24 T body and flathead Merc engine equipped with Elco twin-spark plug heads) to make a

pass down the lakebed to see how it was running. Bert and I were members of the SCTA Road Runners Club, so I had a great interest in the results of his run.

Bert came back to his pit with a long face and said, "Who the hell is that in the yellow and black T roadster? I was running about 125 and he came past me as if I was in second."

We spent the night on the lakebed, sleeping (if you can call it that, what with beer drinking, bench racing, and new arrivals coming into the area with straight-through exhausts blasting our ears) in bedrolls on the lakebed itself. For those who haven't done it, that desert can get as cold at night as it gets hot in the daytime. We almost froze our you-know-whats off.

The owner of the yellow and black roadster turned out to be Regg Schlemmer, a complete unknown to me and, I guess, to Bert at that time. Before the day was over we got to know very well who he was. He was entered as a member of the Gaters Club, and his roadster, driven by Eddie Hulse, set a new Class C roadster record of 136.05mph, beating Randy Shinn's 129.40mph record by almost 6mph. When the first *Hot Rod* magazine came out in January 1948, Schlemmer's roadster was pictured on the cover.

The first issue of *Hot Rod* is viewed by many to be the first publication dealing with racing in general and hot-rod-type cars in particular. To give credit where it is due, *Hot Rod* was the first publication to really put hot

Floyd Clymer published Veda Orr's pictorial recap of dry lakes events of 1946, 1947, and 1948. Veda was the wife of speed shop pioneer Karl Orr. During the war, she published the *SCTA News*, keeping enlisted hot rodders the world over apprised of happenings in the speed community. Veda was a frequent dry lakes competitor as well. *Author photo*

Opposite page, cover of Vol. 1 No. 2 of *National Speedway Weekly*. It must have been exciting in 1934 to find a real magazine which covered real racing.

R.E. "Pete" Petersen (left) and *Hot Rod* magazine Editor Wally Parks at Bonneville in the early 1950s.

Robert Petersen

R.E. Petersen, "Pete" to his friends, moved from his native Barstow, California, home to the Los Angeles area in the mid-1940s to look for work. He found a job at MGM studios as a messenger, but soon worked into the publicity department.

What seemed to be a great spot evaporated when cutbacks at the studio forced him out. Joining a group of ex-MGM staffers, they started Hollywood Publicity Associates and were subsequently hired to publicize the upcoming hot rod show at the Los Angeles Armory.

Petersen had his eye on bigger things and, with Bob Lindsay, founded *Hot Rod* magazine; the first issue, January 1948, made its debut while the Armory show was on. Pete and Bob sold copies of *Hot Rod* on the front steps of the Armory because their ex-partners at Hollywood Associates wouldn't let them sell inside the auditorium.

Hot Rod was joined in September 1949 by *Motor Trend* and in May 1950 by *Cycle*; Petersen Publishing was well on its way to becoming the largest publisher of automotive magazines in the world. Petersen has employed some of the best talent in this business. Some of them stayed for forty years or more (Tom Medley, Erick Rickman,

Bob D'Olivo), and some left earlier to pursue their own interests (Wally Parks, Don Francisco, Bill Burke, Racer Brown, Ray Brock, Jim McFarland, Tex Smith, and others).

Publishing has been good to Pete Petersen, but he had broadened his interests and activities by opening an art gallery in Beverly Hills (specializing in western art), buying and selling real estate, owning the Scandia Restaurant on the Sunset Strip, and operating an aircraft service at the Van Nuys, California, airport which leases business jets.

Pete's contribution to hot rodding is without equal, and in 1994 he and his wife, Margie, put up $15,000,000 of their own money to help start the Petersen Automotive Museum in Los Angeles. The museum is being run under the umbrella of the Los Angeles County Museum of Natural History.

This museum, more than his publishing empire, will be his legacy to this hobby/sport/business. The measure of R.E. Petersen's success was demonstrated this year (1994) when *Forbes* magazine named Petersen as one of the 400 richest Americans; ranking number 350, with an estimated wealth of $375,000,000. Not bad for a kid from Barstow.

rodding on the international car map. Its timing was perfect, and Pete Petersen and Bob Lindsay knew what to do with their opportunity.

Hot Rod became the bible for thousands of young men who read it religiously to learn about the latest speed equipment, how to assemble the equipment to

create a high-performance car, and about who and what was important to all those with similar interests. The "how to" part is what made the magazine so valuable to its readers, as this was something previous publications had ignored. Despite these firsts, *Hot Rod* wasn't the original hot rod magazine.

Seven years earlier a similar magazine, *Throttle*, was published in Los Angeles for one year—1941. There was one issue for each month, but with a special issue between May and June, and a combined November/December issue for a total of twelve for the year. *Throttle* went out of business at the end of 1941 partly because most of its potential readers (and probably, the staff) were heeding a call to military service, but also because of a shortage of paper due to the war. *Time, Newsweek, Life, Saturday Evening Post, Colliers,* and other "big" publications could still get paper, albeit a limited supply, but the smaller publications like *Throttle* were left out.

Jack Peters was the editor and publisher of *Throttle* and wrote most of the copy as well as handling circulation and advertising. Regular contributors were George Rowell, who reported from the San Francisco Bay area starting with the second issue, and Lou Senter, who covered speedway racing starting with the third issue. Senter was later part owner of Ansen Engineering.

Automotive magazines had been published in the U.S. since 1895, but most were trade publications and not generally available to newsstand buyers. These magazines published an occasional feature about racing developments, apparently when the editor or technical editor though it of sufficient merit, but they couldn't be called racing or sports publications by any stretch of the imagination.

Chronogical Listing of U.S. Motor Sport Publications

July 4, 1934	*National Speedway Weekly*	Summer 1953	*Speedways*
Aug. 16, 1934*	*National Auto Racing* (tabloid; part of *Bergen Herald* newspaper)	July 1953	*Goggles and Gauntlets*
		Oct. 1953	*Sports Cars & Hot Rods*
Sept. 19, 1934	*Coast Auto Racing* (changed to *Motor Racing News* 7-16-36)	Feb. 1954	*Car Life*
		Nov. 1954	*Speed*
Jan. 1941	*Throttle*	Apr. 1955	*Rodding and Restyling*
May 1947	*Speed Age*	June 1955	*Official Racing Guide*
June 1947	*Road and Track* (changed to *Road & Track* 1954)	July 1955	*Sports Car Illustrated* (changed to *Car and Driver* 1961)
Jan. 1948	*Hot Rod*	July 1956	*Rod Builder*
Sept. 1949	*Motor Trend*	Aug. 1956	*Motor Guide*
Apr. 1950	*Cycle*	Spring 1956	*Sports Car Pictorial*
May 1950	*Modern Motorcar*	Jan. 26, 1957	*Hot Rod News* (tabloid)
Oct. 1950	*Racing Wheels*	Oct. 1957	*Northwest Rods*
June 1951	*Motor Sports World* (tabloid)	Dec. 1957	*Custom Cars*
July 1951	*Hop Up* (changed to *Motor Life* 1953)	Dec. 1957	*Car Speed and Style*
		Dec. 1957	*Custom Rodder*
Jan. 1952	*Auto Speed and Sport*	July 1958	*Customs Illustrated*
Jan. 1952	*Auto Sport Review*	Feb. 1958	*Foreign Cars Illustrated*
Feb. 1952	*Auto*	May 1958	*Cars and Clubs*
Jan. 1953	*Speed Mechanics*	June 1958	*Rods Illustrated*
Feb. 1953	*Desert Dust*	Spring 1958	*Sports Car Quarterly*
Feb. 1953	*Auto Age*	Dec. 1959	*Cars*
Feb. 1953	*International Car Review*	June 1960	*On the Grid*
May 1953	*Rods and Customs* (changed to *Rod and Custom* with second issue)	Nov. 1, 1962	*Popular Hot Rodding*
		May 1972	*Street Rodder*
		Aug. 1972	*Rod Action*
May 1953	*Honk* (changed to *Car Craft* November 1953)	*National Auto Racing* became *National Speed Sport News* (Chris Economaki)	
June 1953	*Auto Sportsman*		

We don't have a cover, or the first issue of *Coast Auto Racing*, but this page is interesting—and almost two years after the publication was first started.

Most race programs, sold at ticket counters or in the grandstands at oval track races provided a list of entrants and usually a place to record qualifying times and race results, but didn't publish photos of cars or drivers. And many didn't include the race date or location of the track. I guess we have to assume that if you were there and bought the program, you already knew where you were so there was no need for an address.

The earliest publication yet found that was devoted strictly to auto racing was a weekly supplement in the East Patterson, New Jersey, *Bergen Herald* newspaper. It was called *National Auto Racing News*, and this supplement had eight pages of tabloid size, and the inaugural issue was published August 16, 1943. In his editorial, Editor Jos. Cox says, "With this issue of the *Bergen Herald National Auto Racing News*, complying with the insistent demands of our readers and advertisers, we are changing the size of the Auto Racing Edition to tabloid form. The home edition will remain as is."

Mr. Cox went on to say, "Although the *Bergen Herald* is in its thirteenth year, it was only a year ago last May that we started the *National Auto Racing News Edition.*" The way I count it, that makes May 1933 the date that the first newspaper section devoted to auto racing was published. Possibly more important, it is still being published (by Chris Economaki) as the *National Speed Sport News*—still weekly and still in tabloid form.

Although they weren't hot-rod-type magazines, there were two other U.S. automotive magazines before *Hot Rod*. *Speed Age* was first published in May 1947, and *Road and Track* first saw the light of day in June 1947. *Hot Rod* followed in January 1948. *Speed Age* specialized in oval track racing with occasional forays into other types of racing. The editors at *Speed Age* knew a lot more about Indianapolis and NASCAR racing than they did about road racing, sports cars, or hot rods, and the publication did its best work when it stuck to its area of expertise.

Road and Track's bailiwick was coverage of road racing and foreign cars. The publication abandoned the word "foreign" in favor of "imported," claiming that foreign was something that was unknown, or strange, and while imported cars were at first strange to American buyers, as soon as more of them were seen in America they were no longer foreign—but they were still imported. So much for semantics.

Hot rods were not *Road and Track*'s forte either, but the then technical editor and later to become publisher, John Bond, had a strong liking for hot rods and wrote favorably about them on many occasions. The second issue of *Road and Track* also had a feature story by Wally Parks on hot rods.

Although not a hot rod magazine, Petersen Publishing broadened its coverage by introducing *Motor Trend* in September 1949. *Motor Trend* was conceived to cover the world automotive market but with particular emphasis on cars from Detroit. Coverage did include some racing, a considerable number of custom car features, and seemed to consider every aspect of the automobile as fair game for coverage.

By 1951 Petersen Publishing had brought out *Cycle* magazine with Harry Steele as editor, and this expansion from *Hot Hod* to *Motor Trend* to *Cycle* was carefully

His Car Was Hot

Throttle May 1941
—By John Angel

All kinds of stuff, and a Winfield "pot,"
No doubt about it, his car was hot!
He could peel in high, when others could not,
No doubt about it, his car was hot!

Solid panel, fastened by lock,
When asked what he had, he'd say "strictly stock."
But we all knew that that was rot,
'Cause we all knew that his car was hot!

He even got tickets as tickets go,
But not for speeding, for flying so low.
He'd "gow out" in low, 'cause his car was hot!
And still "peeling," eighty feet from the spot.

Winding motor, pipes that "blubber,"
Cracking mufflers, and the scream of rubber.
Tight in second, the same in low,
No doubt about it, his car would go.

Meshing of gears was to him an art,
In a race with him you were "chopped" from the
      start.

He'd "speed shift" to second, and "snap" it in
      high—
His car was hot, and that's no lie!

But all things must start, and all things must end.
Iron will give and steel will bend.
He got his on a Saturday night.
He was feeling good and his motor was tight.

He really shouldn't have tried to pass,
But he dropped in second and gave it the gas.
Headlights were shining in his face,
For once he was going to lose a race!

Even then he could have turned back,
But his car was hot so he wouldn't slack.
A deafening crash that was heard for miles,
And two fast cars were worthless piles.

A wisp of smoke from his motor came,
And soon his car was a sheet of flame.
It has turned over twice and burnt on the spot,
No doubt about it, his car was hot!

---

watched by the *Road and Track* staff at Enthusiasts' Publications. *Speed and Spray* (a racing boat magazine edited by Kent Hitchcock), *Moto* (a pocket-sized fifteen cent motorcycle magazine edited by Bill Bagnall), and *Hop Up* (a small format hot rod magazine) were soon following on the heels of *Road and Track*.

The first *Hop Up*, of which only about 5,000 copies were printed, was July 1951. The second issue was the July issue redone with an August cover date, the first issue having been done to test the market.

A certain amount of hot rod coverage crept into *Speed and Spray* because many of the racing boats had hopped up Ford engines—flathead Ford sixes in the 225 class, flathead V-8s in both 225 and 266 classes, and Ford V-8 60s in the 135 class. The same equipment manufacturers and engine builders worked on these boats almost as often as they did on dry lakes or track cars.

Unfortunately, the *Road and Track* group was expanding faster than finances would allow, and both *Speed and Spray* and *Moto* were dropped. By early 1952 Enthusiasts' Publications was in such poor financial shape that a severe restructuring was called for.

This episode saw the four *Road and Track* owners splitting up. *Road and Track* editor Oliver Billingsley was out, *Hop Up* was given to Bill Quinn and Bill Brehaut for their share of *Road and Track*, (Quinn subsequently bought Brehaut's share), and of the four owners, only John Bond remained at *Road and Track*.

I had gone to work for *Hop Up*, as an advertising salesman, shortly after the first issue was published. After six months on a job I grew to hate, all the while complaining about the editorial coverage in the magazine, Quinn offered me the job of *Hop Up*'s editor. This, in spite of the fact that I had never been an editor, had never written a feature story, and had almost zero knowledge of publishing. It was easier to get a magazine job in those days than it is now.

Quinn had always wanted a "*Motor Trend*-type" magazine, so early in 1953 he set the wheels in motion to accomplish this. The magazine name changed a bit when the words *Motor Life* were added to *Hop Up* (*Hop Up and Motor Life*). The magazine size had already been increased to match *Hot Rod* and *Motor Trend*, and by May 1953 the magazine was called simply *Motor Life*.

Tom Medley was one of the first
employees of Petersen Publishing
Co. and gained fame as the creator
of the monthly cartoon strip "Stroker
McGurk," which was one of the favorite
features of *Hot Rod* magazine. Tom
came to southern California from
Salem, Oregon, and was immediately
drawn to the dry lakes activities. An all-
around talent, Tom also was a great
photographer, was publisher of *Rod &
Custom*, and covered all the hot rod
and custom car activities for several of
PPC's publications. Here he's at El
Mirage Dry Lake on his moderately
customized '36 Ford roadster.
Tom Medley collection

By this time Petersen had noted the change in *Hop
Up* and announced a new pocket-sized magazine to be
called *Honk*, to debut as a May 1953 issue. When Quinn
heard about this, he immediately assumed he had made
a mistake in abandoning the smaller size, yet he still
wanted *Motor Life* to be a *Motor Trend*-type publication.

Quinn's response was quick, and decisive, and resulted in one of the major surprises experienced by Petersen Publishing. Quinn hired Spence Murray and in
a period of two weeks, with a lot of help from Lou
Kimzey, Jack Caldwell, and photographers Gene
Trindl and Ralph Poole, a new magazine called *Rods
and Customs* was finished and printed. The plural use
was dropped for the second issue, and it became *Rod
and Custom*.

Both *Rods and Customs* and *Honk* came out in
May 1953, and after seven issues the *Honk* name was
changed to *Car Craft*. John Christy was the editor. The
production of these magazines prompted a flurry of similar publications; one-shot books from Petersen (Trend
Books) and Fawcett Publications, and numerous
monthly or bimonthly hot-rod-type magazines from the
East Coast, mainly New York.

With rare exceptions the eastern magazines were
poorly done. It was a case of opportunistic publishers
jumping into a field they knew nothing about. The feature material was, to be charitable, lackluster and of lit-

tle interest to anyone other than the builder of the car
and his friends. The staffs hired by these publishers
were clueless when it came to understanding what was
good about hot rods or customs and what was worthless.

Had the publishers themselves been knowledge-
able, they would have known the content of their magazines was no good. Unfortunately, they didn't, and the
magazines were doomed to also-ran status. In spite of the
poor overall quality, these publications gained newsstand space because the publisher had a distributor with
enough clout to get them displayed. Some of these efforts lasted a few years, most were gone after a few
months.

One eastern publication which was done right was
Ziff-Davis' *Sports Car Illustrated*, which came out in
July 1955. In 1961, while Karl Ludvigsen was editor of
SCI the name was changed to *Car and Driver*—the
publisher and the editor believing that *Sports Car Illustrated* was too limiting in both coverage and advertising
potential. Their premise has since been proved correct;
Car and Driver currently enjoys a respected place in the
automotive magazine business.

Three years before *SCI* Petersen Publishing introduced a "sporty car" magazine called *Auto*. With Dick
Van Osten as editor, it was published from February
1952 until April 1953. The magazine was dropped from
the Petersen roster because it seemed to be getting
nowhere.

What Petersen and his management didn't know
is that they had *Road and Track* (it became *Road &
Track* in 1954), "on the ropes." *Road and Track* advertising was down, circulation remained fairly stable but
wasn't increasing, and if Petersen had continued *Auto*
for a few more issues there might not be a *Road &
Track* magazine today.

Bill Quinn had sold *Motor Life* and *Rod and Custom* to Petersen Publishing in 1955, and *Motor Life* was
eventually merged into *Motor Trend* which saw the end
of *Motor Life* as a title. *Rod and Custom* was dropped
and restarted so many times we couldn't keep up with it.

I left Quinn's employ in May 1953 to join John
Morris in operating a machine shop in Glendale, California, and three years later, in March 1956, I went
back to work on *Motor Life* as associate editor, a step
down from the editor's job I had the first time around.

The hot rod/custom car magazine activity as described above, covers only the commercial side of automotive publishing. Both before and after WWII the dry
lakes racing programs were, for all practical purposes,
magazines. They had not only a listing of entries for the
meet, but carried information about who was doing what
to his car, club activities, and related news developments
(state and local legislation) that would affect hot rodders.

These programs and newsletters were circulated only to association members but were sold at the dry lakes meets to anyone interested enough to buy one. Much of this printed material dried up when *Hot Rod* came out in 1948, and it became obvious that the magazine was trying to cover the country and not just southern California.

As soon as these magazines became known around the country, hot rod and custom car activity accelerated faster than anyone could have predicted. Once the enthusiasts across the U.S. found out what was going on elsewhere, they hurried to join those who set the pace and style. While the cars that were built as a result of this new-found knowledge had similarities, there were regional differences, as car features in the magazines would demonstrate.

To get your car into one of the better magazine (you had really made it if your car was also on the cover) was a bragging point that could make your friends envious and put you on a pedestal in their eyes. It is probable, at first anyway, that the editors didn't know what power they had to make or break a car-builder's dream, but it became obvious when they were besieged by car owners wanting their cars on the cover.

If a magazine editor had the best interests of his readers at heart, the vehicles featured in the magazine would be ones that would interest the most readers. If the editor didn't, the cars pictured in the magazine would probably be those owned by his friends.

The magazines served an extremely useful purpose, and when quality was foremost in the minds of the editorial staffs they could be of significant benefit to the reader/builder. Fortunately, most of them were, at least, honest in their attempts to do it right, and if they failed, it was ineptness rather than dishonesty that was to blame.

If anyone tried to follow the vagaries of these magazines' staff members he would likely come to the conclusion that it bordered on incest as staffers went back and forth between magazines published in the same house or even to competitive publications.

I left *Hop Up* (owned by Bill Quinn) in 1953 and returned to it (then called *Motor Life*, and owned by Petersen) in 1956, then went to *Road & Track* in 1958. Dick Day left *Hop Up* to go to Petersen Publishing. Don Werner, who had been editor of *Motor Life* while I worked on that magazine, and Gordon Behn—Petersen's circulation manager—left Petersen to start Argus Publishers Corporation.

Tom Senter, who had worked on *Hot Rod* and in the Petersen book division went to Argus to edit *Super Chevy* and then *Popular Hot Rodding*. Meanwhile, Lee Kelley left Argus to work for Petersen, later hiring Leonard Emanuelson away from *Popular Hot Rodding*. Len was followed to Petersen by Cam Benty, and later Kevin Smith and Greg Brown left Argus to work for *Motor Trend.*

Kevin left *Motor Trend* to become editor of *Automobile*, and Greg went back to Argus to become editor of *VW & Porsche* which was renamed *European Automobile*. Tom Senter and Mike Parris both left Argus for the Ford Motor Company Los Angeles Field Office in the Public Affairs Department.

Ray Brock, who had a lengthy association with *Hot Rod* magazine, left Petersen's employ in 1972 to start *Rod Action*; a move that did not endear him to Pete.

Not all of the magazine personnel jumped ship; as this is written Bill Motta has been with *Road & Track* thirty-five years; Tom Medley, and Eric Rickmann both put in forty-one years with Petersen Publishing before retirement; and Bob D'Olivo holds the longevity record with forty-two years in Petersen's photographic department—and still going.

Bob D'Olivo started as a Petersen Publishing Co. photographer in August 1952 and has been head of the PPC photo department for thirty years. Here he's seen at Bonneville in 1959, Rolleiflex in hand, Hasselblad over the shoulder; one loaded with black and white and one with color (Ektachrome). When the shutter speed and aperture are set right for the blindingly bright light on the salt, a strobe eliminates the deep black shadows under the vehicle. *Author photo*

Dry Lakes and Street Rod Lingo

alcohol—In racing, methyl alcohol or methanol, a very high-octane fuel. Sometimes called "alky" for short.

belly pan—A fabricated underbody piece, usually sheet aluminum or steel, to aid airflow under the car's body.

belly tank—Dry lakes race car with a body made from one of the auxiliary drop tanks carried under the wings of WWII P-38 Lighting fighters. These 315gal tanks were preferred over the smaller 165gal tanks carried by P-51 Mustangs and P-47 Thunderbolts.

bent eight—Slang for a V-8 engine.

binders—Slang for brakes.

BNI—Bonneville Nationals Incorporated (still active).

BTA—Bell Timing Association.

Cal-Neva—California-Nevada Timing Association.

cammer—Any overhead camshaft engine

channeled—Car body, usually a roadster or coupe, which has been lowered over the frame to reduce overall height. This a) reduces wind resistance, b) lowers the center of gravity and, maybe more important, c) makes the car look better.

chopped—Car top which has been lowered by removing horizontal sections of metal from the windshield and door pillars and from the roof rear quarter panels.

cogs—Gears.

dago axle—Ford I-beam front axle which had been rebuilt between the spring-hanger and spindle to lower the front of the car by as much as three inches. Term originated with Ed "Axle" Stewart, who made these axles in his San Diego shop. They were first referred to as "San Diego" axles, then "Diego," and finally Dago, having no reference to a person of Italian heritage.

Deuce—Any 1932 Ford, but particularly the roadster.

drag race—Side-by-side acceleration contest between two or more vehicles. The first known use of the term in print was by Wally Parks in the March 1939 issue of *SCTA Racing News*. But it didn't catch on at that time, and wasn't in general use until after WWII.

dream wheel—A small circular calculator made by cam grinder Ed Iskenderian and used to determine speed based on gear ratio, tire size, and engine revs. Available free to competitors.

drop tank—See **belly tank**

dry lakes—The lowest areas of southern California's Mojave Desert. These collect winter rainfall, creating lakes of water as much as one foot deep. When summer sun and wind evaporate the water they leave a hard, smooth, dry-mud surface. The dry lakes most used by the racers were: Muroc, Harper, Rosamond, and El Mirage. These are not salt lakes.

flathead—An engine with its valves located in the cylinder block rather than in the head. The head itself is a plain, flat casting. The term is used most to indicate a Ford V-8 engine built between 1932 and 1953. It could also indicate a Ford four-cylinder Model A, B, or C four-cylinder engine.

flat motor, flatty—Ford flathead V-8. These are recent additions to the lexicon and were not used by early hot rodders.

four-banger—Any four-cylinder engine, but usually used to denote a Ford or Chevrolet four.

fuel—Generally reserved for anything other than gasoline. Up to about 1950, the term would probably denote methanol. After that, it could mean nitromethane or a mixture of nitromethane and methanol.

gow job—Somewhat obscure pre-WWII term for a car with a modified engine, apparently derived from **gow out**, below. No longer used.

gow out—Early term meaning to accelerate rapidly. One theory has it that the "gow" is simply a mispronunciation of "go." No longer used.

headers—Individual exhaust pipes, usually welded steel tubing but sometimes cast iron, in various shapes and diameters to reduce exhaust back pressure.

high boy—Stock-body roadster, usually a 1932 Ford.

hop up, hot iron—Pre-WWII terms for a car with a modified engine.

hot rod—Post-WWII (after 1945) term for a car with a modified engine. See "Introduction."

juice brakes—Hydraulic brakes (conversion from mechanical brakes), same as **squirt brakes**.

Lakester—Class designation (after 1950) of cars with custom-made bodywork that was streamlined but had exposed wheels.

'liner—Short for streamliner.

Modified—A dry lakes class designation for a car which didn't fit in the roadster class, usually with a single-seat sprint-car-type body but cut off behind the driver. Regulations required that a Modified have a flat area of no less than 400in-sq behind the cockpit.

MRA—Muroc Racing Association

MTA—Mojave Timing Association

overhead—Term applied to engines with overhead valves, but used most often to describe early Ford flatheads (Model A, B, or C, or V-8) with overhead valve conversions.

pot—carburetor

quick change—Specially-made center section for an early Ford differential case which provided two changeable spur gears behind the ring and pinion assembly. By changing theses gears, choosing from a large selection, the overall drive ratio could be selected to provide the most appropriate ratio for a particular situation. The majority of these center sections were made by Ted Halibrand or Pat Warren or, for midget racers, by Ernie Casale.

reversed eyes—The ends of a standard Ford transverse-leaf spring curled down and around the shackle pin. When these "eyes" were reshaped to curl upward, the car was lowered about 1.5 inches, without destroying the spring's effectiveness. In front, though, the clearance in the center between the spring and axle was reduced.

RTA—Russetta Timing Association. "Russetta" is Greek for "red chariot."

rubber—Slang for tires.

salt flats—Large expanse of caked salt at the west edge of the Great Salt Lake Desert in Utah; located just north of Interstate 80 and about ten miles east of Wendover, a town straddling the Utah-Nevada border.

SCTA—Southern California Timing Association.

single stick—Single overhead camshaft engine.

skins—Early slang for tires. No longer used.

speed shift—An extremely fast shift made while keeping the accelerator to the floor. It was mandatory that the synchronization of clutch and shift lever action be perfect, or the selected gear would probably be trashed. A good shift from first to second could leave an uninterrupted pair of black lines from the rear tires, starting from a dead stop to well into second gear.

sprinkler system—Early reference to overhead valves. No longer used.

squirt brakes—Hydraulic brakes (conversion from mechanical brakes), same as **juice brakes**.

stovebolt—Slang (only slightly derogatory) for the inline, six-cylinder Chevrolet engine. The term derives from the fact the cap screws holding the sump, front timing gear cover, and side plate resembled those found on mid-1930s ovens and ranges.

streamliner—Pre-WWII designation of cars whose bodies were special-built and didn't qualify to run in the stock-body roadster class. With two exceptions (one car built by Jack Harvey and one by the Spalding brothers, both in 1939) cars in this class had narrow bodies and exposed wheels. After 1949, when three full-bodied streamliners appeared (Lee Chapel, Xydias and Batchelor, and Howard Johansen's twin-tank), the class included only those cars with full envelope bodywork. The open-wheeled cars then became **Lakesters**.

tail job—Early **Streamliner**, usually using a sprint car body with a pointed tail.

tank—Short for **belly tank** or **drop tank**.

three-on-the-tree—Column-shift mechanism for a three speed transmission (the hot rodders answer to the sporty car set's four-on-the-floor).

time—Hot rodders sometimes say "time" when they mean "speed," because the speed of a race car is calculated from the time it takes to cover a measured distance (see time traps below). So when a rodder says, "My time was 200mph, " he means his time over the distance was equivalent to a speed of 200mph. Through the quarter-mile traps at the dry lakes, his actual time would have been 4.5sec.

time traps—Measured distance over which a car is timed. At the dry lakes, the time traps are a quarter-mile long after a run up to speed of about a mile and a half. At quarter-mile drag strips, the traps are 132ft long, starting 66ft before the finish line and ending 66ft beyond it.

timing tag—Brass plaque, about 2x3.5in, listing entrant, speed, date, location, and timing group. If it was fast enough, the tag would likely be mounted on the instrument panel of the car, otherwise, it was hidden.

Two Club—The 200 MPH Club at Bonneville, for drivers who run two-way averages of 200mph or more.

Unlimited—Pre-WWII class for cars with large engines, such as Marmon or Cadillac V-16s, or cars with supercharged engines.

WTA—Western Timing Association.

Zephyr gears—First and second gears from a Lincoln Zephyr transmission could be fitted into a Ford or Mercury transmission and were popular because of their lower gear ratios (higher gears). A roadster that would do 40mph in first and 70mph in second could achieve probably 60mph in first and 90mph in second with Zephyr gears fitted.

Appendix

Pre-WWII Dry Lake Meet Racing Dates and Locations

DATE	ORGANIZATION	LOCATION	COMMENTS
5-8-32	Muroc Racing Association	Muroc	
7-10-32	Muroc Racing Association	Muroc	
4-30-33	Muroc Racing Association	Muroc	
6-25-33	Muroc Racing Association	Muroc	
9-17-33	Muroc Racing Association	Muroc	
5-6-34	Muroc Racing Association	Muroc	
9-22-35	Muroc Racing Association	Muroc	
5-3-36	Muroc Racing Association	Muroc	
6-28-36	Muroc Racing Association	Muroc	
5-16-37	Muroc Racing Association	Muroc	Meet put on by Knight Riders (Fullerton), Tornados (Santa Ana), and 90MPH Club (L.A.).
9-19-37	Knight Riders	Muroc	
11-7-37		Muroc	Muroc Club Championship Races, sponsored by seven member clubs.
5-15-38	Southern California Timing Assoc.	Muroc	"Sanction No. 1." First meet for newly formed Southern California Timing Association.
7-3-38	Southern California Timing Assoc.	Muroc	"Sanction No. 2." At this meet the U.S. Army forced the racers to leave Muroc, which was then under U.S. Government "ownership" and was to become Edwards Air Force Base. Lake name changed to Rogers.
8-29-38	Southern California Timing Assoc.	Harper	"Sanction No. 3"
10-2-38	Southern California Timing Assoc.	Harper	"Sanction No. 4"
4-30-39	Western Timing Association	Rosamond	First meet sponsored by newly-formed Western Timing Association.
5-28-39	Southern California Timing Assoc.	Harper	SCTA no longer called **meets** "sanctions."
6-25-39	Western Timing Association	Rosamond	
7-23-39	Southern California Timing Assoc.	Rosamond	
8-13-39	Western Timing Association	Rosamond	
9-10-39	Southern California Timing Assoc.	Harper	
10-29-39	Southern California Timing Assoc.	Rosamond	SCTA held only four meets in 1939.
5-5-40	Western Timing Association	Rosamond	
5-19-40	Southern California Timing Assoc.	Harper	Rufi streamliner record, debut of Ralph Schenck Chevy four streamliner and E Eddie Meyer rear-engined V-8 roadster.
6-30-40	Southern California Timing Assoc.	Harper	Otto Crocker "guest timer" for meet.
7- -40	Western Timing Association	Muroc	Invitational meet
8-18-40	Southern California Timing Assoc.	Harper	Otto Crocker now official timer.
9- -40	Western Timing Association	Muroc	Invitational meet
10- 6-40	Southern California Timing Assoc.	Harper	
11-17-40	Southern California Timing Assoc.	Harper	
5-4-41	Western Timing Association		Meet cancelled—lakes still wet from rain.
5-18-41		Russetta	Meet organized by Ray Ingram, who called his timing Russetta—was not an organized racing association.
5-25-41	Western Timing Association	Harper	Rain date for 5-4-41 meet
6-15-41	Southern California Timing Assoc.	Muroc	
6-29-41	Revs Car Club	Muroc	Meet staged by REVS Car Club
7-13-41	Western Timing Association	Harper	
7-20-41	Southern California Timing Assoc.	Muroc	
8-24-41	Southern California Timing Assoc.	Muroc	
9-14-41	Western Timing Assoc.		
9-28-41	Southern California Timing Assoc.	Muroc	
10-19-41	Western Timing Association		
5-17-42	Southern California Timing Assoc.	Harper	
6-14-42	Southern California Timing Assoc.	Harper	
7-19-42	Southern California Timing Assoc.	Harper	

Post-WWII Dry Lake Meet Racing Dates and Locations

DATE	ORGANIZATION	LOCATION	COMMENT
4-28-46	Southern California Timing Assoc.	El Mirage	First official post-WWII meet
6-2-46	Southern California Timing Assoc.	El Mirage	
7- -46	Southern California Timing Assoc.	El Mirage	
8-18-46	Southern California Timing Assoc.	El Mirage	
9-22-46	Southern California Timing Assoc.	El Mirage	
5-25-47	Southern California Timing Assoc.	El Mirage	
7-6-47	Southern California Timing Assoc.	Harper	
8-10-47	Southern California Timing Assoc.	El Mirage	
8-31-47	Southern California Timing Assoc.	El Mirage	
9-21-47	Southern California Timing Assoc.	El Mirage	
10-19-47	Southern California Timing Assoc.	El Mirage	
4-24/25-48	Southern California Timing Assoc.	El Mirage	First SCTA two-day timing meet
5-2-48	Russetta Timing Association	El Mirage	First meet for newly-formed Russetta Timing Association
6-5/6-48	Southern California Timing Assoc.	El Mirage	
6-13-48	Russetta Timing Association	El Mirage	
7-17/18-48	Southern California Timing Assoc.	El Mirage	
7-25-48	Russetta Timing Association	El Mirage	
8-15-48	Russetta Timing Association	El Mirage	
8-28/29-48	Southern California Timing Assoc.	El Mirage	
9-12-48	Russetta Timing Association	El Mirage	
9-25/26-48	Southern California Timing Assoc.	El Mirage	
10-10-48	Russetta Timing Association	El Mirage	
10-23/24-48	Southern California Timing Assoc.	El Mirage	
11-7-48	Russetta Timing Association	El Mirage	
4-24-49	Russetta Timing Association	El Mirage	
5-7/8-49	Southern California Timing Assoc.	El Mirage	
5-29-49	Russetta Timing Association	El Mirage	
6-11/12-49	Southern California Timing Assoc.	El Mirage	
6-26-49	Russetta Timing Association	El Mirage	
7-16/17-49	Southern California Timing Assoc.	El Mirage	
7-24-49	Russetta Timing Association	El Mirage	
8-22/27-49	Southern California Timing Assoc.	Bonneville	First Bonneville Nationals
8-28-49	Russetta Timing Association	El Mirage	
9-24/25-49	Southern California Timing Assoc.	El Mirage	
10-16-49	Russetta Timing Association	El Mirage	
10-22/23-49	Southern California Timing Assoc.	El Mirage	
4-22/23-50	Russetta Timing Association	El Mirage	
5-6/7-50	Southern California Timing Assoc.	El Mirage	
6-10/11-50	Southern California Timing Assoc.	El Mirage	
7-8/9-50	Southern California Timing Assoc.	El Mirage	First one-way record runs (for safety)
8-21/27-50	Southern California Timing Assoc.	Boneville	Second Bonneville Nationals
9-23/24-50	Southern California Timing Assoc.	El Mirage	
10-21/22-50	Southern Califronia Timing Assoc.	El Mirage	

Russetta Timing Association Clubs, 1949

Arabs	Long Beach	Prowlers	San Diego
American Racing Club (ARCS)	Los Angeles	Revs	Los Angeles
		Rodents	San Gabriel Valley
Cam Pounders	San Diego	Road Hogs	San Gabriel Valley
Choppers	Huntington Beach	Rod Riders	San Pedro
Coupes	Inglewood	Rotors	West Los Angeles
Dusters	Long Beach	Screechers	Santa Monica
Gazelles	Burbank	Screwdrivers	Culver City
Glendale Coupe & Roadster Club	Glendale	Smokers	Bakersfield
		Stock Holders	Los Angeles
Hi-Winders	San Fernando Valley	Taft Roadster Club	Taft
Howlers	Long Beach	Throttle Merchants	West San Fernando
Hutters	Whittier	Turtles	Los Angeles
Lancers	Los Angeles	Velociteers	Glendora
Night Hawks	El Monte	Vultures	South Los Angeles
Pan Draggers	Los Angeles		

Southern California Timing Association Clubs, 1948

Club	Location
Albatas	Los Angeles
Almegas	El Segundo
Autocrats	Los Angeles
California Roadster Club	Fullerton
Clutchers	Santa Ana
Desert Irons	El Centro
Detonators	Riverside
Dolphins	Long Beach
Dusters	North Holllywood
Gaters	South Gate
Gear Grinders	Bell
Glendale Stokers	Glendale
Gophers	East Los Angeles
Hornets	Redlands
Idlers	Los Angeles
Lancers	Los Angeles
Low Flyers	Santa Monica
Mad Mechanics	Los Angeles
Milers	Hollywood
Mobilers	Azusa
Night Owls	Riverside
Oilers	Carlsbad
Pacers	Pasadena
Pasadena Roadster Club	Pasadena
Quarter Milers	Redondo Beach
Roadmasters	Van Nuys
Road Runners	Los Angeles
San Bernardino Roadster Club	San Bernardino
San Diego Roadster Club	San Diego
Santa Paula Roadsters	Santa Paula
Serpents	North Long Beach
Sidewinders	Glendale
Southern California Roadster Club	San Diego
Strokers	Whittier
Throttlers	North Hollywood
Trompers	Eagle Rock
Wheelers	Norwalk
Whistlers	Ventura-Santa Barbara

SCTA Club Points Champions | Individual Points Champions

1946
Lancers
Albata
Road Runners
Gophers
Low Flyers

1946
Randy Shinn — Road Runners
Don Blair — Gophers
Tony Capana — Albata
Kenny Lindley — Lancers
Stuart Hilborn — Centuries

1947
Lancers
Road Runners
Low Flyers
Gophers
Gaters

1947
*Doug Hartelt — Lancers
*Emil Dietrich — Gaters
Randy Shinn — Road Runners
Jack Calori — Lancers
Burke & Francisco — Road Runners
Bob Riese — Gear Ginders

1948
Road Runers
Lancers
Low Flyers
Dolphins
San Diego
Roadster Club

1948
Spurgin-Giovanine — Albata
Doug Hartelt — Road Runners
Burke & Francisco — Road Runners
Stuart Hilborn — Low Flyers

Alex Xydias — Sidewinders

1949
Road Runners
Lancers
Sidewinders
Strokers
Dolphins

1949
Burke & Francisco — Road Runners
Xydias & Batchelor — Sidewinders
*Don Waite — Sidewinders
*Marvin Lee — Pasadena Roadster Club
Norm Lean — Dolphins
Reemsnyder & Sullivan — Strokers

1950
Sidewinders
Road Runners
Lancers
Glendale Stokers
Strokers

1950
Stanford Bros & Phy — Road Runners
Bill Likes — Sidewinders
Earl Evans — Road Runners
Xydias & Batchelor — Sidewinders
Ray Brown — Sidewinders

*Denotes tie

NHRA Top Speed and ET Records, 1960–1970

DATE	DRIVER	CLASS/ENGINE	ET-SECONDS	MPH	TRACK
7-03-60	Joe Tucci	A/D/Chrysler	9.06	168.85	Atco, NJ
2-17-61	Dode Martin	AA/D/Chevrolet (2)		174.9	Pomona, CA
2-18-61	Jack Chrisman	AA/D/Chevrolet (2)	9.00		Pomona, CA
5-20-61	Jack Chrisman	AA/D/Chevrolet (2)	8.97		Emporia, VA
7-08-61	Jack Chrisman	AA/D/Chevrolet (2)		175.09	East Haddam, CT
8-06-61	Jack Chrisman	AA/D/Chevrolet (2)	8.78		Caddo Mills, TX
9-04-61	Jim Nelson	AA/D/Chevrolet (2)		175.78	Indianapolis, IN
2-18-62	Glen Ward	AA/D/Chevrolet (2)	8.74		Pomona, CA
5-19-62	Jim Nelson	AA/D/Dodge	8.63	176.12	Memphis, TN
7-07-62	Jack Chrisman	AA/D/Pontiac (2)		176.60	York, PA
8-11-62	Jim Nelson	AA/D/ Dodge	8.59		Pomona, CA
9-03-62	Connie Kalitta	AA/D/Chrysler		180.36	Indianapolis, IN
2-16-63	Don Garlits	AA/FD/Dodge	8.24		Pomona, CA
2-16-63	Steve Porter	AA/FD/Oldsmobile		187.86	Pomona, CA
5-18-63	Norm Weekly	A/FD/Dodge		188.66	Pomona, CA
5-29-63	Don Garlits	AA/FD/Dodge		189.03	Indianapolis, IN
8-04-63	Bobby Langley	A/FD/Chrysler	8.16		Caddo Mills, TX
9-21-63	Don Garlits	AA/FD/Dodge		190.26	East Haddam, CT
9-26-63	Norm Weekly	A/FD/Chrysler	8.03	192.30	Arlington, WA
2-14-64	Jeep Hampshire	AA/DD/Chrysler	8.01		Pomona, CA
2-14-64	Norm Weekly	A/FD/Chrysler		192.32	Pomona, CA
5-16-64	Bobby Vodnik	AA/FD/Chrysler	7.96		Bayview, MD
5-24-64	Jerry Baltes	AA/FD/Chrysler		193.54	Inyokern, CA
6-12-64	Zane Shubert	AA/FD/Chevrolet	7.91		Riverside, CA
7-18-64	Bob Haines	AA/FD/Chrysler		198.66	Fremont, CA
8-01-64	Don Garlits	AA/FD/Dodge	7.78	201.34	Great Meadows, NJ
4-25-65	Danny Ongais	AA/FD/Chrysler	7.59		Carlsbad, CA
4-25-65	Bob Tapia	AA/FD/Chrysler		205.46	Carlsbad, CA
5-16-65	Buddy Cortines	AA/FD/Chrysler	7.54		Dallas, TX
5-22-65	Connie Kalitta	AA/FD/Ford		206.42	Bayview, MD
6-13-65	Jimmy Nix	AA/FD/Dodge		208.32	Richmond, VA
7-18-65	Don Westerdale	AA/FD/Dodge	7.47		York, PA
4-02-66	Tommy Allen	AA/FD/Chrysler		212.76	Carlsbad, CA
9-24-66	James Warren	AA/FD/Chrysler	7.38		Irwindale, CA
9-24-66	Tommy Allen	AA/FD/Chrysler		213.76	Irwindale, CA
9-25-66	Vic Brown	AA/FD/Chrysler	7.26		Bristol, TN
10-22-66	Jerry Ruth	AA/FD/Chrysler		218.44	Arlington, WA
4-01-67	Pete Robinson	AA/FD/Ford	7.08		Phenix City, AL
5-07-67	Don Johnson	AA/FD/Chrysler	6.97		Carlsbad, CA
5-07-67	John Edmunds	AA/FD/Chrysler		226.12	Carlsbad, CA
8-12-67	Hank Westmoreland	BB/FD/Chrysler	6.88		York, PA
9-16-67	Mel Van Niewenhuise	AA/FD/Chrysler		227.85	Arlington, WA
9-16-68	John Mulligan	AA/FD/Chrysler		229.59	Irvine, CA
5-03-69	Jerry Ruth	AA/FD/Chrysler	6.68		Bremerton, WA
9-13-69	Tom Raley	AA/FD/Chrysler	6.64		Atco, NJ
7-11-70	Larry Hendrickson	AA/FD/Chrysler		232.55	Vancouver, B.C.
9-19-70	Tom Raley	AA/FD/Chrysler	6.63		Atco, NJ
10-25-70	Tom Raley	AA/FD/Chrysler	6.53		Dallas, TX

In the ten years listed, elapsed times were reduced by 2.13sec, and top speeds rose 63.70mph. Five years later, the top ET had gone down only 0.75sec to 5.78sec, and top speed had gone up from 232.55mph to 249.30mph, but the era of the Keith Black Hemi was just starting, and drag racing would never again be the same. My thanks to the National Hot Rod Association for preparing this listing.

SCTA Individual Season Champions (Dry Lakes)

Year	Champion	Club Affiliation
1938	Ernie McAfee	Road Runners
1939	George Harvey & Ernie McAfee	Road Runners
1940	Bob Rufi	Albata
1941	Vic Edelbrock	Road Runners
1942	Karl Orr	Albata
1946	Randy Shinn	Road Runners
1947	Dietrich & Thomas	Gators
1948	Spurgin & Giovanine	Albata
1949	Burke & Francisco	Road Runners
1950	Stanford Bros. & Phy	Road Runners
1951	Lindsley & LeSage	Gear Grinders
1952	Fox & Cobbs	Sidewinders
1953	Vesco & Cobbs	Sand Diego Roadster Club
1954	Woods & McIver	Albata
1955	Woods & McIver (tie)	Albata
1955	Fritz Voight (tie)	Gear Grinders
1956	Baldwin & Sommerfeld	Road Masters
1957	Brissette & Eichenhofer	Esquires
1958	Baldwin & Sommerfeld	Road Masters
1959	Alexander & Hrosukoski	Esquires
1960	Bob Myers	San Diego Roadster Club
1961	Nolan White	San Diego Roadster Club
1962	Lufkin & Jones	Road Runners
1963	Nolan White	San Diego Roadster Club
1964	Nolan White	San Diego Roadster Club
1965	Christian-Lemke-Milligan	Rod Riders
1966	Larry Miller	Road Runners
1967	L & L Screw Machine	Road Runners
1968	Hutchinson & Hope	Rod Riders
1969	Geisler-Kehoe	Rod Riders
1970	LeVan Prothero	Rod Riders
1971	Bob Braverman	Rod Riders
1972	The Lindsleys	Gear Grinders
1973	McGee & Geisler	Rod Riders
1974	M. Wolf-B. Haselwerdt	Sidewinders
1975	Jerry Jones	San Diego Roadster Club
1976	Carr-Kaplan	Sidewinders
1977	Carr-Kaplan	Sidewinders
1978	Lattin & Gillette	Rod Riders
1979	Ken Rowe	Lakers
1980	Don DeBring	Sidewinders
1981	Mike Cook	LSR
1982	Anderson & Prothero	Rod Riders
1983	Larry Monreal	Sidewinders
1984	Bickford & Gansberger	San Diego Roadster Club
1985	Dodge Shelby Charger	Rod Riders
1986	Doc Jeffries	San Diego Roadster Club
1987	Don Ferguson, Sr., Jr., III	Rod Riders
1988	Geisler-Stringfellow-Yound	Rod Riders/LSR
1989	Geisler-Young-Toller	Rod Riders/LSR
1990	Berg-McAllister-Robinson	Milers
1991	Dannenfelzer & Richards	Sidewinders

SCTA Top Speed of Season at Dry Lakes

Year	Entry	Driver	Speed
1949	Xydias & Batchelor	Dean Batchelor	180.00
1950	Earl Evans	Bob Ward	166.66
1951	Tom Beatty	Tom Beatty	181.45
1952	Tom Beatty	Tom Beatty	187.50
1953	Tom Beatty	Tom Beatty	199.11
1954	Tom Beatty	Tom Beatty	199.52
1955	Tom Beatty	Tom Beatty	185.56
1956	Culbert's Automotive	Jim Culbert	199.55
1957	Culbert's Automotive	Jim Culbert	205.01
1958	Brissette & Eichenhoffer	Howard Eichenhofer	209.00
1959	Tom Beatty	Tom Beatty	212.26
1960	Quincy-Brisette Bros.	Bob Summers	227.27
1961	Quincy-Brisette Bros.	Burke LeSage	205.94
1962	Quincy-Brisette Bros.	Bob Funk	221.13
1963	Nolan White	Nolan White	197.80
1964	Chevrolet Research	Dick Guyette	213.77
1965	Chevrolet Research	Dick Guyette	218.84
1966	Beatie Bros.	Bill Beattie	199.11
1967	Beattie-Lloyd-Ashe	Greg Ashe	196.93
1968	Johnson & Shipley	Howard Johnson	205.01
1969	Johnson & Shipley	Howard Johnson	237.46
1970	Sadd, Teague & Bentley	Elwin Teague	220.04
1971	Johnson-Haselwerdt-Summers	Monte Wolfe	243.90
1972	Haselwerdt-Wolfe-Johnson	Monte Wolfe	234.47
1973	Sadd, Teague & Bentley	Elwin Teague	235.60
1974	Renaissance-Speedcraft	Jerry Jones	233.16
1975	Baja Bad Boys	Jerry Jones	256.41
1976	Teague, Bentley & Bisetti	Elwin Teague	221.13
1977	Dirt Dancer/Leggitt	Arley Langlo	253.52
1978	Ramjet & Ward	Roger Gates	237.46
1979	Leggitt & Wolfe	Monte Wolfe	267.06
1980	Teague, Bentley & Sturdy	Al Teague	250.00
1981	Ramjet & Ward	Roger Gates	275.22
1982	Carr, Kaplan & Wolfe	Don Carr	275.229
1983	Ramjet & Ward	Roger Gates	275.385
1984	Leggitt & Langlo	Arley Langlo	255.827
1985	Carr-Kaplan	Don Carr	284.630
1986	Carr-Kaplan	Don Carr	286.668
1987	Carr-Kaplan	Don Carr	277.606
1988	Carr-Kaplan	Don Carr	290.979
1989	Carr-Kaplan	Don Carr	273.307
1990	Carr-Kaplan	Don Carr	306.957
1991	Dannenfelzer & Richards	Fred Dannenfelzer	255.246

NOTE: The variations in speed from year to year were caused mostly by lake surface conditions and weather, and in some cases by a team's switch in engines or the addition of a supercharger. Sometimes a car that was fastest one year might not even run the following year.

Index